A Revenue Guide
for Local Government

Second Edition

Robert L. Bland
University of North Texas

International
City/County
ICMA
Management
Association
icma.org

Select ICMA Books

Advanced Supervisory Practices

Budgeting: A Guide for Local Governments

Capital Budgeting and Finance: A Guide for Local Governments

Economic Development: Strategies for State and Local Practice

The Effective Local Government Manager

Effective Supervisory Practices

The Future of Local Government Administration: The Hansell Symposium

Human Resource Management in Local Government: An Essential Guide

Local Government Police Management

Management Policies in Local Government Finance

Managing Fire and Rescue Services

Managing Human Resources: Local Government Cases

Managing Local Economic Development: Cases in Decision Making

Managing Local Government: Cases in Decision Making

Managing Local Government Finance: Cases in Decision Making

The Practice of Local Government Planning

The Practice of State and Regional Planning

Library of Congress Cataloging-in-Publication Data

Bland, Robert L.
  A revenue guide for local government / Robert L. Bland.— 2nd ed.
    p. cm.
  Includes bibliographical references and index.
  ISBN 0-87326-145-3 (alk. paper)
  1. Local finance. 2. Internal revenue. 3. Local revenue. I.
International City/County Management Association. II. Title.
  HJ9105.B57 2005
  352.4'4214--dc22

                          2005005192

Design: Charlie Mountain

Printed in the United States of America,

2010 2009 2008 2007 2006 2005
7 6 5 4 3 2 1
43305
05-092

International
City/County
ICMA
Management
Association
icma.org

The International City/County Management Association (ICMA) is the professional and educational organization for appointed administrators and assistant administrators in local government. The mission of ICMA is to create excellence in local governance by developing and fostering professional local government management worldwide. To further this mission, ICMA develops and disseminates new approaches to management through training programs, information services, and publications.

Local government managers—carrying a wide range of titles—serve cities, towns, counties, councils of governments, and state/provincial associations of local governments. They serve at the direction of elected councils and governing boards. ICMA serves these managers and local governments through many programs that aim at improving the manager's professional competence and strengthening the quality of all local governments.

ICMA was founded in 1914, adopted its Code of Ethics in 1924, and established its Institute for Training in Municipal Administration in 1934. The institute provided the basis for the Municipal Management Series, popularly knows as the "ICMA Green Books." By 1994, the institute had evolved into the ICMA University, which provides professional development resources for members and other local government employees.

ICMA's interests and activities include public management education; voluntary credentialing and standards of ethics for members; an information clearinghouse; local government research and development; data collection and dissemination; technical assistance; and a wide array of publications, including *Public Management* magazine, newsletters, management reports, and texts. ICMA's efforts toward the improvement of local government—as represented by this book—are offered for all local governments and educational institutions.

Acknowledgments

It has been fifteen years since the previous edition of this book was published, and a great deal has changed in the field of revenue policy and administration. A concerted effort was made in this edition to incorporate those changes, beginning with the impact of the terrorist attacks on September 11, 2001. This edition also builds on the expanding base of knowledge in local revenue matters, particularly the linkage to economic development and the impact of tax limitations.

This undertaking was greatly aided by several individuals. I have had the good fortune of having two talented graduate research assistants—Eric Ellwanger and Mark Gooch—in the Master of Public Administration (MPA) program, who have worked at various points on this book. One of the great joys of working in higher education is the intellectual stimulation that comes from our probing and testing of new ideas. I am particularly lucky to be working with one of the most outstanding groups of faculty and professional staff anywhere in the nation: young, energetic, dedicated to improving public management, and teachers par excellence. And I have benefited immensely over the years from interacting with students in a graduate course in revenue policy and administration, where new ideas often find their first exposure and often their most insightful critics. Finally, a number of MPA alumni of the University of North Texas along with other professionals in the field have helped to expand my knowledge as well as providing many timely examples, some of which have found their way into this volume. I particularly wish to thank Lewis McLain for his generosity in assisting in this book's preparation, mostly in ways that he probably doesn't realize.

The editorial staff at ICMA is spectacular. Christine Ulrich and Jane Cotnoir took my feeble prose and reworked it into the more readable narrative that now graces these pages. They deserve particular accolades for their attention to details and editorial guidance extraordinaire. Production of the book was under the capable guidance of Dawn Leland and Charlie Mountain at ICMA. Many thanks for unparalleled professionalism. You have made an otherwise onerous task into a fulfilling professional experience.

As only the families of authors can attest, there are long intervals of isolation, even hibernation. To my wonderful wife, Jane, and children—Becky and husband Wade, Ryan, and Micah—I'm on my way home, really!

Bob Bland
Professor
University of North Texas
Denton, Texas
bbland@unt.edu

About the Author

Robert L. (Bob) Bland is professor and chair of the Department of Public Administration at the University of North Texas, where he teaches graduate courses in public finance, governmental accounting, and budgeting and has been on the faculty since 1982. He is the co-author, with Irene Rubin, of *Budgeting: A Guide for Local Governments* (1997), published by the International City/County Management Association, and of several articles on the municipal bond market, property taxation, and municipal budgeting. On two occasions he conducted workshops in Poland on revenue sources for local governments. Professor Bland received his Ph.D. degree from the Graduate School of Public and International Affairs at the University of Pittsburgh, his M.P.A. and M.B.A. degrees from the University of Tennessee, and his B.S. degree from Pepperdine University's Seaver College.

This book is dedicated to

Charldean Newell, Ph.D., and Chet Newland, Ph.D.—

two of UNT's finest.

Contents

Tables

Figures

Sidebars

Foreword

The fabric of local government finance has undergone dramatic change. Revenue options were once limited but firmly accepted by citizens. As the American economy changed, and as the service sector grew and intellectual property became more valuable, the property tax, long the staple and stable foundation of local government finance, has become less reflective of real worth and less able to keep up with the growing demands for service. It also suffered as a tax that was not convenient to collect and pay, as opposed to a sales tax, which is paid in small increments at the time of purchase, or fees for service, in which the taxpayer can see a more exact relationship between the charge and the good purchased.

The climate for today's local decision makers—managers, assistants, elected officials—and for students of local government is much different. The global market, the increasingly competitive environment for economic development, the reduction of intergovernmental aid, and restrictions on the property tax have forced local governments to be more creative and varied with their revenue choices. The emergence of revenue options—sales taxes, impact charges, and fees for service—has given local governments more choices to meet increasing demands for service. But with those choices have come a new responsibility. Local decision makers now must carefully weigh the implications of each revenue source. Property tax values are sustained by economic activity but can impede economic growth if not applied appropriately. Fees for service provide a direct correlation between the purchase and the benefit received, and grant more user choice; however, policy makers must carefully consider which services are best suited for fees, whether fees should recover all or some part of the cost of delivery, and whether they want fees to encourage or discourage use of a particular service or a particular kind of development.

Striking the right balance between different revenue sources has become a skill that takes and deserves much more time and analysis in order to keep communities solvent, vibrant, and competitive. Professor Bland's *Revenue Guide for Local Government* is a practical blueprint to help local government managers and policy makers align their thinking about the selection and application of the right revenue choices.

Professor Bland correctly reminds us that as the appropriate revenue mix is determined, decision makers must take a thoughtful approach to ensuring the right long-term decisions.

- Leadership is required to gauge and shape public opinion on the services and outcomes desired in communities, and that delicate balance is best achieved when policy and community leaders are engaged and participate in strategic planning for communities so that priorities are clearly articulated, understood, and, to the extent possible, agreed upon.

- Expenditures must be carefully reviewed to ensure that programs are efficiently administered and effectively targeted to do the most good.

- There should be a correlation between the fee or tax paid, the benefit received, and the value perceived.
- There should be a periodic review of revenues to ensure that the mix of options and rates is having the intended consequences in the community and is producing the needed revenue for the local government.
- Finally, it's important to take the long view instead of looking for short-term fixes, because consistency is important for those citizens, both individual and corporate, who live in our communities and whom we wish to attract.

While one mix of revenues will not fit every local government community, Professor Bland's new edition clearly outlines the impact of tax and revenue policies on the local economy, the importance of leaders knowing their community and its needs, and the need for leaders who are willing to make hard choices and right decisions. He offers specifics in an easy-to-read and effective way, clearly outlining advantages and disadvantages. This edition provides an excellent resource for local government leaders as they meet their public service obligations.

J. Thomas Lundy
County Manager
Catawba County, North Carolina
President
International City/County Management Association

1 Revenue policy and the local economy

Why worry about revenue policy?
Revenue policy shapes the local economy
Revenue policy communicates effective leadership

The legal basis for local revenues
Taxing powers
Proprietary powers
Regulatory powers

Early warning signs of revenue shortfalls
Comparison of tax and collection rates within region
Comparison of new business investment within region
Comparison of population changes within region
Evaluating financial condition

Putting it all together: Creating a more resilient local economy
Develop a strategic plan
Avoid tax favors
Diversify the tax base
Increase use of service charges
Limit nuisance taxes
Promote revenue self-sufficiency

Factors shaping local revenue policies

Trends in local government finance
Greater dependence on own sources
Increased intergovernmental competition
Citizen distrust of government
Increased economic uncertainty

Summary

Taxes are what we pay for civilized society.

—Oliver Wendell Holmes Jr.

Revenue policy and
the local economy

The local economy has become increasingly complex. Managers face unprecedented expectations from citizens and council members in a period of declining resources. More fundamentally, today's managers must deliver services at a time when public confidence in government and its ability to perform have reached unparalleled lows. Changes in how governments finance their budgets reflect changes in American values. Occasionally, changes in revenue policy result from direct citizen intervention, as in the case of voter initiatives, or more frequently through such state legislature initiatives as property tax reforms, limitations on local revenue choices, or the addition of new revenue sources for local governments.

This book examines revenue issues from a local manager's perspective. When formulating a revenue policy, a public manager must balance what is economically best, politically expedient, and administratively possible. A manager must also respond to citizens' perceptions of an issue, whatever their accuracy. For that reason, this book also examines revenue issues in terms of their effects on citizens' perceptions. In a more general sense, effective leadership requires that the public administrator both shape and follow public opinion. The recommendations made throughout this book are designed to enhance citizens' confidence in the responsiveness and competence of local government.

Diversity in local revenue policies is not just desirable but politically and socially essential. One strength of our federal form of government is its capacity to accommodate a wide variety of citizens' preferences. While some citizens are quite content with the bare essentials in public services, others prefer more government involvement. Thus, no attempt is made to recommend the one best revenue structure for municipalities or counties. The suggestions offered for strengthening local revenue structures are based on the premise that diversity in the way local governments finance their budgets is the basis for political stability in our society.

Why worry about revenue policy?

No other policy area evokes such strong opinions so quickly as a discussion of taxes, particularly local tax issues. Many citizens believe they pay too much in taxes. Yet when they consider the options, few are willing to sacrifice reduced public services for lower taxes, particularly when they realize the minuscule impact even sweeping reductions in city or county property taxes will have on their monthly budgets. A local tax structure—or, more broadly, a revenue structure (taking into consideration nontax sources)—evolves from a complex mingling of past decisions and chance economic and political events, blended with shifts in community attitudes. Why, then, would a manager ever wade into a politically charged discussion of how a city or county finances its operations?

Revenue policy shapes the local economy

Occasionally local leaders mistakenly assume that all that is needed to achieve economic prosperity is new business investment in their community. But no amount of economic development effort can compensate for poor revenue policies. A city can "give away the farm" in tax incentives and never reap the benefits if its tax structure has remained unchanged since the nineteenth century, and in reality a good many tax structures have not been overhauled since then. A well-designed revenue structure—one that promotes fairness and market neutrality and is administratively cost-effective—is a city or county's most effective tool for attracting and retaining business investment. In fact, tax incentives may be unnecessary if a community's leadership has focused its efforts on building a sound tax structure. Businesses, like citizens, are not averse to paying taxes if they see that local government operates efficiently and that there is a clear connection between the taxes they pay and the quality of public services they and their employees receive.

It is axiomatic that the stronger the local economy, the stronger the local government's revenue base. Investment in prudent tax and revenue policies leads to a stronger economy, which leads to more stable, sustainable revenue yields and thus to less budget volatility. Good tax policy is good economics and provides long-term benefits to the manager willing to invest time and political capital in tackling the sacred cows. Conversely, an inefficient, cluttered tax structure creates a drag on local economic growth. In a real sense, economic prosperity begins with carefully crafted tax policies. This book is about articulating such policies.

Revenue policy communicates effective leadership

Revenue discussions are politically costly because they realign winners and losers in the distribution of the burden. Yet such discussions cannot be avoided—at least not indefinitely. When commenting to the local media on his city's growing budget woes in 2004, Pittsburgh mayor Tom Murphy acknowledged that he had erred in not addressing that city's antiquated revenue policies sooner. Delaying the inevitable pushes local leaders into a crisis mode in which decisions focus on finding ad hoc resolutions rather than long-term, comprehensive solutions. It narrows the choices leaders are willing to consider because their attention is focused on the crisis. Local government leaders' inability to take timely action leads to more drastic actions later, further affirming a cynical citizenry's perception of ineffective government. One distinct, although unexplored, advantage of the council-manager form of government is the appointed career executive's greater political capacity to bring to the table a timely discussion of revenue choices.

Allowing a dysfunctional revenue structure to struggle along heightens citizen cynicism. Everyone knows the structure is broken, yet no one has the political courage to engage citizens in a meaningful dialogue on solutions. Unfortunately, the important discussions emerge only in the crisis that is precipitated by a court ruling or a significant bond downgrading, as was the case in Pittsburgh. The most productive reforms in revenue structure (1) occur in small increments over a long period of time, (2) are guided by a clear set of criteria that are widely shared by the community, and (3) choose economic prudence over political expediency on the general assumption that a strong economy will benefit all stakeholders rather than just the well connected—and then only temporarily.

The legal basis for local revenues

In Western democracies, governments derive their revenues using one of three legal powers: taxing, proprietary, or regulatory. These powers are most typically granted in constitutions or charters but may also come from statutory authority or, infrequently, through court orders.

Taxing powers

Governments levy taxes on any of three **tax bases**—income, consumption, and wealth (or property)—to pay for the cost of their operations. Income-based taxes,

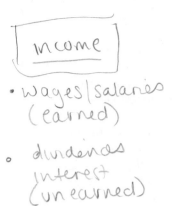
income
- wages/salaries (earned)
- dividends interest (unearned)

such as the personal and corporate income tax, rely on a sophisticated process to determine liability. The tax base may extend only to wages and salaries (**earned income**), as is the case of the widely used local wage tax in Pennsylvania or the federal social security tax; however, state and federal governments usually use a broader definition for their personal income tax bases that includes **unearned**

Recent trends in local revenue structure

Local revenues can be classified as either taxes or nontaxes. The following chart shows the shifts in how municipalities and counties have funded their activities over the last decade. Generally, local governments are depending less on taxes, particularly the property tax, and more on service charges, particularly services charges for current (general) services.

State aid plays a significant role in county finances, owing in part to counties' closer historical connection to state government. Municipalities, by contrast, derive significantly more of their revenue from utility services and, to a lesser extent, from nonproperty taxes, particularly sales, excise, and even variations of the income tax.

	Percentage of total revenue[a]			
	Municipalities[b]		Counties	
Revenue sources	1992	2002	1992	2002
Taxes				
Property	22.4	20.5	27.4	23.9
General sales	5.2	5.7	5.5	6.0
Excise	3.6	3.8	1.3	1.6
Income	4.5	4.2	1.0	1.3
Other	2.4	3.2	1.3	1.8
Total	38.1	37.4	36.5	34.6
Nontaxes				
Current charges[c]	13.7	14.7	16.1	18.1
Utility charges[d]	15.8	15.0	1.3	1.3
Miscellaneous[e]	9.0	8.1	9.3	8.2
Total	38.5	37.8	26.7	27.6
Intergovernmental aid				
Federal	3.6	4.2	2.2	2.9
State/local[f]	19.9	20.6	34.6	35.0
Total	23.5	24.8	36.8	37.9
Total	100.0	100.0	100.0	100.0
Total (in millions)	$232.5	$375,710	$150.4	$260,133
Total per capita	$1,124	$1,618	$669	$1,157

Source: Bureau of the Census, *Government Finances,* 1991–92 and 2001–02 eds. (Washington, D.C.: U.S. Government Printing Office).

Note: Percentages may exceed 100% because of rounding.
[a] Excludes income from liquor stores and insurance trust revenue.
[b] Combines cities and townships.
[c] Includes sewerage and solid-waste collection charges following the Census Bureau classification.
[d] Utilities include water, electric, natural gas, and transit services.
[e] Includes interest earnings, special assessments, sale of property, and motor vehicle licenses.
[f] Local aid represents less than 2% of revenue for both municipalities and counties.

income, such as interest and dividends, realized capital gains, royalties and rents, and alimony.

Consumption-based taxes include an array of taxes usually collected as part of a sales transaction. The **general sales tax** is the broadest-based consumption levy, and it typically includes most consumer goods, food consumed in a restaurant, and selected services such as telecommunications, lodging, and amusements. On the other hand, **excise (or selective sales) taxes** are levied on specific types of transactions at a separate rate from that of the general sales tax and under separate statutory authority. For example, cigarette and alcoholic beverage taxes are nearly universal among the states, and in a few cases, local levies are added. In the case of these "sin taxes," which are designed to discourage consumption, a general sales tax may be levied on top of the excise tax. Other widely used excise tax bases include motor fuels, hotel/motel occupancy, and natural resources at the point of extraction (severance taxes). Frequently, revenue from excise taxes is earmarked (or dedicated) to a particular purpose. For example, motor fuels taxes are almost universally dedicated to highway and street construction or repair.

Wealth-based (or property) taxes constitute a class of levies that fall on the value of assets. For example, an **estate tax** requires determining the value of the deceased person's remaining property. The more familiar **property tax** (or *ad valorem* = "according to the value" tax) is actually levied on several tax bases. Real property represents the largest component and includes land and any improvements (houses, shopping malls, landscaping) to the land. Personal property represents more mobile assets (vehicles, equipment, inventory of raw or finished goods) in the tax base. In some cases, the base may include intangible personal property (stocks, bonds, insurance policies), which poses particularly difficult administrative challenges.

Tax bases may be distinguished by whether the tax is levied on the value (ad valorem) or on a quantity (*in rem* = "against a thing"), such as the motor fuels tax, which is levied per gallon. Ad valorem taxes require more effort, usually by government, to establish the tax base's value and thus the liability of the taxpayer. Unfortunately, taxable value bears only a partial connection to the taxpayer's ability to pay, such as a "property-rich but cash-poor" farmer. On the other hand, in rem–based taxes are more easily administered and thus less open to dispute as to the basis of the **tax liability.**

Proprietary powers

Governments also possess broad constitutional powers to own and operate, even at a profit, various enterprises. The list of such activities is quite astounding: North Dakota owns and operates a state bank; the city of Dallas, Texas, owns and operates a popular FM radio station (WRR); a number of states own liquor stores; Glasgow, Kentucky, operates a fiber-optic network that provides cable television and Internet access to all city residents and much of the surrounding county; and Kenora, Ontario, owns and operates a full-service municipal telephone system (dial-up, wireless, and Internet). Locally owned utilities and transit systems are quite common and, in some cases, profitable. San Antonio, Texas, owns and operates all of the major utility services in the city (water, wastewater, natural gas, and electricity), which collectively provide a substantial subsidy to the city's general fund through interfund reimbursements. Of growing interest among larger cities is the installation of WiFi (wireless fidelity) technology, a citywide broadband wireless network that provides high-speed Internet service to citizens at a fraction of the cost of other modes of service. Several European cities now provide this low-cost technology to their citizens, and it is garnering growing interest among cities in the United States. For example, Chaska, Minnesota, offers its 7,000 homes city-run wireless broadband Internet for $16 per month.[1]

Proprietary activities give rise to **fees-for-service** as opposed to taxes. Whereas taxes represent involuntary conscriptions, service fees culminate in a quid pro quo in which government provides a good or service in exchange for the fee. For example, cities charge private utilities for the use of their rights-of-way; this is often called a **street rental fee**. In this case, the utility company gains access to public rights-of-way to lay its lines or cables and pays rent in exchange. It is interesting to observe how the use of proprietary powers varies among state and local (and even the federal) governments. In the Southwest, for instance, solid-waste collection is usually funded with a monthly service fee paid by households and businesses; in the Northeast such service is more often funded with general taxes.

The accounting and financial reporting requirements for proprietary activities differ from those for tax-supported services. The Governmental Accounting Standards Board (GASB) requires the use of **enterprise funds** to account for services that derive a portion of their income from user charges. Typically, water and wastewater service is accounted for in an enterprise fund, as are other utilities or quasi-business activities of government, including toll roads, airports, public transit systems, docks, golf courses, and even government-owned radio and television stations. Inflows to the fund include the fees charged to users of the service. Outflows include the labor and operating costs incurred in providing the service. Even if a service is not fully self-supporting, maintaining it in a separate enterprise fund provides managers with information on the amount of subsidy required to support the service. GASB now requires that an activity be accounted for in an enterprise fund if it is financed with debt that is backed by fees generated by that activity.

Regulatory powers

The third broad class of constitutionally derived powers comprises those that empower governments to promote the health, safety, and general well-being of a community or state. Sometimes called police powers, this class enables local governments to regulate land use through zoning ordinances, to license various professions or activities, and to inspect and certify the safety of food establishments. The list of state and locally regulated activities is long—from animal control to zoning of land use. In exchange for the cost of regulating an activity, state laws usually permit governments to collect a fee not to exceed that cost.

Although not a large source of revenue for cities and counties, regulatory fees do represent an important source that augments more general revenues. Regulatory fees are treated as general revenue, typically, from an accounting perspective, and thus are accounted for like unrestricted taxes. No effort is made, nor should be made, to fund the building inspection department from its inspection fees or fund the police department from its traffic citations.

Early warning signs of revenue shortfalls

Every local government's revenue structure is unique. No city, borough, township, village, parish, or county has exactly the same mix of revenue sources (property, sales, or income taxes, or service charges, fees, fines, or investment income) or economic activities (retail, wholesale, construction, agricultural, services, manufacturing, or government services). Consequently, the regular business cycles of growth-plateau-recession affect local governments differently. Some communities go unscathed by a recession, while others go into virtual meltdown at the first sign of slowing growth. The severity and length of economic retrenchment also affect local governments differently. Universal indicators of pending revenue problems have little utility. Indicators such as changes in bond ratings or local unemployment rates lag economic trends and thus fail to provide managers with sufficient advance warning to anticipate revenue crises and take remedial action.

Comparison of tax and collection rates within region

One indicator that does anticipate revenue crises well in advance is a comparison of the local government's principal **tax rates** with those of comparable governments (cities with cities, towns with towns, counties with counties) in the region. Local governments operate in a highly competitive environment at the substate level. Business investment becomes significantly more mobile at the regional level, as discussed in greater depth in Chapter 3. For example, cities with an extraordinarily high **property tax rate** but without other offsetting benefits may expect fiscal problems.

In the 1980s, leaders in Fort Worth, Texas, recognized that the city's property tax rate (operating and debt service combined) of over $0.90 per $100 assessed value was uncompetitive with the prevailing rates of the more than 100 cities in the region. In 1988, city leaders made a bold decision to form a public-private alliance to develop a transportation-manufacturing hub around Alliance Airport; this partnership would also anchor the city's economic development initiatives to the **agglomeration economies** that result when firms in a given industry cluster in hub cities to take advantage of the resources (skilled labor, technical support, specialized service providers) that are concentrated in the same area. The city's bold venture has contributed to a steady decline in its property tax rate since 1996 and to a more attractive environment for business investment.

An extraordinarily high tax rate, particularly for the property tax, by itself does not portend revenue problems. For example, largely residential communities typically have higher property tax rates than surrounding governments with more diversified tax bases. In part, the high rates may be an unwitting strategy to preclude business development. A community of single-family residences provides offsetting benefits, such as the preservation of property values, that compensate for the burdensome tax rate.

Another indicator of potential revenue problems is abnormally high tax or fee delinquency rates relative to those of the region. Like private businesses, governments must manage their receivables—those from both taxes and service fees, and particularly those from utility fees. Delinquency rates typically follow the business cycle, increasing during economic downturns and then declining as local economies improve. From a long-term revenue perspective, delinquency rates that exceed the norm for the region portend a problem. If the prevailing property tax **collection rate** is 95 percent for a region, local governments with significantly lower rates (higher delinquency rates) may be in the early stages of a revenue crisis. Again, these early warnings must be evaluated on a case-by-case basis. If a large property owner accounts for most of the delinquency, this is an unreliable indicator. However, persistent and growing delinquency rates for both property taxes and utility service charges suggest a more systemic revenue problem that may necessitate the kind of bold response made by Fort Worth, Texas.

Comparison of new business investment within region

For local governments with more diversified tax bases, a lag in new business investment when compared with investment in surrounding communities provides a red flag in the development of the community's revenue structure. An aging infrastructure, the high cost of land, a lack of skilled labor, and the unavailability of supporting industries (agglomeration economies) may contribute to the out-migration of capital. (The economies of agglomeration are derived from wholesaling facilities, a skilled labor pool, and specialized professional services such as accounting, data processing, and legal counsel that serve the unique needs of a particular industry.) Whatever the cause, a central city or mature "inner-ring" city whose economic development and business reinvestment lags that of newer, outlying communities will eventually confront a revenue crisis. The key to remaining competitive is to design an economic development plan that builds on a city's or county's strengths, capitalizes on new investment opportunities, and revitalizes existing industries. Cities that succeed in economically reinventing themselves will forestall having to take draconian budget measures to realign their operations with a declining tax base.

Comparison of population changes within region

Population shifts provide a third indicator of looming revenue problems. A community experiencing extraordinary increases or decreases in population compared with surrounding communities (a benchmark) inevitably will encounter a revenue crisis. Research has found that when population declines, revenue yields decline more quickly than local government expenditures.[2] This is because expenditures tend to be fixed, at least in the short run. Revenue yields decline much more quickly than long-term commitments for debt service, pensions, or maintenance of existing public facilities.

The age of the population making the shift also has a significant bearing on a community's economic fortunes. Generally, mobility is highest among young professionals and young families. These groups also make the greatest demands for consumer goods (vehicles, furniture, housing) and are most willing to incur debt for those goods. As households age, mobility declines. The economic aging of a community parallels the social changes that occur and vice versa. A community's tax policies, such as property tax relief for seniors, send powerful messages to citizens as to the type of community it wishes to become. It should come as no surprise that a city or county that extends favorable property tax terms to seniors will over time become a tax haven for seniors and will see growth in the consumer services that serve that age bracket (medical care, assisted living facilities, florists, and funeral homes).

Of the three tax bases available to government—property, consumption, and income—the property tax base is the most sensitive to population changes.[3] When population declines, residential and commercial property values, which represent the bulk of the typical local government's property tax base, plummet. Rapid population increases also strain the local revenue structure when infrastructure and service capacity cannot increase quickly enough to meet the new demand. Communities with stable populations or only moderate rates of population growth experience the least strain; those with the highest rates of population change, whether from growth or from decline, experience the most strain.[4]

Smaller, more rural municipal and county governments, particularly those on the urban fringe, are least able to accommodate rapid increases in population. Revenue effort (revenue collected per capita) will increase the most in these communities because they have the least excess capacity in public facilities and fewer economies of scale in service delivery. From a planning perspective, smaller rural governments are usually least prepared to cope with growth.[5]

Evaluating financial condition

While the foregoing ad hoc indicators suffice as early warning tools, a more comprehensive approach can be found in the Financial Trend Monitoring System (FTMS), as discussed in ICMA's *Evaluating Financial Condition: A Handbook for Local Government.*[6] Built around three clusters of factors—financial, environmental, and organizational—the FTMS provides a mechanism for monitoring trends in up to forty-two areas and tracing changes in each over time. Unfortunately, the system is labor- and data-intensive, and often local governments with the greatest revenue risks have the least budget slack with which to support such ongoing analyses. The other problem is the "compared to what" question.

Red flags

You know revenue problems loom in the near future when . . .

Persistent budget deficits continue even during periods of economic growth

Delinquency rates for taxes and utility charges remain high even during periods of economic growth

High vacancy rates in housing and/or business persist even during economic expansions

Population and housing stock age at faster rates than they do elsewhere in the region

Legislators repeatedly postpone replacement of aging infrastructure

Business investment, especially new plant construction, remains stagnant

Tax rates steadily increase

Conflict during budget preparation increases

Little open space remains available for new development.

Another concern for conducting municipal financial analysis is the lack of normative standards for the financial characteristics of a local government. What, for example, is a healthy per capita expenditure rate, level of reserves, or amount of debt? The credit-rating industry has many benchmarks for evaluating local government, but these benchmarks have to be considered in combination with more subjective criteria, such as the diversity of the government's tax base or its proximity to regional markets.[7]

An ideal benchmarking mechanism remains illusive; however, for the purpose of anticipating a revenue crisis, simple regional comparisons will suffice. At a regional level, a city or county with an extraordinarily high property tax and/or delinquency rate, lagging business investment, and lagging population growth has a high probability of incurring a revenue crisis in the future. The key is to recognize the warning signs early and, like the city of Fort Worth, take corrective action to reverse these unfavorable trends.

Putting it all together: Creating a more resilient local economy

A strong revenue structure begins and ends with a strong local economy. Adopting and tenaciously pursuing prudent revenue policies is the key to strengthening the local economy. In other words, a perpetual feedback loop exists between a local government's revenue policies and its economy.

Where should local leaders begin? The answer depends on the severity and duration of the fiscal problems confronting the jurisdiction. The late Charles Levine, a noted public administration scholar, developed a typology for understanding the various strategies governments use to cope with fiscal stress.[8] Levine's presentation, represented by a 2×2 table, focused on the spending side for strategies to redress the budget problem; however, the revenue side cannot be ignored if a more resilient local economy is to emerge. Figure 1–1 adapts his table to the revenue side and recommends different strategies depending on the severity of the revenue problems. Assuming that local governments will take appropriate actions on the spending side to mitigate the adverse budget trends, the following discussion elaborates on the recommendations summarized in Figure 1–1 to examine the actions that governments should pursue on the revenue side.

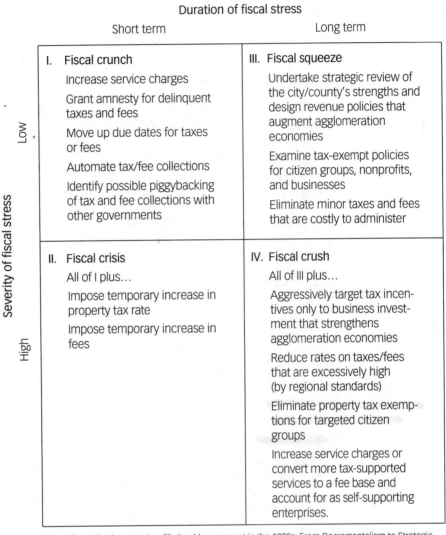

Source: Adapted from Charles H.Levine, "Police Management in the 1980s: From Decrementalism to Strategic Thinking," *Public Administration Review* 45 (November 1985): 695. © Blackwell Publishing Ltd.

Develop a strategic plan

Revenue problems do not develop suddenly, and it follows that their resolution requires a long-term plan, a carefully crafted strategy, and continuous attention. Neglecting to assess objectively the impact of local taxes and fees on the economy is an invitation to a revenue crisis in the future. The first task is to undertake a strategic planning process to assess the local government's economy. What are the economy's strengths and weaknesses? Are there clusters of related businesses or is there the potential to build clusters of related businesses (agglomeration economies)? What other opportunities exist for strengthening the economy? What threats exist to undermine it? How do current tax and fee policies affect the economy?

On the basis of this analysis, local leaders can develop a multiphased plan for building on the community's economic strengths and ameliorating its weaknesses, and for capitalizing on opportunities while mitigating the threats. Part of the plan may incorporate the principles of good revenue policy discussed in Chapter 2. For example, one of the consequences of agglomeration economies is that a local government, especially a smaller one, may become more vulnerable to economic cycles in that particular industry or business sector. A rural community that builds its economy around the farm implement industry will experience large swings in its tax and fee bases. Such a community's plan should include economic development measures that diversify the tax base, ideally introducing countercyclical industries to offset the adverse effects from downturns in its preeminent business sector.

Local governments facing a fiscal crunch or crisis may focus on longer-term strategies to sustain the viability of their local economies. They may focus on revenue policies that support an adequate supply of public services while encouraging reinvestment in the local economy. On the other hand, governments facing a squeeze or crush will need to take more intentional and immediate measures to attract business investment, diversify the tax base, and sustain an adequate level of public services.

Once a plan is in place and is, ideally, formally adopted by the council, local leaders have a standard against which to judge the merits of revenue proposals as they are formulated. How will freezing tax liabilities for senior citizens help accomplish the community's economic goals? The plan provides a reference point for legislators, managers, and citizens in evaluating the merits of revenue proposals, and a standard for discarding economically imprudent ideas. Unfortunately, local governments are "creatures of the state" and do not hold complete sway over their destinies, as Californians demonstrated with Proposition 13. Our world is interdependent, and policies in one jurisdiction ripple through to affect other jurisdictions. But even in this environment, Torrance, California, took swift and aggressive action to mitigate the effects of economically imprudent state actions. It added a utility user's tax after the passage of Proposition 13, increased service charges, and pursued an aggressive economic development plan using tax increment financing to attract new commercial and industrial development.[9] The result has been a more stable revenue structure for the city over the long term.

Avoid tax favors

As politicians know, everyone is a special case, and the quickest way to win political support is to provide tax relief to one's constituency. But as discussed more extensively in the next chapter, one of the most destructive actions any government can take is to extend permanent tax favors to a particular sector, industry, or segment of the population. Besides the blatant inequity it introduces, such action also interferes in the market by skewing decisions to benefit from the tax treatment and not necessarily to achieve greater productivity. In short, governments that feel compelled to hand out tax favors invite increasing inefficiencies into their local economies. Eventually those inefficiencies stagnate new economic initiatives and emerge as chronic revenue shortfalls.

Yet, as discussed in Chapter 3, tax incentives are essential tools that local governments use to shape their economies, and if local leaders enter into economic development without a well-articulated plan, these tools will not be used constructively. The key is to use tax favors to strengthen the long-term economic viability of the community, and that requires careful, thoughtful, and thorough planning and the political discipline to stay the course.

Diversify the tax base

Tax diversification has two dimensions: diversification of tax sources and diversification of the tax base. In addition to the property tax, local governments should have available one other broad-based tax source, such as a general sales tax or a personal income tax. Both sources have greater **income elasticity** than the property tax, which means that they yield greater amounts of revenue as the local economy grows. (The property tax is generally income inelastic, which means that its revenue yield does not keep pace with economic growth. This results from assessment practices that fail to keep pace with market values.) Balancing an income-inelastic source with a more elastic source results in a more stable overall revenue yield.

A diversified property tax base maintains a balance among residential, commercial, industrial, and vacant property. When a tax base is weighted too heavily toward one type of property, revenue yield becomes more vulnerable to economic cycles. Similarly, the local sales tax base should be diversified among a variety of retail and service industries. A city or county that strategically plans its economic development will identify new investment opportunities that simultaneously complement its unique strengths while diversifying its residential, commercial, and retail tax bases. For example, San Antonio, Texas, with a large concentration of military bases, has attracted tourism and financial services that build on its strengths while also diversifying the tax base. Although diversifying revenue sources almost always requires legislative approval, an existing tax base can be diversified through local initiative.

Increase use of service charges

Service charges promote revenue stability by reaching beneficiaries of local services who would otherwise escape taxation (e.g., owners of tax-exempt property), and by reducing the need to expand local government staff and facilities to levels beyond citizens' preferences and needs. Service charges promote economic efficiency by ensuring that public services are used by those who value them the most. Moreover, services provided on a fee basis are less likely to be wastefully used than are services financed through general tax revenues.

Economists are fond of noting that the pricing system is a far more precise measure of citizens' preferences than the ballot box. Financing public services solely from general tax revenues results in wasteful consumption because the service is effectively "free" to any one user, and local governments must expand staffing levels and facility capacity to meet a potentially wasteful level of demand. User charges serve to limit the use of public services, thereby reducing the need to expand government staff and facilities beyond what consumers are willing to pay for them. For example, customers who are charged for the amount of water they consume will use less than they would if water were financed with general revenues. Other local services that could be effectively financed through user charges include solid-waste services, utilities, highways, parks and recreation, planning and land use, information services, transportation, and public health.

One final note on the productivity gains from service charges. Public managers tend to overemphasize productivity gains on the supply side—improving worker performance to reduce cost—and to underemphasize the demand side—reducing wasteful consumption of local services. Even if a manager succeeds in improving production efficiency, the demand for the service is not thereby reduced: the pressure remains to provide higher levels of service than what citizens would be willing to pay if the service were provided on a fee basis. The significant productivity gains in local government are on the demand side. Only by eliminating wasteful use of public services will a local government realize significant savings.

Limit nuisance taxes

One common consequence of patchwork tax reform is the adoption of narrowly based taxes, particularly excise taxes, such as on admissions to entertainment events, on specific products (e.g., cigarettes and tires), or on employees for the privilege of working (occupation privilege taxes). These taxes are generally costly to administer and have small revenue yields. Yet local governments find it difficult to abandon them because they provide just enough revenue to make a difference in the local budget. Local governments in this position should develop a plan to gradually eliminate these taxes, replacing them with broader-based taxes or service charges.

Promote revenue self-sufficiency

Accepting state or federal aid places a local government at risk of becoming too dependent on those funds. One drawback of dependency is the local government's increased vulnerability to changes in funding policies—changes in either the amount of funding or the formulae used to allocate grant funds.

The distortion of local budget priorities is another consequence of dependency on grants. Most local governments find the inducements too great to pass up a grant; once the grant is in place, the federal or state government's priorities move to the top of the local agenda, and local priorities are supplanted or delayed. This centralization of policy making and priority setting undermines the diversity of spending patterns that has been a hallmark of local government. Grants also increase spending by local governments by typically requiring a local match.

A policy of self-sufficiency does not mean that local governments should shun all grants-in-aid. Grants serve an economically efficient function by compensating recipients for locally produced services that benefit the region or nation. Self-sufficiency does mean, however, that local governments should minimize their dependency on grants, and one way they can do this is by linking grants to specific programs or projects and then varying service levels in the targeted areas according to the availability of grant funds. Another recommendation is that grants be accounted for in separate funds or, at the least, in restricted accounts within a fund. Linking available money in the fund to particular activities provides a defensible basis for terminating the program once grant funds are exhausted.

Factors shaping local revenue policies

As a result of changing economic and political conditions, local governments are undergoing major transformations in the methods they use to finance their operations. Figure 1–2 shows the principal forces shaping the revenue structures of local government.

Legally, local revenue policies are most directly shaped by state laws defining the revenue-raising powers of municipalities and counties, as discussed at length earlier in this chapter in the section on the legal basis for local revenues. The discretion of these jurisdictions to raise revenues is the most visible indication of autonomy given to local governments by a state. Federal mandates also shape revenue policies through limits on local discretion, such as a maximum franchise fee of 5 percent on the gross revenues of cable television providers. Grant conditions, such as formulae

Figure 1–2

External influences on local government finance.

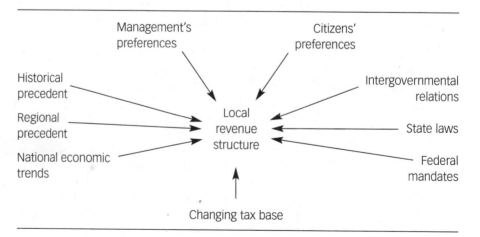

favoring the use of tax over nontax revenue sources, are a more indirect form of federal control.

Politics also shapes revenue systems. For example, intergovernmental competition for new business dictates that local governments keep their property tax rates in line with those of surrounding jurisdictions. Local governments with **overlapping tax bases**, such as counties and school districts whose boundaries overlap with those of a city, all compete for revenue from the same property tax base.

Some local governments develop reputations for innovative administrative procedures or policies. Innovations spread regionally once they have proven to be successful. A manager will more likely convince the council to adopt an impact fee on new development or a charge for refuse collection if other jurisdictions in the area are doing the same. Regional precedent can be especially important in revenue policy, in which a bad policy recommendation can be politically costly.

Historical precedent is an equally forceful factor in shaping a revenue structure. An approach that was successful in the past usually provides a politically expedient solution to a current problem.

One widely accepted hypothesis in public finance is that people "vote with their feet" by moving to communities that provide a preferred package of public services at an acceptable cost.[10] If this is the case, then past policies tend to be perpetuated. Citizens preferring communities with more parks and recreation services or higher-quality public schools will continue living in communities where those priorities exist. As a result of sorting out by citizens' preferences, local government policy, including revenue policy, tends to be self-reinforcing.

Finally, **cyclical** and **sectoral changes** in the regional, national, and even international economy affect the local revenue structure. Cycles of prosperity followed by decline are a fact of life and bear directly on local budgets. More subtle are the sectoral changes that occur as economies progress through various stages of development, such as from manufacturing to service-based industries.

Trends in local government finance

Changes in state and local tax bases have had a significant impact on revenue practices. The shift from a manufacturing to a service-based economy has prompted widespread efforts by both state and local governments to revamp their tax policies in order to capture more of the benefits from growth in the service sector. The influence of these external forces has created the following four trends in the revenue structures of local governments:

1. Greater financial self-sufficiency
2. Increased intergovernmental competition for new business investment
3. Citizen distrust of government
4. Increased economic uncertainty.

Greater dependence on own sources

The decline in federal aid has ushered in what Robert Kleine and John Shannon, two noted public finance experts, have called the "finance-it-yourself" fiscal era.[11] At its peak in 1978, federal aid represented about 26 percent of own-source revenue for cities and 19 percent for counties. However, by 2002 it had declined to 4 percent and 3 percent, respectively. This has imposed a significant realignment in the revenue structures of local governments.

State aid has not replaced lost federal aid but has declined along with it. The combined loss of federal and state aid has required local officials to choose between curtailing services and increasing their own revenue. The decline in aid has also exacerbated local officials' traditional mistrust of state and federal aid policy.

In retrospect, governments that shunned almost all federal aid may have taken a more politically prudent, although in the short term financially costly, course of action.

Declines in state and federal aid have not been accompanied by reduced constraints on local governments. In fact, state restrictions on local revenue matters may have increased as the federal government withdrew from local affairs. For example, nearly every state now places a limit on the property tax rate or levy that local governments may impose. As state control has increased, city and county officials have found themselves caught between the standardized revenue policy imposed by state law and the preferences of citizens, which vary from community to community.

In addition to becoming more dependent on their own revenue sources, local governments have become more prominent partners in the federal system. Since the federal government began turning more responsibility back to subnational governments, municipalities and counties have assumed greater responsibility in directing and financing public services, such as for terrorism preparedness in the post–September 11 era, and therefore greater responsibility for raising the revenues needed to finance those public services.

Increased intergovernmental competition

Although local governments have always formulated revenue policy with an eye toward other jurisdictions, declining federal aid and taxpayer resistance have created an unprecedented level of interlocal competition. This competition occurs on three fronts: (1) competition for tax revenues, (2) competition for the tax base, and (3) exportation of the tax burden.

Cities, counties, and independent school districts may have the authority to tax the same parcel of property. When overlapping governments levy a tax on the same tax base, as in the case of the real property tax, competition for revenues inevitably follows. Each government considers its budget needs to be more pressing than those of the overlapping governments, and each sets its tax rate independently, without regard for the aggregate impact on the property owner. The result is an overburdened taxpayer. **Tax competition** is also in evidence when a local government tries to lock in voter approval for a general obligation bond issue before other overlapping jurisdictions have an opportunity to ask voter approval for competing bond issues.

Competition for business investment has also assumed unparalleled proportions. As state and local governments cultivate reputations for providing favorable business environments, interlocal competition undoubtedly lowers tax burdens on businesses. Intensified interlocal competition has spurred public officials' efforts to shift more of the local revenue burden to nonresidents—a sort of "beggar thy neighbor" strategy. **Tax exportation** has become particularly commonplace at the state and local levels through such measures as hotel and motel taxes, entertainment taxes, taxes on the income or purchases of commuters, and taxes on businesses selling their products or services to customers outside the taxing jurisdiction.

To what extent should a local government export its tax burden? The principles of social equity would say it should do so only until it recovers the cost of serving nonresidents. Political reality dictates a more aggressive response. Regrettably, the current environment compels local officials to maximize opportunities for tax exportation. Most local governments have at least one economic strength—tourism, natural resources, a cultural or commercial center—that can be used to budgetary advantage. Those local governments with opportunities for tax exportation will tailor their tax policies so as to maximize their competitive advantage.

Citizen distrust of government

Tax revolts are nothing new in the United States. After all, hatred for the crown's taxes precipitated the Revolutionary War. Like previous tax revolts, the most recent tax limitation movement is motivated in part by the public's perception that it has no control over government policies, especially those dictating taxing and spending. While public opinion polls consistently indicate that citizens regard local government as giving them the most for their money, the polls also reveal a long-standing dislike for the property tax.

Local governments have been quick to respond to citizens' objections to the property tax. Both municipalities and counties have shifted away from it to other sources of revenue during the past decade. That the greatest increases have occurred in non-tax revenue sources—especially current service charges—indicates public officials' awareness that citizens do not wish to have their tax burdens increased.

Increased economic uncertainty

Three principal economic events at the regional, national, and international levels affect local revenue structures:

1. Cyclical shifts in the economy brought on by recession, inflation, and expansion

2. Sectoral shifts brought on by changes in technology and economic development (principally, in the United States, the movement away from manufacturing and toward an information- and service-based economy)

3. Population movement across regions or national borders brought on by changes in job markets and technology.

The most obvious factor affecting local government revenues is the business cycle in the regional and national economies: economic growth followed by decline, price stability followed by inflation, and low interest rates followed by rising rates. The ability of local government revenue structures to withstand these cycles depends in part on the degree of diversification in both the property tax base and revenue sources. As noted previously, cities and counties with more diversified property tax bases and more diversified revenue sources will generally have more stable revenue yields and thus more stable operating budgets over the business cycle.

As a result of the sectoral shift in the U.S. economy, local governments luring high-growth industries will achieve stronger revenue positions, the qualification being that not all high-growth industries affect local budgets the same way. Clearly, some areas win as a result of this shift while others lose. The success stories have received extensive press coverage: California's Silicon Valley, Route 128 around Boston, North Carolina's Research Triangle, and Austin, Texas, are just a few of the more notable examples in the computer industry.

Population shifts—from central city to inner-ring to outer-ring suburbs, or from the frostbelt to the sunbelt and back to the frostbelt, or across national borders—are the third major influence on the revenue yield of a local government's tax base. When population declines, revenue yields decline more quickly than local government expenditures. This is because expenditures tend to be fixed, at least in the short run.

These three external forces—cyclical, sectoral, and population shifts—create continuous strains on local revenue structures that require prudent action by managers. No quick and easy solutions exist, although diversifying the tax base, increasing the use of service charges, reducing dependence on nuisance levies, and prudent dependence on intergovernmental aid provide a beginning point for moderating the effects of these outside forces. The remainder of this text offers more specific strategies for fine-tuning a local government's revenue structure.

Summary

This chapter has examined the importance of monitoring a local government's revenue structure. The key to a strong and stable revenue structure is the local economy. But that economy is largely shaped by the revenue policies adopted over time.

The chapter identified several advance warning signs of looming revenue problems that managers should monitor. Each indicator is inexpensive to track and is relatively easily measured, and heeding these signs can provide immeasurable returns if the community's leadership musters the political courage to take aggressive but purposeful action to redress economically unhealthy trends.

The chapter has summarized the basic legal powers that local governments use to raise revenues, and it has reported on recent trends in tax and nontax sources for municipalities and counties. Several trends are now apparent in the policies governments use to finance their operations.

First, in order to create a more resilient economy and with it a more stable revenue structure, local governments must begin with a plan to strengthen their economy and then use that plan to guide their revenue decisions. They must avoid extending tax favors indiscriminately, diversify their tax sources and tax bases, increase the use of service charges, limit the use of nuisance taxes, and reduce the cost of revenue administration.

Second, local governments will continue to assume more responsibility for raising the revenues needed to finance their services. Those local governments in the strongest financial position will be able to export a greater share of their tax burden.

Finally, research has found that when population declines, revenue yields decline more quickly than local government expenditures. Among revenue sources, the property tax is the most sensitive to population changes. It is also reasonable to expect that as the mobility of the nation's population increases, the instability it creates for governmental budgets will also increase.

---

1 See the Web page of the city of Chaska, Minnesota, at www.chaska.net.

2 George E. Peterson and Thomas Muller, *The Economic and Fiscal Accompaniments of Population Change* (Washington, D.C.: The Urban Institute Press, 1980), 100.

3 Peterson and Muller, *Economic and Fiscal Accompaniments,* 102.

4 Helen F. Ladd, "Municipal Expenditures and the Rate of Population Change," in *Cities under Stress*, ed. Robert W. Burchell and David Listokin (Piscataway, N.J.: Center for Urban Policy Research, Rutgers University, 1981), 351–367.

5 Richard J. Reeder, *Rural Governments: Raising Revenues and Feeling the Pressure,* Rural Development Research Report no. 51 (Washington, D.C.: U.S. Government Printing Office, 1985), 10.

6 Sanford M. Groves and Maureen Godsey Valente, *Evaluating Financial Condition: A Handbook for Local Government,* 4th ed., rev. Karl Nollen-

berger (Washington, D.C.: International City/County Management Association, 2003), 3–11.

7 Ibid, 3.

8 Charles H. Levine, "Police Management in the 1980s: From Decrementalism to Strategic Thinking," *Public Administration Review* 45 (November 1985): 691–700.

9 Gregory D. Saxton, Christopher W. Hoene, and Steven P. Erie, "Fiscal Constraints and the Loss of Home Rule: The Long-Term Impacts of California's Post–Proposition 13 Fiscal Regime," *American Review of Public Administration* 32 (December 2002): 423–454.

10 Charles M. Tiebout, "A Pure Theory of Local Expenditures," *Journal of Political Economy* 64 (October 1956): 416–424.

11 Robert J. Kleine and John Shannon, "Characteristics of a Balanced and Moderate State-Local Revenue System," in *Reforming State Tax Systems,* ed. Steven D. Gold (Denver: National Conference of State Legislatures, 1986), 33–34.

2 Revenue policy choices: Principles to guide managers

The three pillars of support

Choices that promote fairness

Equity in theory
Equity in practice
Equity in action: The good, the bad, and the really ugly

Choices that strengthen the local economy

Tax neutrality in theory
Tax neutrality in practice
Tax neutrality in action: The good, the bad, and the still ugly

Choices that facilitate effective administration

Notification
Collection
Enforcement

Putting it all together: Designing a balanced revenue system

Summary

Our plans miscarry because they have no aim. When a man does not know what harbor he is making for, no wind is the right wind.

—Seneca

Revenue policy choices:
Principles to guide managers

Strengthening a community's economy begins with an assessment of the taxes and fees currently in use. Are they consistent with the community's economic goals? Do they promote a diverse tax base, encourage the development of countercyclical industries, and bring greater revenue stability to the budget? Are there opportunities for increased use of benefits-based levies and for reducing or even eliminating nuisance taxes? Do certain groups receive unjustified tax favors?

Managers need specific criteria to guide their planning and deliberations toward policies that strengthen the local economy. This chapter synthesizes public finance research addressing the criteria that should guide local revenue policy making. These criteria fall into the three general categories—the pillars of support for a sound local economy: equity, neutrality, and effective administration.

The three pillars of support

Not only does a revenue structure reflect a community's values, but citizen attitudes toward local government are shaped largely by the perceived fairness of the revenue structure. Fairness, or **equity**—the fair distribution of both the tax burden and the benefits from public services—is the first pillar.

Neutrality of tax policies is the second pillar. Tax neutrality requires placing the long-term economic health of a community above any short-term political advantages. Taxes alter the way markets function by prompting producers, consumers, workers, and investors to find ways to reduce or eliminate their tax liability. The less interference by taxes in the marketplace, the more neutral those policies and, by implication, the more productive the market's operation—up to a point. No economy operates perfectly—that is, with perfect competition, free flow of information, and freedom of entry or exit by participants. Economists refer to tax avoidance behaviors collectively as dead-weight losses to the economy. The goal is to minimize interference from tax policies while creating a return to the community, in the form of tax revenue, for its investment in public goods and services.

The third pillar is effective administration. Not all revenue options that have economic or political merit are feasible for local use when the cost to government to administer the tax or the cost to taxpayers to comply with the tax is taken into account. For example, charging a fee for the use of municipal parks has economic merit but lacks feasibility, given the high cost of collecting the fee. In fact, municipal parks, like a number of other public services, possess benefits that spill over well beyond individual users, making their financing solely from benefits-based sources less attractive.

Equity, neutrality, and effective administration are principles to guide local managers in formulating revenue policies for their communities. But as will become evident, even with the aid of these principles, local leaders are left with the unsavory task of making tradeoffs among them. Gains in equity often come at the expense of lost neutrality and increased administrative complexity. In the political context in which local managers operate, much of their time is devoted to resolving the conflicts that arise. The formulation of revenue policy occurs in an imperfect world with incomplete knowledge; the prudent manager takes full advantage of those occasional opportunities when balance can be achieved in the tradeoffs made among these three pillars of tax policy.

Choices that promote fairness

Few issues rankle taxpayers more quickly than the conviction that they bear an unfair tax burden relative to the burden of others. Especially at the local level where the linkage between tax burden and public service is the closest, managers have a particular obligation to constantly monitor the fairness of the tax burden. But how can fairness be measured or otherwise gauged?

Equity in theory

From a theoretical perspective, equity is measured along two dimensions that often are at odds with one another. **Horizontal equity** refers to the distribution of the tax burden among persons or businesses in comparable circumstances. For example, households that live in comparably valued housing should incur the same property tax liability, assuming that housing value is the basis for establishing comparability.[1]

Horizontal equity is a deeply held value in the United States. "No taxation without representation" implicitly appeals for fair treatment for persons in similar circumstances. But on what basis should tax burdens be measured? Current annual income provides the most commonly used indicator of the relative impact of taxes on a household's available resources (effective tax rate = tax liability/current income). Some economists argue, however, that a broader measure, such as lifetime income, is justified because many decisions with tax consequences (e.g., the purchase of a home or vehicle) are made from a long-term perspective.[2] Since most tax policies focus on current income, however, that is the more appropriate measure of relative tax burdens.

Many of the deductions and personal exemptions allowed on the federal income tax seek to establish horizontal fairness for the current tax year. Adjustments are made for family size (personal exemptions) and extraordinary medical expenses. However, a number of state constitutions include a **uniformity clause** that, in varying degrees, compels even treatment of all citizens, or at least those citizens in comparable situations, and preclude state and local governments from making adjustments for individual circumstances. The Pennsylvania Supreme Court has ruled, for example, that the state's uniformity clause precludes extending personal exemptions or deductions and requires that personal income be taxed at a flat, as opposed to a progressive, tax rate.

Whereas horizontal equity considers the burden for each cross section of the income spectrum, comparable to the balance sheet in financial reporting, **vertical equity** takes a more dynamic look at how that burden varies across the spectrum of income, comparable to the income statement. Vertical equity refers to the variation in tax burdens among taxpayers in different circumstances. As circumstances change, how much should taxpayers' burdens change? Three possibilities exist: regressive distribution, proportional distribution, or progressive distribution.

In a **regressive distribution,** the relative tax burden declines as income increases. For example, in the case of the sales tax, it is well known that while higher-income households pay more in sales taxes, their effective tax burden is less than that of lower-income households. Thus, sales taxes are generally acknowledged to be regressive.

On the other hand, a **progressive distribution** means that the effective tax burden increases across the income spectrum, resulting in both absolute and relatively

Progressive:
Federal
Income
Tax

Proportional.

higher tax burdens for higher-income households. Progressivity can be achieved through incrementally higher tax rates, which is the case with the federal and most state income taxes. Alternatively, it can be achieved by targeting the sources of income and consumption of higher-income households, as New Hampshire and Tennessee have done with the unearned income tax, or by imposing a luxury excise tax that targets the purchases of the wealthy.

Lying between regressive and progressive taxes is a **proportional distribution,** in which the effective tax rate remains flat across the income spectrum. On the surface, a flat-rate income tax should exhibit proportionality, but because of the federal tax's progressive rate structure, the value of the deductibility of state and local income taxes increases with income, making an otherwise proportional state or local tax effectively regressive.

Equity in practice

Theories of equity provide valuable benchmarks for evaluating taxes, but they do not offer prescriptive guidelines for designing an equitable tax structure. Two basic principles in public finance offer a more prescriptive basis for tax policy: the benefits-received principle and the ability-to-pay principle.

At the local level, the **benefits-received principle** offers the most defensible basis for tax equity: those who benefit from a public service should bear a pro rata share of the cost of the service. The simplicity of this principle largely explains its appeal. Even in the case of public goods and services, to the extent that beneficiaries enjoy private benefits, they should bear part of the cost. Charges for services or utilities and fees for licenses all find their justification in the benefits-received principle, and all share pricelike properties with their counterparts in the marketplace.

Benefits Based Tax
- motor fuel tax
- hotel/motel occupancy tax

Taxes administered in accordance with this principle are called benefits-based taxes. Motor fuels and hotel/motel occupancy taxes, for example, possess benefits-received properties to the extent that they are dedicated to funding activities that benefit taxpayers. In the case of motor fuels taxes, revenue is typically dedicated to highway, street, and bridge construction. In the case of occupancy taxes, revenues may be dedicated to promoting tourism, hospitality services, or convention services. Even the property tax has some benefits-received properties. For example, as crime declines or the quality of parks and recreation services improves, property values rise. This rise is particularly evident in neighborhoods known to have better schools. Increased property values represent a return (benefit) from investment in public service that can then be recaptured through the property tax. In fact, as property values increase, tax rates may decline and still generate the same amount of revenue.

The **ability-to-pay principle** resonates deeply with Americans: those with the greater ability to pay, usually measured in terms of annual income or wealth, should bear a greater share of the burden for financing government. The progressive rate structure of the federal and several state income taxes is predicated on this principle, which implicitly recognizes that "from those to whom much is given, much shall be required." Since its inception in 1913, the federal income tax has always had a progressive rate structure, and calls for a flat rate structure must overcome a century of precedent. Yet, as a practical matter, presidents and congresses struggle with finding the right degree of progressivity, and rates have generally converged since the Tax Reform Act of 1986.

Moreover, local and even state taxes based on the ability-to-pay principle encounter significant difficulty when higher-income households avoid the burden by "voting with their feet" and moving next door to a lower-tax jurisdiction.[3] The ability-to-pay principle brings into stark reality the complexity of tax policy and the inevitable tradeoffs that must be made. As discussed later, equitable tax policies often lack economic neutrality, making them unwise for local governments. The general sense among public finance experts is that taxes predicated on the ability-to-pay principle are better left to the states and even better left to the national government.

Equity in action: The good, the bad, and the really ugly

Ultimately, defining a fair revenue structure is a political decision. Yet there is general agreement on the fundamental elements.

1. Benefits-based levies are the most defensible in terms of fairness.

2. Tax favors to particularly vocal or well-connected groups undermine the perceived equity of the revenue structure.

3. Revenue policies should ease the burden on the poorest and not punish the wealthiest.

4. Tax fairness varies among local communities, depending on their age and income distribution and their preference for public services.

When in doubt, use benefits-based levies   Local governments have numerous opportunities for expanding their use of benefits-based charges and fees (discussed in Chapters 8 and 9). With the notable exception of landfills for reasons explained more fully in Chapter 8, utility services, including indirect costs, should be fully funded from service charges. Managers should look carefully at using block-rate and peak-period pricing structures for utility services. Charges for the use of public rights-of-way provide another benefits-based levy that can generate significant amounts of revenue. Although politically difficult, recreation services should be partially financed from charges on users, at the very least to minimize a wasteful use of the service, such as registering for a free recreation program and then failing to participate.

On the tax side, greater use of motor fuels taxes should be encouraged at the local level through more lenient state enabling legislation. Gasoline taxes not only provide a viable revenue source for local streets and highways, but also make good equity sense for financing public transit. Commuters benefit from public transit through reduced highway congestion and greater convenience, and short of levying tolls for road and bridge use, motor fuels taxes provide the local government with the most appropriate mechanism for capturing the individual benefits from the enhanced convenience. In order to minimize the incentive for motorists to purchase gasoline in neighboring cities with lower tax rates, motor fuels taxes must be levied regionally—and preferably as an added levy to the state tax that is allocated to the county of origin and distributed among the county's municipalities on a population basis, analogous to the strategy used by North Carolina with its local sales tax (see Chapter 5).

Cities and counties should also have access to the hotel/motel occupancy tax, with the revenue dedicated to promoting tourism, conventions, and the like. Some states allow local governments to use the revenue for historic preservation, county fairs, and the arts, both visual and performing. It is also reasonable for local governments to receive a portion of the hotel/motel tax for truly public goods and services, such as police and fire protection, general management, planning, and other property-based services, because nonresident guests benefit from these services and should share in paying for their costs.

Everybody is a special case when it comes to taxes   Managers know the truth of this axiom and, unfortunately, so do politicians—especially those looking for a cheap strategy for securing voter support. The problem is that such favors undermine the tax system's horizontal equity and contribute to the public's cynicism about government. As discussed in the next section, special tax relief also undermines the tax system's neutrality and introduces significant incentives for unproductive or even counterproductive market behavior. Once Pandora's box of special tax favors is opened, there is no closing it. And new opportunities for granting such favors appear regularly, including

- Classifying property by type of use (residential, commercial, industrial, agricultural) and then applying a separate assessment ratio or tax rate to each class, with those classes that are perceived to have a greater ability to pay incurring the more punitive ratios or rates.

- Freezing tax liability for certain classes of property owners, usually senior citizens, again on the misguided assumption that ability to pay is linked to age of household.

- Granting partial or full exemptions from the tax base or from tax liability for certain classes of consumers, producers, property owners, or income sources. State and local tax codes, not to mention the federal code, are riddled with such exemptions, known as **tax expenditures.** Often these exemptions are permanent, although some are temporary. One special privilege that gained popularity during the 1990s was **sales tax holidays** for school-related purchases timed to precede the beginning of the school year (see sidebar in Chapter 5). On the assumption that the sales tax was imposing an unfair burden on families buying clothes and supplies for their school-age children, several state legislatures implemented a sales tax holiday of two or three days, temporarily exempting such purchases from the sales tax.

While tax expenditures should generally be avoided, they have a legitimate place in the local manager's toolbox, particularly for economic development purposes as described in Chapter 3. The key is whether the favor (tax expenditure) is part of an overall plan for achieving certain economic goals or an attempt to garner political favor with a particularly vocal group of voters. The latter undermines the long-term economic health of the community and inevitably leads to woeful ends. Cities like Detroit, Newark, Philadelphia, and Pittsburgh, once economically robust, now must face the consequences of special favors granted in past years.[4] Their experience should serve as a clarion call to local governments everywhere that the long-term cost of special tax favors far exceeds the lost revenue. Fairness in tax policy makes good sense not only politically but also economically.

The humane side of revenue policy   While local governments are ill-suited to pursue redistribution of income on the tax side, they have a responsibility to protect their most vulnerable citizens by finding innovative mechanisms for targeting relief to the poorest households. For example, while it is administratively awkward to attach a means test to the property tax, tax relief can be targeted through a state-funded income tax credit for extraordinarily burdensome property taxes, called a **circuitbreaker program,** or through a partial **homestead exemption** (less preferable because it doesn't target relief to those who need it). These options are described more fully in Chapter 4. Local governments should maintain a utility relief fund, paid for by donations from users, to target utility fee subsidies to qualifying households. Some governments offer free or significantly reduced admission charges to recreation programs during off-peak periods. Conversely, local tax policies should not single out the wealthier households for discriminatory taxation. As already noted, the openness of local economies means that people and their wealth will move to lower tax areas that offer adequate public services. As discussed in the next section, pursuing good tax policy is a tightrope walk that balances fairness with neutrality.

Fairness is a community-based standard   A politically acceptable revenue policy reflects the political environment of the community—and changes with it. For the public manager, the challenge is to assess the political environment and then design a budget that complements it.

Figure 2–1 combines revenue effort and capacity to depict four types of communities according to their political environment.[5] Revenue capacity indicates the ability of a local government to raise revenue, and it is usually measured in terms of per capita income or per capita wealth of the property tax base. In other words, if residents have low personal income or low property wealth, the local government's revenue capacity is limited. Revenue effort, or the actual amount of revenue raised by a local government, is measured in terms of revenue per capita. A high revenue effort indicates a comparatively high tax or service charge burden.

A **caretaker community** has a low revenue capacity and a low revenue effort. Expenditures are for basic services only. Citizens expect and want nothing more. Caretaker communities generally obtain their revenues from a modest property tax, a limited number of license and permit fees, and possibly some service charges. Smaller, more rural communities often fall into this category.

A **growth community** also maintains a low revenue effort but has the capacity for more. Typically, growth communities pursue laissez-faire economic policies on the assumption that such policies will create a more favorable business environment and thus more economic development. While per capita property wealth and personal income levels could support a much larger public sector, growth communities prefer a modest revenue effort and modest level of locally provided public services.

By contrast, an **arbiter community** has a relatively high per capita revenue effort but a low capacity to provide the required revenues. Therefore, the manager must arbitrate among competing interest groups who want a share of an already stretched local budget. Citizens expect a diverse and significant number of services, but available resources are limited, possibly because of the erosion of the local tax base. This type of community makes heavy use of the property tax, but increased dependence on the tax is limited by intergovernmental competition. Other broad-based taxes, such as an income or a sales tax, may be used. Arbiter communities also pressure state legislatures to pass enabling legislation giving them access to tax revenues from nonresidents who use local services. Older central cities and counties dominated by manufacturing may fall into this category.

Figure 2–1
The relationship of political environment to revenue structure.

	Revenue effort	
	Low	High
Revenue capacity — Low	Caretaker community Keeps cost of government down	Arbiter community More public services are expected, but resources are limited
Revenue capacity — High	Growth community Creates favorable business climate	Consumption community Maintains quality public services that preserve community appeal

A **consumption community,** which is usually an upper-middle-income area, values locally produced public services and is willing and able to pay for good services. Residents value publicly provided amenities and are willing to preserve them at any cost. Consumption communities rely primarily on the property tax and possibly the sales tax but also make extensive use of service charges and regulatory fees.

Like households, communities age. They evolve as their population changes, but it is difficult for the revenue structure to keep pace with the demographic-driven changes. Young families, which are the most mobile households, seek growth-oriented communities where public services are plentiful and affordable. Consumption and borrowing characterize these households and thus shape their communities. As these families reach middle age, however, they find less satisfaction in the consumption of goods and more satisfaction in the consumption of services—namely, those services that enhance the quality of life, providing security, stability, and even serenity. Community services begin to reflect these new caretaker values, as typified by communities that exclusively serve active senior citizens.

But aging rarely proceeds gracefully or uniformly. Some communities become more diverse socially, ethnically, and economically. Arbitration among competing interests becomes the norm and brings a unique set of revenue challenges for the public manager.

Choices that strengthen the local economy

Every bit as important as the more frequently debated issue of fairness is neutrality, the second pillar of sound public finance. Neutrality addresses the impact of tax and revenue policies on the local economy. Achieving neutral tax policies requires extraordinary care that cannot be found on the cutting-room floor of political compromise. Tax neutrality is intentional. It places the community's long-term economic viability ahead of short-term political accommodation. Unfortunately, the nation's current political environment does not bode well for tax neutrality, but the unique vantage point of professional managers enables them to push the neutrality question onto the public agenda and shape the debate in ways that ensure that important questions get addressed.

Why is neutrality important? Taxes affect the way we behave. Some consequences are intended and positive. Consider the effect of individual retirement accounts on Americans' willingness to save, or the effect of cigarette taxes on the consumption of tobacco, especially by younger consumers. "Business friendly" tax policies attract employers. On the other hand, some consequences are unintended and negative. For example, taxes on improvements discourage inner-city property owners from upgrading their property, and taxes on property at the urban fringe where property values are rapidly increasing encourage speculators to convert farmland to housing development. California's Proposition 13 is a poster child for the consequences of ignoring the effects of tax policy on the economy, as it has penalized new arrivals to the state, discouraged long-term owners from selling their property unless they plan to move out of state, and discouraged investment in new construction.[6] (See Chapter 3 for more on the fallout from Proposition 13.)

Tax reform requires careful assessment of the short- and long-term consequences for the economy. Every tax has economic consequences, some more obvious than others. The public manager's task is to ensure that those consequences are understood and that, where possible, negative consequences are mitigated in order to strengthen, rather than weaken, the community's economy.

Tax neutrality in theory

From a public finance perspective, taxes introduce inefficiencies into a perfectly competitive market. Welfare economics holds that consumer satisfaction is maximized when markets are left to operate without outside interference. They produce just enough goods and services to meet consumer demand, and they allocate those goods and services to those who value them the most. This is the familiar Pareto Optimum.[7] Any interference in this ideal state, from taxation or regulation, diminishes this optimality and results in economic losses—fewer goods and services available at less than optimum prices. Consumer welfare is less than optimal.

But the ideal state does not exist and doubtless never will. Consumer goods and services produced through competitive markets represent only some of the products that communities and societies need. For example, a whole range of **public goods and services,** from national security to land use controls, are demanded by citizens. Because these services lack marketplace properties (as they are nondivisible and nonexcludable), they must be produced through nonmarket mechanisms. Most Western democracies have chosen a representative government with majority rule to produce and allocate such goods and services.

Public goods make up only a portion of the services and products governments produce. For varying reasons, mostly because of the lack of a profit incentive, local governments also provide an array of what are called **private goods and services,** such as utilities, recreation, parks, public transit, and education. Sometimes a government provides services, such as libraries, that otherwise could be provided by the private sector, but their social and cultural benefits to the community make profiting from their sale inappropriate. Most citizens regard such services as **merit goods**—that is, goods that merit subsidization by the community. The mix of public, private, and merit goods varies widely among cities, counties, and states—each the product of an admixture of history, local preferences, and necessity.

But the production of these nonmarket goods and services requires that governments, through some collective decision process, collect the resources needed for their production. In theory, taxes provide governments with the funding needed for public and merit goods, whereas service charges and fees more typically finance private services and goods produced by government. Of course, such a tidy distribution of funding is not the case in reality.

While all taxes diminish the market's efficiency—their very presence affects the market and is therefore not neutral—some taxes create more inefficiencies than others. The challenge is to design a tax structure in which unintended interference is minimized (keeping in mind that some changes caused by tax policies, such as increased business investment from a **tax abatement,** are intended).

One final observation. Not only does the choice of the type of tax (the tax base) affect markets, but so do the tax rates themselves. Arthur Laffer, widely regarded as the father of supply-side economics, conjectured that as tax rates increase, tax yields increase at a decreasing rate and at some point begin to decrease[8] (see Figure 2–2). The implication of the Laffer curve, or what is now called the "revenue hill," is that for governments with tax rates beyond the peak, any reduction in rates results in *increased* yields, in which case tax reductions will pay for themselves.

One study of the revenue hills for four major cities found that Houston, New York City, and Philadelphia were at or just beyond the peak of the hill and that reductions, especially in the property tax rates for Houston and New York City, would result in increased revenues. Only in Minneapolis was the property tax rate below the peak of the revenue hill.[9]

Figure 2–2
The Laffer curve.

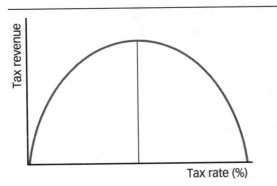

Courtesy of Investopedia, Inc. ©2003. Available at www.investopedia.com

Tax neutrality in practice

The pragmatic question then arises: how can the adverse market effects of taxes be identified and then minimized? Four principles for strengthening the local economy may provide useful guidance to public managers as they grapple with difficult tradeoffs:

1. The broader the base and the flatter the tax rate, the fewer distortions a tax will introduce into the local economy.

2. Given their quasi-market character, benefits-based taxes and charges interfere the least in the economy.

3. Neutrality is more adversely affected by tax rate differentials than by the absolute level of the tax rate.

4. Particular care is required in the design of local business taxes.

The broad, flat expanse of neutrality One of the axioms of tax policy holds that broad-based taxes are more neutral than narrow-based taxes, and that a flat rate is more neutral than a progressive or differential rate. Obviously, this rule runs counter to the equity-maximizing principles of ability to pay and progressive rate structures. Where neutrality is the goal, however, communities are best served by taxes that fall on all income, consumption, or wealth.

Of course, exemptions and exclusions are usually offered—some for administrative reasons, others for social and political reasons. Whenever such tax expenditures are introduced, the subsidized activity will be encouraged, shifting economic activity toward the favored sector or activity. Thus, seniors whose property assessments are frozen will stay in their larger homes; nonprofits that are exempted from local property taxes will gravitate toward more expensive property that otherwise would be used for taxable purposes. Market participants gravitate to locations where their costs are minimized, assuming that quality remains constant.

The property tax that pays for education in most states poses an interesting case in point. Prior to 1993, Michigan's school districts set their own tax rates, creating a patchwork of varying tax rates and revenue yields.[10] In the summer of 1993, in response to the disparities in funding levels between property-rich and property-poor school districts, the Michigan legislature abolished the local school tax and in its place instituted a two-tiered statewide rate of 6 mills on primary homes and 24 mills on all other property, including second homes and businesses. The two-tiered structure significantly reduces rate differentials and makes school property tax rates a non-issue in business location decisions. This reform enhances the neutrality of the property tax. (The downside to Michigan's approach is the local school districts' loss of autonomy, a price many would regard as not worth the gain of neutrality.) Variations of the Michigan approach will likely emerge in other states.

Complicating an understanding of how a tax proposal affects the market is **tax incidence.** Who ultimately bears the burden of a tax? While the law establishes tax liability—owners of record in the case of the property tax, buyers (or sometimes vendors) in the case of the sales tax, wage earners in the case of the personal income tax—the economic burden can be shifted either forward to consumers in the form of higher prices or backward to owners in the form of lower profits. How a tax burden is shifted depends on (1) whether the tax falls at an intermediary point in the transaction process and (2) whether market conditions allow shifting forward or backward.

Sin taxes, such as taxes on tobacco and alcohol products, are largely shifted forward to the final consumer because demand remains fairly price inelastic, particularly among long-term consumers. By contrast, when the state of Texas tripled the fee for vanity license plates, thinking that the revenue yield would increase commensurately, demand for the license plates plummeted and increased yields never materialized. A substitute product was available—non-personalized plates—and consumers showed their price sensitivity by shifting to the lower-priced alternative.

The tax on business property poses a more complex situation. While the owner bears **legal liability** for the tax, the owner can shift the burden forward in the form of higher rents if the market allows it. But in the case of rental property, if comparable housing is available at a lower price in a nearby jurisdiction, renters will move there, so the landlord must either lower rents or risk losing tenants. If the landlord cannot shift the cost of the tax forward, the only other direction is backward as lower profits. But a lower profit, or even loss, on the rental property means that it is a less valuable business enterprise; that is, it has lost value. Consequently, changes in the property tax are **capitalized** into values: the cost of a tax increase is borne as a reduction in property value and vice versa for a tax reduction. In competitive markets, changes in the property tax result in inverse changes to values: a tax increase results in property values declining by a commensurate amount, and a tax decrease results in property values rising. One of the consequences of Californians' ratification of Proposition 13 was a reduction in the cost of owning property in California and thus an immediate increase in the value of property there, resulting in an immediate windfall to all property owners who saw the value of their homes and businesses increase.

Still the best for the money: Benefits-based levies Because they function like prices in the marketplace, benefits-based levies are as valuable a tool for achieving neutrality as they are for achieving equity. In addition, tying expenditures to service charges in particular, or even to benefits-based taxes, reduces the pressure on government to expand public services beyond the real demand for them.

When it comes to tax rates, keep an eye on the Joneses Interjurisdictional differences in tax rates, particularly highly visible rates like those of the property tax, are factors in the location decisions of industries and, to a lesser extent, of commercial and residential owners. Small rate differences, when compared in present value terms, can have significant cumulative effects on the corporate bottom line. As implied by the Tiebout hypothesis, interlocal tax competition imposes a quasi-market discipline on local budgets and, if ignored, can result in the erosion of a community's tax base. Thus, city and county leaders must constantly scrutinize their rates to ensure that they are competitive. In some cases, higher tax rates may be a strategy, intentional or otherwise, to bar commercial and particularly industrial development and preserve the "residential" environment of a town. Every business has a critical point at which differences in tax rates among local governments in a metropolitan area become significant to its location decision. However, sensitivity to those differences increases in areas with higher tax rates. That is, in metropolitan areas characterized by high property tax rates, small differences in rates at the municipal level can have significant implications for where businesses choose to locate.

Consumption and income-based taxes pose special challenges for local governments because of the potential for **border-city** and **border-county effects.** For example, two cities sharing a border or within commuting distance will experience such effects if one has a significantly lower sales tax rate than the other. Retail stores will prefer to locate in the lower tax jurisdiction, thereby drawing consumers from neighboring communities to shop in their city. Similar effects occur with local income and, to a lesser extent, property taxes. The greater the disparity in tax rates, the more sensitive workers and consumers become to the effects of the tax. Towns around Tucson, Arizona, advertise on billboards their lower sales tax rates for shoppers. In its final report, the Philadelphia Tax Reform Commission estimated that 172,889 jobs left the city between 1971 and 2001 because of increases in the wage tax rate during that period relative to the rates levied by surrounding municipalities.[11]

Some states have designed local enabling legislation that precludes border-city effects. As discussed more fully in succeeding chapters, North Carolina has taken a particularly laudable approach toward the local sales tax, as has Maryland in the case of the local income tax. Counties levy a uniform sales tax in North Carolina and share the revenue with municipalities based on either their pro rata share of the county's population or property value. Similarly, counties in Maryland levy a personal income tax, collected by the state, with limited discretion in the range of local rates that may be levied. By placing limits on local discretion over taxes, these states have eliminated the inefficiencies of border-city effects without compromising local autonomy.

With the growing popularity of Internet sales, a new set of tax issues has arisen. In 1998, Congress imposed a moratorium on local and state taxes both on the sales of products over the Internet and on fees subscribers pay for various Internet services. In 2004, that moratorium was renewed by Congress through 2007, although the act allows the seventeen states that already collect sales taxes on Internet access to continue doing so. The loss in state and local sales tax revenue from the moratorium on emerging Internet services is growing rapidly and is expected to reach $45 billion by 2006. In terms of tax neutrality, the moratorium created the e-commerce equivalent of a border-city effect by making online purchases tax exempt but on-site purchases of the same products taxable. If such disparities persist, a disproportionate share of the retail market will shift to the Internet and further undermine the sales tax bases of state and local governments.

For two special types of communities, tax competition is less of an issue. The first type is communities with established agglomeration economies. These communities have a competitive niche, which allows them to attract additional economic activity and with it a lower tax rate to sustain the same level of public services.

The second type is communities that are able to shift taxes to nonresidents through a practice called tax exportation. Some taxes are specifically intended to maximize this practice by shifting the tax burden either to nonresident consumers as higher prices, as in the case of hotel/motel taxes, or to nonresident owners as lower profits, as in the case of taxes on stock transactions; however, more of the local tax burden is borne externally than is commonly realized. For example, the Texas state comptroller estimated that 15 percent of that state's general sales tax, 27 percent of the property tax on industries, and 54 percent of the property tax on oil and natural gas is exported to nonresident consumers or producers.[12] Some communities have extraordinary opportunities for tax exportation either as a result of natural advantages, as in the case of Maui County, Hawaii, or through agglomeration economies, as in the case of Branson, Missouri. No rules, in theory or in law, set the appropriate amount of tax exportation.

When it comes to local taxes on business, go with the Joneses   Businesses represent tempting targets for revenue-pressed governments, particularly those experiencing a fiscal crisis or crush (see Chapter 1). Since businesses are able to pass their tax liability on to consumers (forward shifting) or investors (backward shifting), it becomes politically expedient for these governments to shift more of the tax burden on to businesses. And since businesses don't vote, they represent to the imprudent political leader the perfect candidates for discriminatory tax treatment. But businesses do "vote"—by moving their investment to more favorable tax jurisdictions. Unless a community has unique resources—Alaskan oil, Colorado ski slopes, Florida beaches, for example—virtually all business investment is mobile, and in an era when information is the coin of the realm, that mobility has only increased.

Where businesses are concerned, local governments should avoid imposing two types of taxes: corporate income taxes and gross receipts taxes on business sales. As discussed in Chapter 7, corporate income taxes introduce serious equity and neutrality problems. Only a few cities still attempt to collect a true corporate income tax, and then on declining tax bases. Gross receipts taxes are more prevalent because of their relative ease of collection. Unfortunately, they can have a **tax pyramiding** effect, which occurs when a production process has multiple stages (raw materials are converted to intermediary goods, which in turn become finished goods that are sold to wholesalers and then, finally, to retailers). The problem occurs because, unlike the general sales tax, the gross receipts tax is applied at each stage of the production process. The portion of the tax that is shifted forward creates a cascading (or pyramiding) effect, with taxes falling on top of taxes. To avoid such tax effects and gain a competitive advantage in the market, businesses have an incentive to vertically integrate the production process, which may not be the most efficient means of operation. Because of these effects, gross receipts taxes have nonneutral consequences and so compromise the efficiency of business production.

For business taxation, the following guidelines should be considered:

- Any tax on business should be widely used in that state or region. If a city or county is the only one to impose a particular tax on business, the tax almost certainly will have a detrimental effect on that community's long-term economic growth.

- Taxes on the less mobile components of production—land, buildings, and equipment—have the least detrimental effect on markets. Statewide taxation of that property, while undermining local autonomy, greatly enhances tax neutrality through the imposition of a uniform tax rate. As an alternative, regional tax base–sharing arrangements, such as in Minneapolis/St. Paul and more recently in Racine County, Wisconsin, offer appealing approaches to reducing interlocal tax competition and enhancing regional tax neutrality.[13]

- Statewide sales taxes on business purchases will be less detrimental to local economies than if local governments define the tax base.

- Although no examples exist, business taxation seems a prime candidate for greater cooperation between a state government and its cities and counties. As discussed in Chapter 3, business investment benefits more than just the jurisdiction in which the new development occurs. The state-local partnership required to attract and retain business investment could also design more equitable and neutral tax policies.

Tax neutrality in action: The good, the bad, and the still ugly

This chapter has thus far considered two key components to tax policy: equity and neutrality. Much to the frustration of tax analysts and legislators, these two compo-

---

Tips for would-be tax reformers

Initiatives to reform the local tax structure always begin with the highest aspirations and noblest intentions but frequently end in disappointment. As discussions for tax reform progress, participants come to realize the complex tradeoffs that must be made, and too often they conclude that the political costs are not worth the economic gains. The following tips, while lowering aspirations, may elevate results:

The more heavily a tax is used, the more apparent its economic and political defects become. Increasing rates on existing taxes without correcting the deficiencies of the existing tax structure exacerbates hidden flaws.

Because of their visibility, higher tax rates on a relatively narrower tax base have a more detrimental effect on economic growth than more moderate rates on a broader tax base. Tax reformers should look first to broadening the existing tax base before raising tax rates.

An axiom of public finance is "an old tax is a good tax" because the marketplace has adjusted to accommodate the tax. In general, improving the equity and neutrality of existing taxes is preferable to introducing a new tax unless the inequities and inefficiencies of the existing taxes are greater than those of a proposed new tax.

Tax reforms that occur incrementally over time generally have a better chance of succeeding politically than sweeping tax reforms introduced over a short period.

One of the easiest reforms is the elimination of nuisance taxes that have low revenue yields and high administrative and/or compliance costs. Taxes on entertainment and per capita or occupation privilege taxes have relatively low revenue yields and high administrative costs, and they impose unfair burdens, especially on lower-income households.

Excise taxes, especially "sin" taxes and those borne by nonresidents, usually arouse the least political opposition.

Because tax reform almost always comes with considerable political costs to leaders, successful tax reforms require strong political support from elected officials who have an abundance of credibility with voters. The key is to clearly and convincingly articulate the benefits from the reforms, whether through improved public services on the expenditure side or reduced inequities and inefficiencies on the revenue side.

Low tax rates do not guarantee economic growth, as a number of states are discovering. On the other hand, nonneutral tax policies do guarantee that a state or local government's economy will never grow to its fullest potential. For the tax reformer the lesson is this: In the long term, the greatest gains toward economic prosperity come from increasing tax neutrality rather than from reducing tax rates, all other things being equal.

A well-designed tax structure can make tax incentives unnecessary. An equitable tax structure that minimizes adverse economic effects, such as border-city/county effects, is a government's most effective tool for creating a favorable business environment.

nents often exist in tension with one another. Gains in equity come at the expense of reduced neutrality, and vice versa. And both often create additional administrative costs and compliance complexity for taxpayers. For example, considering family size or inordinate casualty losses may promote horizontal equity, but it may also reduce neutrality by narrowing the tax base, and it adds significantly to compliance costs by requiring more documentation. Flat rate, broad-based taxes are regressive. Progressive income taxes discourage work and penalize investment in income-producing ventures, which adversely affects economic well-being. What should local managers do?

No perfect solution

- First, there is no perfect tax source. Each suffers from its own set of deficiencies, some more than others.

Locally, neutrality rules

- Second, at the local level, primary consideration must be given to tax neutrality—that is, to tax and revenue policies that minimize market distortions and maximize economic growth. Failure to give neutrality priority condemns a community to lackluster growth or even decline, in which case any efforts to promote fairness are doomed as well.

Avoid special tax favors

- Third, special tax favors that are not part of a comprehensive economic development plan, while gaining political favors in the short term, increase inequities and lessen neutrality—a double negative. A written, formally adopted plan for promoting economic growth can prove particularly helpful in managing persistent demands for tax favors.

Horizontal equity trumps vertical equity

- Fourth, policies that promote horizontal equity merit priority over those that promote vertical equity at the local level. Redistribution of income is part of a civilized society, but because of the openness of state and particularly local economies, those efforts result in economic decline as production capabilities shift to more favorable tax environments.

Benefits-based levies!

- Finally, benefits-based levies offer the best option for promoting horizontal equity and tax neutrality. They reduce overconsumption of an otherwise "free" good or service by providing consumers and public managers with an awareness of the true cost of its production.

Choices that facilitate effective administration

+ service delivery by – overhead costs in tax admin.

The new reality in local public finance dictates that jurisdictions channel more funds into service delivery by minimizing overhead costs in tax administration. The third pillar of sound economic policy considers both the government's cost to administer taxes and the taxpayers' cost to comply with them.

Figure 2–3 depicts the phases that governments typically go through when collecting taxes and service charges. The specific issues involved in collecting each type of revenue are discussed more extensively in succeeding chapters. The following sections summarize the general principles that guide revenue administration.

Notification

Notification of tax liability comes either indirectly through self-reporting by taxpayers, as in the case of most state and federal income taxes, or directly as an invoice from the governing jurisdiction, as in the case of property taxes and utility service charges. Notification includes a due date (or dates if payments may be split over several periods) and the **penalty and interest** for late payments. Late payment of tax liability always involves a penalty in addition to interest for the time lapsed since it was due. Failure to receive notification of a tax liability does not absolve the taxpayer of liability. Governments operate on the assumption that its citizens are responsible for knowing their obligations and fulfilling those obligations faithfully.

Figure 2–3
The flow of information in the tax administration process.

notification ⟶ collection ⟶ enforcement

Even before notification can be made, legal liability for the tax or charge must be established. For example, in the case of a property that was sold during the year, is the current owner or the previous owner liable for the tax? This issue becomes particularly problematic with more mobile property such as vehicles and manufactured housing. Utility charges for service to rental properties pose their own set of challenges. Local governments typically require a larger **security deposit** for service to such properties until the user establishes a record of timely payments.

Establishing legal liability also poses challenges where **tax overlapping** exists—that is, where multiple jurisdictions tax the same property, consumption spending, or household income. If the overlapping governments use somewhat different tax bases, taxpayers can easily become confused as to their liability.

Political boundaries add to the complexity of tax liability. For example, some properties straddle two or more taxing jurisdictions. **Apportionment** becomes an issue in the case of an income tax on a wage earner who works in one state (or county) but lives in another. Taxes on business activity (e.g., locally levied sales and excise taxes), especially for businesses with a **taxable nexus,** or connection, in multiple jurisdictions and in jurisdictions where income is the base, pose significant apportionment issues, especially when they are allocated on the basis of the consumer's point of residence and not the more typical **point of sale.**

The final general issue in notification of liability involves the attachment of a **tax lien.** State laws typically impose a blanket lien on fixed assets, usually real property, as collateral for pending tax liability. Such a lien is usually automatic, which is to say that it affixes to each property title as of a particular date and does not require specific action by the taxing jurisdiction. The lien remains attached until the liability is paid in full. Usually the asset cannot be sold with an outstanding lien attached to the title. In some cases, such as with special assessments (see Chapter 9), governments must formally file documentation affixing a lien for an obligation. As discussed below, a lien becomes particularly useful when taxes or charges for services become delinquent and payment is not likely to be forthcoming.

Collection

The process of levying taxes or service charges creates **accounts or taxes receivable** for the local government. The goal is to collect all receivables by their due date. Unfortunately, as in business, governments encounter bad accounts, some that result from bankruptcy and others from evasion. Although the collection rate can vary with the business cycle, governments should normally achieve rates of at least 95 percent of the current liability for each revenue source. Lower rates risk undermining taxpayer confidence in the tax system and, more generally, in the management capabilities of that jurisdiction.

The cost of administering a tax or any revenue source should never exceed 5 percent of the revenue collected. A key to reducing collection costs is to share notification, collection, and enforcement of tax liabilities with overlapping governments: centralized tax collection and enforcement programs provide economies of scale. For example, state governments should collect local sales and income taxes in tandem with state taxes, funneling local taxes back to the local government. (The exception is the truly rare case in which the state does not collect the tax on its own, such as Alaska, where a local but not a state sales tax is levied.) Cooperative arrangements for revenue administration almost always result in lower unit costs and more uniform enforcement of the law.

[handwritten margin notes:]

Dairy Queen in Rochelle

≥ 95% Collection rate!

≤ 5% Administration rate.

From a local government's perspective, the most obvious problem with state administration is the perceived loss of political autonomy, although local autonomy rests on powers far more fundamental than tax collection. In fact, the reduced costs of centralized revenue administration greatly outweigh any political costs from perceived reductions in local autonomy. Centralized administration also lowers taxpayers' compliance costs by making it possible to complete only one tax return for two or more taxing jurisdictions.

From a state perspective, the primary concern with centralized administration is whether taxpayers differentiate state from local tax liability. If they do not, then the state tax burden appears much greater, placing state government in an undesirable political position. Whether such blurring of liability occurs depends on the clarity with which the tax return differentiates between state and local liability. Several states have successfully overcome potential problems by designing exemplary tax returns. Maryland's personal income tax return is probably the best example (see Figure 7–3).

An alternative is **outsourcing** collection and/or enforcement. For example, Pennsylvania local governments rely on third-party firms to collect and enforce payment of the earned income tax levied by municipalities and school districts. In Texas, local governments generally contract with law firms that specialize in collecting delinquent property taxes. As in all types of outsourcing, there is the danger that contractors will focus on easier accounts—a practice that is often referred to as "creaming"—unless the contract is structured to prevent this from occurring.

Finally, as briefly discussed in the previous chapter, each revenue source responds differently to the business cycle, resulting in income elasticities that can vary significantly over time. Tax yields that increase at rates greater than growth in the economy, usually measured as changes in personal income, have income elasticities greater than 1.0, and yields that do not keep pace with economic growth have income elasticities of less than 1.0. Figure 2–4 shows the income elasticities of the property tax and general sales tax over time for the city of Forth Worth, Texas.

Figure 2–4

Relative income elasticities of the property and sales taxes for Fort Worth, Texas.

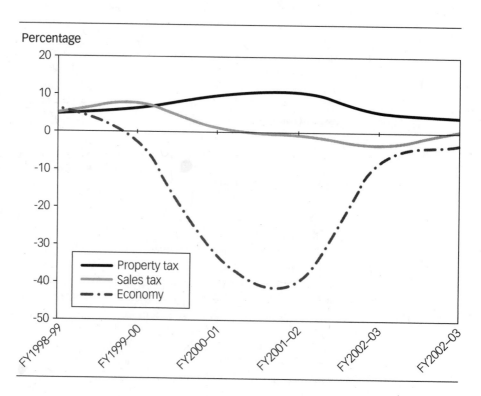

An income-elastic revenue source performs well during upswings in the economy but leaves governments short of revenue in the downswings. As noted in Chapter 1, a diversified tax base and multiple tax sources can help offset these cycles in tax collections, producing a more stable stream of income for budget purposes.

Enforcement

The integrity of a tax system depends ultimately on its enforcement. A government's vigilance in auditing and collecting delinquent receivables conveys its commitment to fairness and the uniform application of the law, whereas cutting corners on revenue enforcement undermines the community's confidence in the management capabilities of its leaders. As with collections, enforcement offers some opportunities for coordination with overlapping jurisdictions, thereby reducing administrative costs to all participating governments and compliance costs to taxpayers.

Tax liens represent powerful enforcement tools, enabling local governments to foreclose on delinquent taxpayers. State laws specify the procedures, but they typically require due notification to the taxpayer (assuming his or her whereabouts are known) of the delinquent tax liability. If the taxpayer fails to settle the claim within a reasonable period, the taxing jurisdiction petitions a court to issue an order giving the jurisdiction title to the property on which the lien is attached. If the order is granted, the jurisdiction then sells the property for the outstanding taxes. In recent years, a number of states have adopted provisions giving the previous property owner a grace period following foreclosure in which he or she can reclaim the property. Some states also grant special protection to homesteads (i.e., primary residences), a practice rooted in the principles of frontier justice.

One controversial enforcement measure is the widespread practice among local governments of offering **amnesty** to delinquent taxpayers and, more commonly, for traffic fines. (Amnesties have never been widely used by states or the federal government.) Amnesties usually proliferate during tight budget periods when local governments are looking for additional revenue at little political cost. Often the penalty portion of the delinquent charge is reduced or eliminated as a reward for payment during the amnesty period. Amnesties are always accompanied by threats to redouble enforcement after the amnesty period. If the threat is credible, such strategies do produce an infusion of delinquent payments. Scofflaws, of course, weigh the probability of being caught against the cost of paying the delinquent tax or fee. Investment in a professional, dedicated team of enforcement officers obviates the need for amnesty programs and minimizes the incentives for the gamesmanship they encourage.

Putting it all together: Designing a balanced revenue system

Local government managers are finding formal revenue policies valuable as guides both for themselves and for local governing boards. Maureen Godsey has identified some of the benefits from such statements:[14]

1. By making explicit the important assumptions underlying revenue practices, a policy statement helps management and members of council achieve congruent expectations about how the government finances its operations. If annual tax increases are not to exceed 5 percent, the statement should make that explicit.

2. A revenue policy provides continuity in the procedures used to fund services. Management and members of the governing board may move

on to other positions, but the policy remains to familiarize incoming officials with the practices deemed to be in the public interest by previous administrations.

3.   A policy statement saves time for executives and legislators. For example, once agreement is reached on the fraction of costs to be recovered in service charges for park and recreation services, setting a fee for new services becomes relatively simple. A policy statement also brings a second, related benefit: those seeking an exception to the policy bear the burden of demonstrating why such an exception should be granted. A general policy statement on fees also makes it politically easier to adjust individual fees annually to bring them into compliance with the policy.

Summary

equitable

neutral

effective

The three pillars of tax policy—fairness, neutrality, and effective administrative—provided the framework for the discussion in this chapter. In the quest for good tax policy, fairness ranks high with taxpayers and ratepayers. Unless taxes and user charges are *perceived* as imposing a fair burden, citizens' dissatisfaction with local government will persist. Fairness in tax policy is most readily achieved through (1) using benefits-based levies to a greater extent; (2) minimizing the use of tax favors (such as freezing liability, exempting part of a tax base, or imposing preferential tax rates); (3) easing the burden on the poorest and not punishing the wealthiest; and (4) recognizing that perceptions of fairness vary by community, and that even within a community, those perceptions change over time as the age and social composition of the community changes.

Issues of tax neutrality bring to the fore a discussion of the policy choices that strengthen the local economy. Failure to consider these choices or their adverse effects on an economy inevitably leads to economic stagnation and even decline. Every tax has economic consequences, some more disruptive than others. The public manager's task is to make sure that those consequences are understood and, if at all possible, mitigated through careful design of the policy. Generally, neutrality is enhanced through (1) expanding the tax base and relying on a flat (single) rate of taxation; (2) using benefits-based levies where possible; (3) minimizing border-city/county effects by avoiding interjurisdictional rate differentials, particularly for local sales and income taxes; and (4) giving particular care to the design of local business taxes. A well-designed revenue structure is a local government's most effective business recruitment and retention tool. No amount of tax favors for new business investment can compensate for tax policies that interfere excessively in the local market.

The third pillar of sound public finance is administratively effective policies—that is, policies that limit the cost of administration (notification, collection, and enforcement) to no more than 5 percent of the revenue yield and minimize costs for taxpayers to comply with the law. Local governments, in particular, can benefit from the piggybacking of tax collection and enforcement. Administration of revenues must ensure near universal compliance.

1 In fact, Californians, when they ratified Proposition 13 in 1978, introduced a new measure of comparability. Under the amendment's bizarre rules for property taxation, horizontal equity exists only for homes purchased in the same year and for the same price. Otherwise, two houses standing side by side with equal market value may have markedly different tax liabilities, especially if one house was purchased before 1975, the base year for establishing value under Proposition 13, and the other was purchased at the peak of the California housing boom in the 1990s. The tax liability for the more recent buyer could be many times greater.

2 Gilbert E. Metcalf, "The Lifetime Incidence of State and Local Taxes: Measuring Changes during the 1980s," in *Tax Progressivity and Income Inequality,* ed. Joel Slemrod (Cambridge, U.K., and New York: Cambridge University Press, 1994).

3 Charles M. Tiebout, "A Pure Theory of Local Expenditures," *Journal of Political Economy* 64 (October 1956): 416–424.

4 *Final Report,* Philadelphia Tax Reform Commission, November 15, 2003. Available at www. philadelphiataxreform.org. One widespread practice among older cities is the ad hoc practice of fractional assessments (discussed in Chapter 4)—the more favorable valuation of residential property relative to commercial and industrial property, thereby shifting the tax burden to the latter types of property.

5 The four types of communities used in Figure 2–1 were first proposed by Oliver P. Williams. He did not use them in the context they are used here—namely, to demonstrate the types of linkages between revenue structure and political environment—although his typology has been adapted for this purpose. See Oliver P. Williams, "A Typology for Comparative Local Government," *Midwest Journal of Political Science* 5 (May 1961): 150–164.

6 Lenny Goldberg and David Kersten, "Huge Disparities Found in California Commercial Property Taxes," *State Tax Notes* 31 (May 10, 2004): 437–457; Gregory D. Saxton, Christopher W. Hoene, and Steven P. Erie, "Fiscal Constraints and the Loss of Home Rule: The Long-Term Impacts of California's Post–Proposition 13 Fiscal Regime," *American Review of Public Administration* 32 (December 2002): 423–454; Carol Douglas, "Proposition 13—25 Years Later," *State Tax Notes* 30 (October 20, 2003): 222–226.

7 Ronald C. Fisher, *State and Local Public Finance,* 2nd ed. (Chicago: Richard D. Irwin Co., 1996), 35–38.

8 Victor A. Canto, Douglas H. Joines, and Arthur B. Laffer, eds. *Foundations of Supply-Side Economics—Theory and Evidence* (New York: Academic Press, 1982).

9 Andrew F. Haughwout et al., "Local Revenue Hills: Evidence from Four U.S. Cities," National Bureau of Economic Research (NBER) Working Paper 9686 (Cambridge, Mass.: NBER, May 2003). Available at www.nber.org/papers/w9686.

10 Paul D. Ballew, Richard H. Mattoon, and William A. Testa, "School Reform and Tax Reform: A Successful Marriage?" *Government Finance Review* 10 (August 1994): 32–35.

11 *Final Report,* Philadelphia Tax Reform Commission, 33.

12 Carole Keeton Strayhorn, *Tax Exemptions and Tax Incidence* (Austin: Texas Comptroller of Public Accounts, January 2003), 47. Available at www.cpa.state.tx.us./taxinfo/incidence03.

13 James M. Fiacco and Christine A. Cramer, "A New Model for Fiscal Regionalism: Greater Racine's Plan for Overcoming Fiscal Disparity," *Government Finance Review* 20 (February 2004): 24–29; for the Twin Cities Metropolitan Area Fiscal Disparity Program, see www.house.leg. state.mn.us/hrd/pubs/fiscaldis.pdf.

14 W. Maureen Godsey, "Establishing Financial Policies: What, Why, and How," in *Practical Financial Management: New Techniques for Local Government,* ed. John Matzer Jr. (Washington, D.C.: International City Management Association, 1984), 27–33.

3 Strategic revenue choices: Using tax policies for economic and social purposes

Taxes and economic development: Finding the balance

The inefficiencies of local tax incentives
Why do local governments get involved in economic development?

Factors affecting business location decisions

Primary determinants
Property taxes
Local income and sales taxes

Tax relief for business investment

Types of tax incentives offered by local governments
Tax abatements
Tax exemptions
Tax increment financing

Tax incentives for professional sports and the arts

Why government financing?
Civic symbolism
Guidelines for using tax incentives
Questions to ask about economic development proposals

Tax relief for citizens

Broad tax relief measures
Targeted tax relief measures
Do tax limitations work?

Revenues and disaster management

Summary

Appendix: Policy statement for tax abatement—Plano, Texas

Now the Israelites had been saying, "Do you see how this man keeps coming out? He comes out to defy Israel. The king will give great wealth to the man who kills him. He will also give him his daughter in marriage and will exempt his father's family from taxes in Israel."

—I Samuel 17:25

Strategic revenue choices: Using tax policies for economic and social purposes

Not only do local revenue policies provide the resources to fund local government services, but they have become key elements in two politically powerful but potentially antithetical trends: encouraging business investment and providing tax relief for citizens. The former finds expression in the growing array of economic development incentives offered by state and local governments. The latter is seen in such measures as tax limitations, beginning with Proposition 13 in California in 1978, and, more recently, as targeted relief to select groups of citizens, particularly senior citizens.

This chapter examines these powerful influences on local revenue structures and their effect on the economic landscape. It begins by examining the role of local taxes and tax incentives in economic development. These measures for promoting investment, particularly tax incentives, are only one type of tool in a local government's increasing array of measures that includes industrial development bonds, one-stop service centers, subsidized loans, preemployment training, publicly financed infrastructure, and public financing to renovate existing facilities. The following discussion is limited to the relationship between local tax policy and economic development, and specifically to these issues:

1. What criteria do businesses use when making location decisions?

2. What effect does a local government's tax burden have on the location decisions of businesses?

3. What effect do locally financed tax incentives, such as tax abatements and tax increment financing, have on new business investment decisions?

4. How effective are targeted incentives—for example, for tourism development and sports stadiums?

The chapter then addresses the effects of tax limitations on local economies. Do tax limits reduce spending? Do they have an adverse effect on economic growth and social equity? The chapter concludes with a discussion of the special circumstances created by natural disasters and the threat of attack by terrorists.

Taxes and economic development: Finding the balance

Pursuing an aggressive economic growth policy makes good political sense. A successful economic development initiative communicates to industries making location decisions that the business environment is a favorable one. If one industry is attracted to a community, other related industries are likely to follow. Economic development initiatives also express to voters that public officials are concerned about job opportunities and are making efforts to expand them.

However, a more fundamental objective underlies the effort to attract business investment: to improve the local government's revenue condition by expanding its tax base. Investment in plant facilities and equipment expands the property tax base and creates new employment opportunities. New jobs bring more workers—or at least help to retain the existing workforce—and that further expands the local tax base. If the municipality or county has access to an income tax or a sales tax, it will reap even greater revenue returns from economic development as a result of the increased income and consumption.

Three factors have escalated competition among states, cities, and counties for new business: the increased mobility of business; stagnant growth, particularly in the economy's manufacturing sector; and the federal government's decision to reduce grants and shift more service responsibility to the subnational levels.

The inefficiencies of local tax incentives

From a political perspective, providing tax breaks to businesses is a win-win proposition. Businesses reduce their operating costs, and the local community expands employment opportunities for its citizens, augments its tax base, and promotes its reputation for having a favorable business climate.

However, from an economic perspective, the use of tax abatements, **tax credits,** and tax increment financing by local governments is inefficient for two reasons: (1) it represents government interference in the marketplace, and (2) the benefits from new job opportunities that inevitably spill over into surrounding or overlapping governments are paid for by taxpayers only in the jurisdiction providing the tax incentives.

Market interference   A locally financed tax abatement lowers the cost of production for qualifying firms, which makes the jurisdiction more cost competitive with another city or county. However, even in the absence of a government-provided incentive, a business will choose the location for new investment that minimizes its production costs. Energy-intensive firms search for locations with lower energy costs; labor-intensive firms seek out locations with low labor costs; and technology-dependent firms locate in areas with an ample supply of technologists. The point is that for any one firm, not all locations are equally desirable alternatives. Every jurisdiction has a unique set of attributes that makes it more attractive to some industries than to others. Economic incentives interfere in the decision-making process by enhancing a community's locational advantages beyond what would have been the case in the absence of such incentives. By interfering in the market process for choosing a location, economic incentives lure business investment to less than optimal locations. Ideally, a local government should limit its economic development efforts to attracting those firms whose operating costs would have already benefited by locating within its borders, but such efforts have gone well beyond these limited bounds.

Spillover benefits   People and money move unhindered across state and local borders. If a city uses a tax-incentive package to attract a new business, the cost of those incentives is borne by local taxpayers, but the benefits may accrue to a much broader area. For example, job creation financed by a city creates **spillover benefits** for job seekers from surrounding areas, too. No economic development initiative has ever successfully included a residency requirement for job beneficiaries.

Revenue windfalls that can accrue to overlapping governments are another type of spillover benefit. For example, state and federal governments reap increased income tax revenue from a firm's increased profitability as a result of locally financed tax relief. State sales tax revenue also increases as businesses and households increase their consumption. In other words, a locally financed tax incentive may represent a subsidy to overlapping governments at the expense of taxpayers in the originating jurisdiction.

Why do local governments get involved in economic development?

Given the inherent inefficiencies of locally financed incentives for economic growth, why do so many jurisdictions use them? As noted in Chapter 1, local government managers must formulate decisions and make policy recommendations in the context of *public perceptions* that business "pays its way" and that a **tax incentive** will more than "pay for itself" in the long term as new jobs and additional business investment follow.

Research supports these perceptions. In a study of midwestern states, William Oakland and William Testa found that, on average, businesses pay 2.4 times in taxes what they receive back in tax-supported services. The minimum ratio in their sample was 1.9, meaning that in the worst case, businesses pay almost $2 in taxes for every $1 in tax-supported benefits they receive.[1] Tax incentives provide local governments with a mechanism for better aligning the tax burden incurred by businesses with the public benefits they receive.

A second reason for the popularity of programs promoting growth is the need to signal a hospitable business environment. Tax incentives are a highly visible indication of the government's effort to keep existing jobs and attract new ones.

A related reason is that businesses may pressure local leaders to offer incentives, playing one local government against another.[2] Municipalities in economic decline are especially vulnerable to such pressure: they can afford neither the tax incentives nor the political consequences of refusing to offer them.[3]

The issue for city and county administrators and legislators has become not *whether* to influence the location decisions of businesses but rather *how* to create a favorable business environment. Interlocal competition for business investment and the mobility of business capital have made tax incentives a standard tool in the local economic development toolbox.

Defining a favorable business environment raises two fundamental questions: (1) how do local taxes affect business investment and (2) under what circumstances should local governments offer tax incentives? Both issues have been the focus of research, and studies can be found to support almost any position on these questions. One reason for conflicting findings is the complexity of the issues. Isolating the effect of local taxes or tax incentives on business location patterns requires highly sophisticated techniques and theories. Anecdotal analyses that compare the number of jobs or the size of the business tax base before and after completion of a major business investment but that do not simultaneously control for other factors should be disregarded. The next two sections examine these issues in more detail.

Factors affecting business location decisions

Although business leaders often contend that local tax decisions have a significant bearing on their investment decisions, the general conclusion among researchers is that, at the state level, taxes matter little to business location decisions.[4] The exception may be in those states in which business taxes are abnormally high, although exceptions abound here as well, such as California and Alaska. However, once a firm has narrowed its location choice to a particular region, tax burden becomes more important, although not paramount to the final choice. Firms that are otherwise indifferent to two or more possible sites may consider the effective local tax burden of the finalists in their evaluation.[5] Thus, at the margin, a local government's tax burden does affect business investment decisions.

However, no firm rule can be offered because a lower tax burden does not necessarily lower the cost of doing business in a jurisdiction. If lower taxes mean fewer public services, particularly those used by businesses, operating costs may be much higher because businesses must absorb the cost of providing those services. For

Summary of research on local taxes and business location

In the initial search for possible sites, taxes have virtually no bearing on the location decisions of firms. As the number of possible sites is narrowed, differences in the effective tax rates of local governments increase in importance.

Nontax factors such as labor supply and cost, energy cost, transportation networks, space availability, agglomeration economies, and education level of the workforce are more central to the final location choice of a firm than are tax-related factors.

The effect of local taxes on business investment decisions varies with the type of business. Firms in manufacturing and wholesale trades appear to be more sensitive to effective property tax rates

(property taxes as a percentage of the property's market value) than firms in other types of industries.

Inordinately high local tax burdens may exert an indirect effect on business investment by promoting the emigration of labor. Manufacturing firms, followed by retail and service industries, then leave in order to be closer to the labor supply.

In the long term, above-average property tax burdens cause property values to decline as businesses and households relocate to lower-tax areas. If a competitive level of public services is to be maintained, governments with declining property values must levy even higher tax rates, precipitating further decline in the tax base.

example, low expenditures on roads and transportation systems may mean highway congestion, limited access, and thus higher shipping costs for a firm. Another reason for the relative unimportance of tax burdens is that state and local taxes usually represent a small component of the cost of doing business. One study found that differences in after-tax rates of return for a typical firm were negligible across fifteen different localities in eleven different states.[6] And tax expenses are deductible for federal income tax purposes, further lowering their marginal costs.

Therefore, if the state and local tax burden does not play a major role in business location decisions, the questions become what factors *are* primary in those decisions and where do property and other taxes enter in?

Primary determinants

Like households, businesses seek locations that satisfy their preferences for public and private services. Although no two firms will use the same criteria when selecting a location site, research indicates that central to the site-selection decision are the supply and cost of labor, proximity to suppliers and to markets, the presence of other firms in the same industry (creating the potential for agglomeration economies), and, increasingly, the quality of life.[7]

The three reasons most frequently cited by business executives for relocating a plant are the lack of space to expand at the existing site, the need to modernize the plant, and the need to move closer to a labor supply.[8] In central cities, land costs are generally higher and space is less available, which prompts the out-migration of businesses.[9] Labor-related factors also surface repeatedly in research as an important consideration in business location choices. For example, higher levels of unionization are associated with lower levels of business investment.[10] Labor supply also affects the concentration of business investment: as the supply increases, so does the concentration of business establishments.[11]

Agglomeration economies also influence business location patterns.[12] As noted in Chapter 1, firms in the same industry tend to locate in a common geographic area in order to reap the economies that come from sharing the costs of specialized services. Such economies explain the concentration of the motion picture industry in the Hollywood area and live entertainment in Branson, Missouri, as well as of software development and computer hardware manufacturing in Austin, Texas. Agglomeration economies also lower labor costs because firms that require a technically specialized workforce can tap into a common pool of skilled labor.

Less frequently cited factors influencing location choice include the average level of education attainment in a community (probably an indication of the level of productivity of the workforce), energy costs, weather (with warmer states experiencing greater rates of employment growth), and transportation networks. Finally, all analyses of business location decisions assume that those decisions are made rationally. In reality, personal considerations also enter in. For example, business executives may include in the decision criteria their own preferences for proximity to recreation sites, good schools, and other amenities that shape the quality of life.

Property taxes

The relationship between property taxes and business investment is a primary concern for local government managers. As noted earlier in the chapter, research indicates that taxes increase in importance as the location choice is narrowed from a regional to a local level.

Several studies have examined the effect of property taxes on employment growth and on property values. In a summary of these research findings, Therese McGuire concluded "that high local property taxes deter economic growth."[13] This is consistent with other studies that found, over the long term, that cities with higher-than-average property tax burdens do have lower property values. For example, Katharine Bradbury and Helen Ladd's analysis indicates that if the per capita property tax burden in one city is twice that in another, per capita property values will be about 15 percent lower in the higher-tax city, all other things being equal.[14] These researchers concluded that part of the reduction in the base probably represents the decision of some potential residents (households and firms) not to move into the city, the decision of some other firms to let their city property depreciate as they invest elsewhere, and the decision of some city residents to disinvest in their residential structures by reducing maintenance. This decrease in investment occurs simultaneously with a fall in the price of land and stops once the after-tax rate of return to investment is again equalized across jurisdictions.[15]

For cities experiencing declining property values, an even higher tax rate must be imposed if a comparable level of services is to be provided. For businesses (and households) seeking to maximize after-tax profits, the greater the differentials in property tax rates, the more important the tax becomes to their location decisions. Conversely, cities and counties experiencing rising property values can levy a lower effective tax rate and still provide the same level of services.

As is typically the case in economic analysis, particularly with decisions that involve a significant capital outlay, short-term market effects differ from long-term effects. In general, higher-than-average property taxes probably do not discourage business or household investment in the short term. One reason is that the deductibility of property taxes from federal income taxes reduces the adverse effect of interlocal differences in tax rates, especially if local governments offset their lower property tax burdens with higher sales or excise taxes. Another reason is that most businesses, especially retail outlets that follow population and income migration, are immobile in the short term.

Other studies indicate that various industries respond differently to local property tax burdens. For example, capital-intensive industries, such as manufacturing and wholesale trade, will be likely to weigh property taxes more heavily in their location decisions.[16] Firms in the construction, retail, finance, real estate, insurance, and service industries, on the other hand, have demonstrated no sensitivity to property taxes in their location patterns. Most likely these firms are less sensitive to property taxes because they follow consumer markets, whereas manufacturing and wholesale trade firms are more conscious of the cost of production, which includes local taxes.[17]

Local income and sales taxes

On the basis of an exhaustive review of the research literature, McGuire concluded,

> I find it difficult to be convinced that taxes are an important factor in explaining differences in business location decisions and economic activity *between states or regions*. . . . I simply do not think that the evidence allows us to comfortably advise lawmakers that reducing the corporate income tax rate or personal income tax rate will revive a flagging state economy (emphasis added).[18]

However, the picture becomes more complicated at the local level, where decisions about where to build or work are nowadays made separately from decisions about where to live. McGuire found that higher sales and personal property tax rates had a negative effect on local employment growth on the nine general-purpose local governments in the Washington, D.C. area.[19] In a comparative study of four major U.S. cities, researchers found that changes in income (New York City) and wage (Philadelphia) tax rates adversely affected job creation.[20] Specifically, between 1971 and 2001, New York City lost 331,000 jobs owing to income tax increases, and Philadelphia lost 173,000 jobs owing to increases in its wage tax rate—now the highest in the nation at 4.4625 percent of gross earnings. In both cases, the impact of these taxes is heightened because surrounding local governments do not levy comparable taxes.

The effect of local sales taxes appears less certain, however, possibly because the local tax is frequently piggybacked onto a state levy and collected as one tax liability. Also, rarely do local sales tax rates reach the relatively high rates in larger urban areas that local property and income tax rates reach.

These studies indicate that local taxes do affect business location decisions in the long term. If a municipality or a county imposes a higher tax burden than surrounding governments, some disinvestment by existing businesses and less new investment by nonresident firms will result. Local managers must be concerned about the competitiveness of their government's tax burden, particularly local income and property taxes. Local governments with tax burdens consistently higher than those of surrounding governments will experience a decline in the per capita value of their tax base. Lower property values mean either higher tax rates or reduced services, both of which prompt even further disinvestment by remaining households and businesses.

A related issue in local tax policy is whether high nominal tax rates drive business away—the so-called **announcement effect.** For example, a city may impose a property tax rate that is 20 mills higher than that of surrounding jurisdictions but may offer much more generous homestead exemptions. Does this discourage business and household investment? Unfortunately, no analysis has directly examined this issue at the local level, although one study found that no announcement effect exists for state corporate or personal income tax rates.[21] It is less certain whether such an effect exists at the local level. A high nominal tax rate does not necessarily imply a high tax burden, and most business executives are sophisticated enough to recognize that fact.

One other issue involves whether local governments that rely more heavily on the sales tax have relatively lower property tax burdens. That is, do local sales taxes create a **substitution effect** for the property tax? A study of Texas's ninety-three largest cities found that those cities with higher per capita sales tax burdens did not have lower per capita property tax burdens, at least not for the portion of the property tax used for municipal operations.[22] However, a modest substitution effect was found for local excise taxes and general-purpose service charges, greater use of which does result in an offsetting reduction in the property tax burden. The difference may lie in the underlying economics of these taxes. Trends in the sales and property tax bases are much more closely linked to trends in the local economy. Rising sales tax revenue occurs concurrently with increases in property values. An increase in sales tax revenues may allow local governments to lower property tax *rates,* but because of increases in the property tax base, the burden may not be reduced.

The preceding discussion offers some justification for local governments to keep their taxes competitive with those of surrounding governments. Over the long term, local governments that maintain above-average property and income taxes will experience a decline in their property tax base, even though other factors, such as education levels and quality of life, have a greater effect on business location decisions than taxes. For example, in a national study of cities over 30,000 in population, it was found that the percentage of the population with college degrees is a key determinant of economic growth, particularly for urban areas in the Northeast and upper Midwest.[23] The researchers speculated that more skilled workers may react more readily and acquire new skills more quickly as a local economy changes.

The next section considers an equally politically charged issue of the cost-effectiveness of tax incentives in influencing the location decisions of firms.

Tax relief for business investment

The fundamental purpose of incentives is to reduce the cost of doing business. Lower costs increase a firm's competitive position and may increase profitability. Incentives for business investment fall into two general categories: (1) tax incentives, such as tax abatements, tax increment financing, tax exemptions, and tax credits; and (2) nontax incentives, such as subsidized loans, industrial development bonds (IDBs), land acquisition, site preparation, preemployment training, and publicly provided infrastructure. The following discussion is limited to tax incentives.

Tax incentives can be used to negotiate benefits for the local government. For example, after city officials in Dayton, Ohio, were approached by a savings bank for a tax abatement on a proposed office complex in the downtown area, they negotiated the inclusion of a provision in the abatement agreement that increased the number and amount of loans the bank was to award for home improvements in the city. It is also quite common for tax incentive agreements to include employment requirements, such as a percentage of new hires who reside within the city or county.

However, public finance experts disagree about the cost-effectiveness of tax incentives. It is indisputable that tax concessions improve the competitive position of a local government, but are the costs of tax concessions, measured in forgone revenue, worth the benefits from the business investment? Are tax incentives essential to attracting new business investment? A 2003 assessment of the numerous research studies on the effectiveness of tax incentives concluded that "the economic case against such incentives is far from clear."[24]

Initially, local and state governments targeted their economic development initiatives to stimulating reinvestment in blighted areas using federal aid designated for that purpose. With the decline in that aid, local and state governments have increasingly broadened their use of incentives to include nonblighted areas as a general strategy to increase business investment. Meanwhile, states are reducing their own economic development expenditures by giving local governments the financial responsibility to provide incentives on their own and the discretion to determine the type and amount of incentives they will offer. In so doing, states avoid mandating

Summary of research on locally financed tax incentives

Tax incentives are economically most easily justified in marginal cases, where a firm is otherwise indifferent to the choice between two or more possible locations. Yet even in these instances, competing local governments tend to offer nearly comparable incentives that effectively cancel each other out.

Tax incentives are politically most appropriate for state and local governments with relatively high and persistent rates of unemployment. Unfortunately, these governments are the least able to bear the cost of tax incentives, particularly when competing with more prosperous jurisdictions.

To the extent that local taxes on businesses exceed the benefits in public services those businesses receive, tax incentives provide local governments with a mechanism for more equitably aligning the tax burden on business, particularly for mobile sectors. Thus, tax incentives make the most sense, politically and eco-

nomically, for high-tech industries and services and the least sense for retail and residential development.

Once agglomeration economies become established in a jurisdiction or region, the economic and political necessity for tax incentives declines.

Local governments with taxing powers limited to the property tax are less able to recover the cost of a tax incentive through increased revenues than those with access to an income tax or a sales tax.

Local governments in economically linked metropolitan areas retain fewer benefits from tax incentives within their jurisdiction. For example, a tax abatement offered by a central city will produce spillover benefits in surrounding suburban communities that supply some of the labor force. The smaller the geographic size of a jurisdiction, the more benefits are exported to surrounding communities. The same is true for rural communities surrounded by an unincorporated area.

that local governments provide such aid while knowing that interlocal competition will compel them to make concessions available. However, recent trends indicate that local governments recognize the cost associated with development and are awarding tax concessions more selectively than in the past.

In general, political expediency requires that local governments offer some type of tax incentive if for no other reason than to indicate a "favorable business environment." For public managers, however, the issue is more complex: what does it cost in tax incentives to lure new business investment without alienating existing businesses?

Types of tax incentives offered by local governments

Next to IDBs, tax concessions are the most frequently used incentive for promoting economic growth. Unlike development bonds or public financing for infrastructure, the effects of which are long term, tax incentives immediately improve a business's income statement by reducing operating costs. Of course, if all competing firms in an industry receive the same tax incentives, competition will lower prices for the firms' products rather than increase profits.

Tax incentives are also relatively easy to implement and enjoy widespread public approval when presented as aids to job creation. As mentioned earlier, most people assume that incentives more than pay for themselves. Whether this is true, however, must be determined on a case-by-case basis and only after careful analysis of the economic impact of the firm's investment.

The accompanying sidebar summarizes the range of tax incentives used by state and local governments. The following sections focus on the three most popular locally provided incentives: abatements, exemptions, and tax increment financing.

A typology of tax incentives

One way of classifying tax incentives is by the component in the basic tax equation (tax base × tax rate = tax liability) targeted by the incentive. Ultimately, all incentives are intended to influence tax liability, but some do so by manipulating the tax base, others by manipulating the tax rate, and still others by directly altering tax liability.

Tax base	Tax rate	Tax liability
Tax abatement	Split tax roll	Tax credit
Tax assessment freeze	Tax rate freeze	Tax levy freeze
Tax (freeport) exemption		Tax dividend
Tax increment financing		Tax rebate
Tax holiday		Tax amnesty
Tax base sharing		

Tax abatements

Tax abatements, the most popular incentive and the least costly to administer, temporarily reduce the property tax burden of a business. Abatements work in several different ways depending on the parameters of state law. One common method is to exempt all or a portion of the taxable value of the new investment in a building and equipment for a specified number of years (usually ten to fifteen), after which the property is assessed and taxed at the prevailing rate. An alternative involves freezing the tax liability at its predevelopment level for the abatement period. In exchange for this tax benefit, developers must make contractually agreed-upon improvements in the designated area, which may include hiring from the local labor pool.

Missouri was the first state to authorize abatements in 1943. According to the National Association of State Development Agencies (NASDA), at least twenty-eight states now sanction the use of tax abatements by local governments, although four states limit the benefits to a particular type of industry.[25] Table 3–1 summarizes the practices in the twenty-eight states on the basis of information reported by NASDA and collected from Web sites. State statutes vary in the conditions they impose for awarding abatements; such variations are found in

1. The types of firms qualifying for an abatement
2. The conditions necessary to designate a geographic area as qualifying for an abatement
3. The approval process
4. The terms of the abatement agreement.

Qualifying businesses Most states allow participation by a broad range of industries, especially if the state limits abatements to blighted areas. Where such limitations are in effect, all types of firms—retail, service, warehousing, and manufacturing—that locate in the designated areas usually qualify for an abatement. In some cases, even residential property qualifies. Iowa and Illinois restrict their abatements to new firms moving into a local jurisdiction from another state or country or to an existing firm expanding its production capacity by adding to an existing facility.

Designation of qualifying areas Historically, the purpose of tax abatements was to encourage redevelopment in economically depressed or blighted areas. That purpose is still apparent, as seen on Table 3–1, but the trend among states

Table 3–1
Statutory provisions governing the use of tax abatements.

State	Local governments granting abatements	Maximum abatement period (years)	Types of taxes abated	Special features or conditions
Alabama	M, C	10	P, S	State and local sales taxes abated on qualifying businesses
Arizona	7 foreign trade zones	Not specified	P	Reduction of 80% of state property tax liability in free trade zones: Mesa, Nogales, Phoenix, Sierra Vista, Tucson (2), and Yuma
Arkansas	M, C	Not specified	P	Requires payment in lieu of taxes of at least 35% of abated tax liability
Connecticut	M	5	P	17 targeted communities may abate up to 80% of the liability for qualifying businesses
Florida	M, C	10	P	Requires voter approval to authorize abatement policy
Illinois	M, C	10	P	
Indiana	M, S	10	P	
Louisiana	Parishes	5 or 10	P	
Maryland	29 enterprise zones	10	P, I	80% of liability abated for first 5 years, then declines by 10% each year for remaining 5 years
Michigan	M, C	12	P	
Minnesota	M, C, S	10–12	P	
Mississippi	M, C	10	P	
Missouri	M	25	P	Limited to Urban Redevelopment Corps in blighted areas. Abate 100% for first 10 years, then up to 50% of value for remaining 15 years

Table 3–1
Continued

State	Local governments granting abatements	Maximum abatement period (years)	Types of taxes abated	Special features or conditions
Montana	M, C	9	P	Uses a state-mandated sliding scale for percentage of tax abated
New Jersey	M	5	P	
New Mexico	M, C	30	P	
New York	New York City	25	P	
North Dakota	M, C	15	P	
Ohio	M, C	15	P	Requires state certification that benefits exceed costs
Oklahoma	M, C	5	P	A 2002 constitutional amendment allows counties, with voter approval, to use up to ¼ the revenue from a previously exempt project for economic development
Oregon	Enterprise zones	15	P	
Pennsylvania	M, C, S	10	P	
Rhode Island	M	10	P	Alternatively, the tax rate may be frozen
South Carolina	C	5	P	May abate for up to 20 years if a fee is paid in lieu of taxes
South Dakota	C	5	P	
Texas	M, C	10	P	
Vermont	M	10	P	State administered
Virginia	M, C	15	P	Alternatively, qualifying high-tech equipment may be taxed at a lower rate at the discretion of the local government

Source: Based on information in National Association of State Development Agencies, *Directory of Incentives for Business Investment and Development in the United States: A State By State Guide* (Woodbridge, Va., 2002). Available at www.nasda.com.

Note: C—counties, M—municipalities, S—state, P—property, I—income.

is clearly toward relaxing the definition of blight and even authorizing tax abatements for purposes other than redevelopment. For example, the Michigan legislature passed the Technology Park Development Act, allowing local governments to designate large undeveloped parcels of land as technology parks; improvements in these parks qualify for a 50 percent abatement from property taxes for up to twelve years.

The Texas tax abatement law includes any area where abatement will contribute to the economic development of the city or town.[26] And even among states that limit abatement benefits to economically blighted areas, considerable variation exists in the definition of blight. For example, New Jersey limits participation to those municipalities designated by the state as urban aid cities. Ohio limits benefits to economically depressed areas but allows cities and counties to determine what constitutes a depressed area.

Approval process   State laws usually give municipalities and counties the authority to designate areas qualifying for abatement. A source of considerable disagreement and litigation, however, is the participation of overlapping local jurisdictions, such as school districts and special districts, in abating their taxes in the designated areas. Those on one side of the issue say that all local jurisdictions should bear the cost of encouraging redevelopment of an area because all will enjoy the future revenue benefits from the increased property value. Those on the other side of the issue contend that maintaining or improving the urban environment is a municipal responsibility and not a school district's.

As might be expected, states handle this issue differently. In general, southern states, including Alabama, Mississippi, South Carolina, and Texas, prohibit school districts from participating in tax abatement programs. Other states, like Illinois, leave it to the discretion of overlapping governments.[27]

Louisiana is the only state in which the state's commerce department may authorize an exemption from *local* property taxes for new or expanding firms without the approval of the local governments affected by the decision. At the other extreme, Maryland compensates local governments for up to half the lost revenue from property tax credits granted to firms locating in enterprise zones, to the extent that funds are appropriated by the state legislature.

Terms of abatement agreements   Once a reinvestment district is designated, local governments granting abatements usually enter into agreements with developers that specify the improvements both government and business are to make. Abatement of taxes is conditional on the developer making the specified improvements or restorations. In Texas, contracts must include

- The amount of exemption and method of calculating it
- A list and description of improvements to be made by property owners
- Limitations on the property's use
- Provisions for access and inspection by city personnel
- Provisions for recovering lost property tax revenue in the event that the owner fails to honor the contract's terms.[28]

The maximum length of the abatement period varies from state to state. Among the states granting comprehensive coverage, New Mexico has the longest abatement period at a maximum length of thirty years; however, most states specify limits in the ten- to fifteen-year range. In those states offering more than one abatement program, such as Louisiana, separate limits apply to each program.

State laws also vary with respect to the type of taxable property that can be abated. Ohio, for example, exempts new buildings or improvements to existing buildings but

Resources on the Internet

The following professional organizations maintain Web sites that offer reference materials useful to the community and economic development director. Community development associations foster investment in infrastructure, housing, and educational opportunities with the goal of enhancing the community's quality of life. Economic development associations, by contrast, foster investment in job-creating activities. Additionally, while economic development relies primarily on local resources (tax expenditures), community development initiatives tend to rely more heavily on federal (Housing and Urban Development, or HUD) and, to a lesser extent, state grants-in-aid.

Community development

American Planning Association (APA); www.planning.org

Council of State Community Development Agencies (COSCDA); www.coscda.org

National Association for County Community and Economic Development (NACCED); www.nacced.org

National Association of Housing and Redevelopment Officials (NAHRO); www.nahro.org

National Association of Towns and Townships (NATaT); www.natat.org

National Community Development Association (NCDA); www.ncdaonline.org

Economic development

Economic Development Research Group; www.edrgroup.com/index.shtml

International Economic Development Council (IEDC); www.iedconline.org

National Association of Development Organizations (NADO); www.nado.org

National Association of State Development Agencies (NASDA); www.nasda.com

National Congress for Community Economic Development (NCCED); www.ncced.org

---

levies taxes on the current assessed value of the land and on all tangible personal property, such as machinery, equipment, and inventory. Florida, by contrast, exempts both improvements to real property and all tangible personal property.

The usual pattern is to abate taxes on the entire property value but to require payments in lieu of taxes (PILOTs) on the predevelopment value of the tax base. These payments are subject to negotiation and constitute one of the provisions in the abatement agreement. Some states limit abatements to less than 100 percent of the value of improvements made in the postdevelopment period. For example, Connecticut abates only 80 percent of the property taxes owed on qualifying improvements. Maryland law imposes a graduated scale: for the first five years, a property tax credit of 80 percent of the tax owed is given, declining by 10 percent each year from the sixth through the tenth year of the abatement period. Iowa's local governments can abate 75 percent of the property taxes in the first year after construction; the maximum abatement declines by 15 percent each year for the remainder of the abatement period.

Tax exemptions

Tax exemptions permanently exclude from taxation particular types of transactions or property. For example, building materials used in construction may be exempted from a local option sales tax. A common form of property tax exemption—a **freeport exemption**—extends to inventory items, both raw materials and finished goods, that move across state borders for fabrication or sale. Most states now extend some sort of partial exemption for goods in transit, but the parameters vary. For example, in Texas the freeport exemption is a **local option** for cities, counties, and school districts. One, two, or all three overlapping local governments may extend an exemption, which is available on all inventories brought into the state for "fabrication, assembling, manufacture, storage or processing" and then exported outside the state within 175 days. If the local governing body adopts the exemption by ordinance, Texas law provides that it can never be revoked. By targeting exemptions to businesses with inventories, local governments can stimulate significant agglomeration economies. A community that serves as a transportation hub—either by highway, railroad, or airline—may use its competitive advantage to become a center for warehousing, for example.

Of the three types of tax incentives, exemptions are the most powerful at stimulating growth. At the same time, they are the least amenable for targeting economic development efforts because they almost always exist as a blanket provision (covering all inventory, all sales of a particular type) in state law. Any business that meets the provisions of state law qualifies for the exemption, which thereby reduces the local government's capacity to target its development efforts to shape its economy toward specific goals.

Tax increment financing

Tax increment financing (TIF)—also called tax allocation financing—is authorized in at least forty-eight states.[29] In 1952 California became the first state to adopt a TIF statute; it continues to lead the nation in the number of local governments using this approach to redevelopment. Although state laws vary in detail, all have the same basic approach: the increases in property tax revenue resulting from the redevelopment of an area are dedicated to financing development-related costs in that area.

TIF divides tax revenue from the area into two categories: taxes on the predevelopment value of the tax base (the tax increment base) are kept by each taxing body, while taxes from the increased value of property resulting from redevelopment (the tax increment) are deposited by each jurisdiction into a tax increment fund, which is usually maintained by the city. Unlike property owners granted a tax abatement, property owners in a **tax increment district (TID)** incur the same property tax rate as owners outside the district. Preferential treatment is granted only in that taxes from the TID are dedicated to financing public improvements in the district.

Money in the tax increment fund is usually used to repay TIF-backed bonds issued to finance public improvements in the redevelopment area. The Tax Reform Act of 1986 reclassified TIF-backed bonds as private-purpose bonds, making their interest payments subject to federal income taxation.

Typically, TIF bonds are sold to provide up-front financing for the purchase and preparation of land in the TID, including preparing the land for industrial, commercial, or residential development and for the installation of public infrastructure, such as streets, lights, water and sewer lines, curbs, gutters, and landscaping. Once prepared, the land is sold to developers at a price that is often below the local government's cost of preparing the site, a technique known as a **land write-down.** The predevelopment costs, including write-downs, are recouped through the tax increment fund over the life of the project.

The underlying assumptions of the TIF approach to economic development are that locally financed improvements will draw private investment into the TID and that without those improvements, private investment would not occur. Whereas a tax abatement draws business investment into a designated area by lowering the property tax burden, TIF lures such investment by providing a ready-made site for construction usually at a subsidized price. In the absence of TIF, developers have to bear the site preparation costs up-front. With TIF, developers still pay for site preparation, but the cost is spread over several years and is repaid through property taxes on the tax base increment dedicated for such purposes.

Pros and cons of tax increment financing

Supporters say:

It can provide financing for projects that otherwise would not be economically feasible.

The city loses no tax revenue.

Property owners in the redevelopment zone pay their full share of property taxes; property owners outside the zone are not required to pay for the redevelopment.

The TIF bonds are not included in a city's general debt obligations (in some states).

Development is financed from increases in tax revenues that it generates, not from a subsidy from other areas of the city.

Once the TIF bonds are retired, the city and all other affected taxing units get the advantage of the full tax base and increased tax revenues.

Projects must be well planned and economically feasible in order to attract bond investors; ill-conceived projects won't get off the ground.

No voter approval is required, nor is approval of other units (in most states); a city council may act unilaterally.

Opponents say:

While the projects appear to be self-financing, in reality taxpayers outside the redevelopment zone subsidize the projects by paying for increased service needs (fire, police, schools) that emerge as a result of redevelopment.

There is no voter accountability.

Cities often abuse the program, "capturing" taxes on development that would have occurred without the TIF project or using captured tax revenue to provide basic city services.

If the increment does not materialize as planned, the city must find some other source of funds to prevent a bond default.

TIF debt is more expensive to service since it is not backed by the full faith and credit of a city.

It is difficult to alter development plans once the bonds have been issued since bond buyers require assurances that limit flexibility.

Cities often stretch the definition of "blight" to ridiculous extremes, thus allowing the use of TIF in areas that don't need publicly subsidized assistance.

Other taxing units are forced to give up a part of their tax revenues to a city (in most states) without being given any authority over how the money is spent.

Source: Mary Alice Davis, "Tax Increment Financing: Texas Tries a New Urban Development Tool," Special Legislative Report no. 82 (Austin: Texas House of Representatives, House Study Group, June 11, 1982), 6–7.

Although TIF is more complex and costly to administer than tax abatements, it is generally preferred by private firms. A tax abatement increases the net income of a firm, which is then partially taxed away by state and federal income taxes. With TIF, a firm can deduct the entire cost of its property taxes from its federal, and usually state, income taxes and still reap an advantage: a portion of its property tax liability is used for public improvements that directly benefit the business.

Like tax abatements, TIF poses a ticklish political problem for local government officials in that it gives preferential treatment to property owners in a particular area. The accompanying sidebar summarizes supporters' and opponents' views on TIF.

Several analyses of the effectiveness of TIF at increasing the taxable value of a city or county have produced mixed results.[30] A report by the Wisconsin Legislative Audit Bureau evaluating that state's TIF program identified two major abuses by cities.[31] First, some cities and villages had designated TIDs in areas that would have been developed anyway, thereby effectively capturing the tax revenue of overlapping governments. Second, the report noted that some TIF-backed projects were only indirectly linked to promoting economic development. Legislation was subsequently adopted that excluded from TIF the project costs for the construction of municipal buildings; the construction of facilities financed by user fees, such as stadiums and convention centers; and general government operating expenses.

One of the more rigorous analyses of the impact of TIF found that among Illinois municipalities, increases in commercial property investment within a TID came at the expense of reduced investment in commercial property outside the TID.[32] This result was not found for industrial development. An earlier study of Indiana municipalities found that investment in TIF stimulated increases in property values in the TID and in surrounding areas.[33] Chicago, designating a TID exclusively for industrial development, actually lowered the value of the land.[34] Some researchers found that restricting TIDs to industrial development imposes significant costs on property values, but that allowing mixed uses (i.e., residential and commercial development) for the land "gives owners the discretion to develop the property in whatever way they see fit and the financial benefits of this flexibility will result in increased demand."[35]

The primary source of opposition to TIF lies in its effect on overlapping local jurisdictions that levy property taxes on the TID. In all but one state, only cities, towns, and villages have the statutory authority to create a TID; California also authorizes counties to establish redevelopment districts. Under most state laws, overlapping local jurisdictions must share in the cost of redevelopment by forgoing the tax revenue captured by the TID.[36] Without TIF, cities bear the full cost of redevelopment while overlapping jurisdictions, such as counties and school districts, reap revenue windfalls from increased property values.

State laws specify the procedures that cities must observe when creating a TID or redevelopment district. The next five sections discuss these procedures.

Proposing the TID Although all states that permit TIF restrict use of this incentive to "blighted" areas of a city, state laws vary in their definition of blight and in the rigor with which they construe those definitions. Most state laws specify a percentage of substandard or older housing that must be present for an area to qualify as blighted.

Once a city proposes the creation of a TID, all states require it to notify overlapping local jurisdictions and hold a public hearing where affected individuals and governments may express their opinions on the proposed district.

Cities usually designate the TID and then function as developers by making the public improvements needed to draw private investment into the area. If redevelopment in the TID would not have occurred without tax increment financing, then overlapping jurisdictions have nothing to lose from such an incentive. However, officials of overlapping jurisdictions, particularly school districts, often complain that cities and towns designate areas for redevelopment that would have undergone redevelopment without TIF backing, thereby "capturing" tax revenue that otherwise would have been collected by the school district.

State laws sometimes limit the amount of a city's property tax base that can be included in reinvestment districts. For example, Wisconsin restricts the equalized value of all TIDs in a municipality to 5 percent of its equalized tax base.[37] (Equalized property value is the assessed value adjusted to a common fraction of appraised value. See Chapter 4 for a discussion of fractional assessments.) For smaller communities, this limit means that, in effect, only one TID can be created within the municipality. Texas law permits designation of up to 15 percent of a city's real property tax base in TIDs.

In some states, the full tax increment does not have to be committed to the tax increment fund. By agreement, overlapping local jurisdictions may retain a portion of the tax increment for their own general fund. For example, a school district may annually retain 20 percent of the tax increment and remit only 80 percent of the incremental funds to the city-maintained tax increment fund. Several states compensate school districts for revenue lost through the creation of a TID. For example, the Minnesota school aid formula guarantees local districts a fixed amount of funds per student, so any deductions from the property tax base increase state payments. The state thereby indirectly pays about 30 percent of the cost of TIF.[38]

Preparing a redevelopment plan   Critical to the success of a TID is the preparation of a plan that guides the implementation of projects in the redevelopment district and formally identifies the commitments made by both public and private sector participants. Most states require cities and towns to adopt a plan for redeveloping the TID that identifies the proposed projects and their estimated costs. Typically local governments must create a board of directors whose primary responsibility is developing detailed project and financial plans for the improvement district. Wisconsin requires that a five-member board be appointed for a proposed TID, including a private citizen as well as representatives from the school district, the county, the city, and the vocational-technical district.[39]

According to the Illinois Department of Commerce and Community Affairs, a redevelopment plan should include

- A description of the land uses proposed for the district
- An itemization of the public improvements to be undertaken
- Commitments and plans by private developers for the area
- An estimate of the cost of redevelopment
- Sources of financing
- Nature and terms of bonds that may be issued
- Boundaries and recently assessed value of the TID
- A projection of the assessed value on completion of redevelopment.[40]

The project plan may also include a description of any changes in zoning, planning, or building codes required by improvements; maps of the project area; estimates of nonproject costs; and methods of relocating households or existing businesses displaced by the project.[41] The financial plan should include realistic estimates of the proposed public expenditures; the costs of site preparation including acquisition, relocation, and demolition; and the cost of project administration.[42]

Adopting an ordinance creating the TID   Once public hearings have been completed and input from other local governments has been provided (if appropriate), the city must formally establish the TID by ordinance. The Texas State Property Tax Board recommends that the ordinance

- Define the boundaries of the TID
- Set the termination date of the TID
- Name the redevelopment district
- Create a TIF fund
- Make two findings of fact: (1) that the public improvements in the district will enhance private investment in the area and (2) that the area qualifies for redevelopment as defined in state law.[43]

Once the TID is established, the predevelopment value of its tax base is determined and then all affected local and state agencies are notified of that value. The city council may also adopt an ordinance authorizing the issuance of TIF bonds.

Implementing and administering redevelopment Funding for acquisition and preparation of land in a TID has historically come from TIF-backed bonds. In some states, such as Minnesota, these bonds represent general obligations of the city. In other states, such as Texas, state law precludes cities from backing these obligations with their full faith and credit. The tax increment plus any other revenues from the sale or operation of facilities in the TID may be pledged as the source of funds to repay the TIF bonds. A common practice is for cities to enter into formal agreements with developers to undertake the construction of various projects in the TID.

To reduce the risk that tax increment revenue will be insufficient to repay outstanding TIF bonds, cities in Minnesota enter into assessment agreements in which developers in a TID agree to pay property taxes based on a minimum value of the development regardless of the actual value.[44]

Another issue is whether the predevelopment tax base represents a minimum for establishing revenue owed to overlapping jurisdictions.[45] Conceivably, property values in a TID could drop below the predevelopment base, and thus overlapping local governments would receive less tax revenue after development was initiated than before. The unresolved legal issue is whether cities have to make up the difference in lost revenue to overlapping governments.

Some states require cities to summarize for all affected local governments the activity of the TID during the preceding year. The report must provide information on the amount and source of revenues in the tax increment fund, the amount and purpose of expenditures from the fund, the amount of principal and interest due on outstanding TIF bonds, and the tax increment base and current appraised value of property in the district.

Terminating the TID Most states place a maximum life on either TIDs or the bonds used to finance redevelopment. Illinois limits the life of redevelopment districts to twenty-three years or until all project costs are paid, whichever comes first. Wisconsin limits TIDs to twenty years or until the city's bond obligations have been satisfied. Texas places no constraints on the life of TIDs but limits TIF-backed bonds to twenty years.

Tax incentives for professional sports and the arts

Professional sports stadiums and performing and visual arts centers that demand tax-supported assistance present special challenges to local governments. Even the spreading use of subsidies for outdoor displays—Cincinnati's pigs, St. Louis's arch—raises questions about the extent of public support for such community symbols. Just how long is the "arm of economic development"?

Such symbols have their origins in antiquity. The Athenians built the Parthenon and the Romans the Coliseum, both monuments to the cultural accomplishments of their respective city-states. But the past twenty-five years have witnessed a significant increase in public funding in the United States for such initiatives under the guise of economic development. Between 1989 and 2001, sixteen major league baseball stadiums were built at a current dollar cost of $4.9 billion, two-thirds of which came from government subsidies.[46] Between 1993 and 2002, nine professional football stadiums were constructed, almost all with substantial tax subsidies, mostly sales and hotel/motel tax revenue. Performing and visual arts centers also receive dedicated tax revenue to subsidize their operations or capital improvements. Americans for the Arts (www.artsusa.org), a national advocacy organization, estimates that 4,000 local arts agencies exist in the United States, with one-fourth of them public agencies funded by city or county government. The most common form of local tax support is a hotel/motel tax, although occasionally local governments may dedicate a portion of the property tax or sales tax for local arts and historical preservation. For example, the city of Denton, Texas, dedicates 3 percent of its 7 percent hotel/motel tax to the arts.

But do these investments provide economic returns greater than their cost in public subsidies? The resounding answer from numerous studies, particularly of the economic benefits of professional sports teams, is *no*. But if they are not justified economically, what then is the justification for such massive public investments in these facilities?

Why government financing?

Public financing of stadiums and arts venues is justified for either of two reasons: (1) the facilities provide public (collective) benefits that merit subsidization or (2) their effects on economic growth (job creation, increases in property values, growth in personal income) merit a subsidy from local or state government. For true public goods, or even merit goods with substantial collective benefits, tax support is justified up to the value of the collective benefits. But professional stadiums and arts complexes, however meritorious, do not meet the criteria of nondivisibilty and nonexcludability described in Chapter 2. Admission tickets are required to their events, and nonsubscribers are excluded from enjoying any direct benefits. Thus, they do not qualify as pure public goods.

A more convincing case can be made that because of the intangible benefits they provide a community, such as civic pride and enhanced quality of life, these facilities qualify as merit goods and so a partial subsidy is justified. A professional sports team or symphony orchestra, like a library or a museum, enriches the life and character of a community, meriting some public funding. Two studies have examined the intangible benefits of these venues and reached opposite conclusions. In an analysis of attitudinal data for residents in the Indianapolis area, one study found that "attendance is an important element in determining pride."[47] Those who attend sporting and cultural events derive more pride from the event than those who do not attend. The researchers concluded that "financing mechanisms should place more of the burden of paying for an asset on those who attend than on the general public."[48]

In a cross-sectional analysis of the fifty-three U.S. cities with National Football League (NFL) franchises, Gerald Carlino and Edward Coulson estimated the impact that these professional teams had on wages and rental rates for housing for the 1993–1999 period.[49] Using the economic theory of implicit pricing, they examined whether the presence of an NFL team added to the quality of life in the host city. If wages are lower and rents higher in host cities, then consumers are implicitly responding to the enhanced quality of life brought by the team by accepting lower wage rates and bidding up the cost of housing, other things being equal. Carlino and Coulson found that wages are not lower in NFL cities but that rents are, on average, 8 percent higher. For the average city in 1999, they determined that the intangible value that hosting an NFL team brings to a city's quality of life is $139 million per year. However, they cautioned that their results "do not constitute a blanket endorsement for stadium subsidies,"[50] acknowledging that other factors correlated with the presence of an NFL team may partially or fully explain the higher rents. The aggregate nature of their analysis also means that individual effects will vary widely among the fifty-three cities.

In terms of the second justification for public subsidies—the impact of sports stadiums and arts venues on economic development—the research is conclusive: not only do the benefits to economic growth fall short of the cost of the subsidy, but these venues may even have an adverse effect on economic growth.[51] Whether measured by job creation, changes in consumer spending, or revitalization of a blighted area, independent analyses consistently show that public investment in stadiums, in particular, has no effect on economic growth.

Part of the reason is that household spending for entertainment is limited. If people buy more tickets for professional sports, they simply reduce spending for other entertainment purposes, and the result is no net economic gain for the region. Only 5 to 20 percent of the fans at professional athletic events are from outside the area.[52] While some visual or performing arts events may have a strong regional draw, it is unlikely that, on the average, the percentage of out-of-area patrons is any greater. Thus, athletic and arts events, on average, are not effective mechanisms for exporting the burden for financing stadiums and performance halls. Of course, rare events like the World Series or the Super Bowl offer significant opportunities for tax exportation.

Finally, the benefits to economic development of professional athletics and the arts are constrained by the absence of significant **multiplier effects.** Local governments, especially those in metropolitan areas, can expect that for every $1 in new investment by a manufacturing firm in their area, there will be a $2 impact on the local economy.[53] New investment, especially by firms that export goods and services outside the region, means more hiring and consumption, which generates further hiring and consumption by other businesses and households in the area. However, professional sports have a multiplier effect of at most 1.25.[54] Because of their limited season, use of lower-skilled labor in service areas, and limited opportunities for agglomeration economies, investment in athletic and arts events does not have the same multiplier effects as investment in manufacturing or technology.

Civic symbolism

Why do leaders in local governments acquiesce to the demands of owners of professional teams for new and increasingly more costly stadiums? Why do cities feel compelled to build and operate concert and opera halls, theaters, and art museums? In fact, cities and civic leaders, from pharaohs to presidents, have always erected monuments as a visible legacy of their leadership. Seen in a historical context, sports stadiums and arts centers serve much the same function, particularly in Western culture, where benefits to the whole are valued over the immortalization of individual leaders. Beyond the civic pride, quality of life, and "bragging rights" that these venues bring to a community, they serve as permanent reminders of a community's past accomplishments and as proclamations of future expected achievements. Just as the arch defines St. Louis and the Eiffel Tower Paris, so too does Bass Hall symbolically herald Fort Worth's cultural achievements and Jacobs Field Cleveland's athletic triumphs.

Regardless of what team owners and arts proponents may say, the value of stadiums and arts venues is symbolic, not economic. These facilities have tangible value—albeit political—particularly for those leaders responsible for their development and construction. But Americans' general lack of historical perspective and preoccupation with economic growth complicate the local leader's task of rationalizing the construction of new facilities. Not surprisingly, when put to a vote, such initiatives result in highly contentious elections with each side making dubious claims about expected benefits and costs. When such facilities are seen as civic symbolism, arguments faulting their lack of value for economic development fall by the wayside. But promoting them as symbolic tributes to a community's accomplishments poses political hurdles that the more pragmatic would prefer to avoid.

Guidelines for using tax incentives

Every local government has a unique set of attributes that make it a more attractive location for some types of industries than for others. The following points are summarized from discussions in this chapter:

- Before launching an economic development program, local leaders should develop a **strategic plan** that identifies (1) their community's economic strengths, weaknesses, opportunities, and threats; (2) goals, measurable objectives, and strategies for achieving those objectives; and (3) measurable benchmarks for assessing the progress toward achieving the community's economic development goals. Local leaders should commit to regularly (annually) reviewing the strategic plan and revising its elements where warranted.

- A local government offering tax incentives should have access to at least one broad-based nonproperty tax, such as a general sales tax or an income tax, in order to capture more revenue benefits from economic growth.

- The larger the jurisdiction, the better the match between those taxpayers bearing the cost of the incentives and those benefiting from the increased economic activity; by implication, counties are better suited for providing tax incentives than are cities, towns, or villages.

- Economically declining jurisdictions are the most vulnerable to "giving away too much" when negotiating with a business contemplating the relocation or expansion of an existing facility.

- For urban areas already benefiting from agglomeration economies, it is not necessary to use tax incentives to attract other firms in the same industry.

- Tax incentives are most justified for industrial and technology development because of the greater multiplier effects and greater up-front investment costs. Incentives, both tax and nontax, for commercial and retail development have no economic justification because commercial development follows population migration.

- In the long term, locally financed tax incentives may prove counterproductive because they shift the cost of services to other taxpayers, who then have an incentive to move to a lower-tax jurisdiction.

Governments using tax incentives as a tool for promoting growth should carefully assess their strengths and weaknesses and then target their recruitment efforts toward firms that would benefit the most from locating or expanding there. For example, the city of Arlington, Texas, systematically evaluated itself on three dimensions: (1) local operating conditions (e.g., water availability, sewer treatment, telephone service, fuel availability, electric power availability, highway accessibility); (2) cost of business (e.g., taxes, construction cost, utilities, labor costs); and (3) quality of life (e.g., education, housing, cost of living, retail activity, medical services, cultural activities).[55] Such an evaluation can provide direction for a local government's economic development initiative and can become the basis for a policy on tax incentives.

A city's strategic plan for economic development has a profound impact on the way the city works with other organizations and other governments. Robert Agranoff and Michael McGuire have identified three patterns of collaborative management in cities pursuing economic development: (1) jurisdiction-based management, in which local managers seek out partnerships with other local governments that can help them achieve their strategic goals for economic development; (2) donor-recipient jurisdictions, which emphasize mutual gains and share program administration with other levels of government while working to influence state and federal regulations and procedures; and (3) top-down jurisdictions, which are more likely to accept state and federal regulations and procedures as given and work within them.[56]

Questions to ask about economic development proposals

Few governments have a clearly defined set of criteria for evaluating economic development proposals or for agreeing on the conditions under which they will award tax incentives.

Local governments must begin by asking the right questions of each firm that requests a tax incentive. What effect will the proposed project have on job creation? What effect will it have on the local property, sales, and income tax bases? The appendix to this chapter shows the policy statement on abatements for Plano, Texas. Each applicant for an abatement must respond to the questions listed in the second section of the statement. The request is then evaluated by a Joint Committee on Tax Abatement according to the procedures specified in the fourth section of the statement.

While the Plano approach is commendable because the same criteria are used to systematically evaluate each request, such information must be used cautiously. Firms tend to grossly overestimate the economic benefits of their presence in a community—especially if they have reason to believe that doing so will help them get a break on their property tax bill. Before extending an incentive, the local manager should carefully consider the following questions:

- Do independent analyses verify the expected benefits from the development? What are the estimated tax yields and level of job creation for the development? Are the estimates realistic?

- Is the proposed development consistent with the local government's strategic goals?

- Does the development add to existing agglomeration economies? Does it have the potential to stimulate the creation of new agglomeration economies?

- Does the contract extending incentives specify the conditions for receiving and retaining the incentive, and does it give local governments extending an abatement the power to verify compliance with the agreement and the performance measures agreed to by the contractor?

Tax relief for citizens

While local governments have pursued tax relief for business through targeted tax incentives, citizens have grown increasingly resistant to paying more taxes, particularly property taxes. The groundswell began in 1978 when Californians ratified Proposition 13, rolling back property tax rates to a combined maximum of 1 percent and limiting annual increases in taxable values to 2 percent or the purchase price in the event the property was sold during the preceding year. Subsequent **tax and expenditure limitations (TELs)** have drawn on the California approach, and while each has its own unique set of constraints and targets for relief, they can be grouped into broad-based limits and more targeted limits. Although states have always imposed limitations on the taxing capabilities of local governments, such as capping the maximum property tax rate, the following discussion focuses on more recent efforts to constrain locally imposed taxes.

Broad tax relief measures

Four states—Colorado (1992), Missouri (1996), Nevada (1996), and Oklahoma (1992)—responded to citizens' pleas for tax relief by adopting a requirement that increases in tax rates could not be made without voter approval. Colorado's Taxpayer Bill of Rights (TABOR) not only requires voter approval for any increases in local tax rates but also restricts revenue growth in local governments to inflation plus population growth, unless voters approve otherwise. Missouri's famous Hancock Amendment requires voter approval not only on taxes but also on fees, one of the more sweeping local revenue limitations in the nation. Eight states limit annual increases in the taxable value of property (tax base), but six states—Arizona, California, Florida, Maryland, New York, and Oregon—apply the limits to individual properties. A few states extend voter approval to require approval by an extraordinary majority. In 1986 Californians approved Proposition 62, requiring two-thirds approval by voters for any new general fund taxes, and in 1996 they approved Proposition 218, extending the extraordinary majority requirement to new fees and assessments.

A number of states cap tax rates, particularly for the property tax. Although many states have constitutional limits on the maximum rates that particular types of local governments can impose, such as $1.50 maximum property tax rate for general law cities in Texas and $2.50 for home-rule cities, Proposition 13 unleashed citizen efforts to limit the combined tax rates of overlapping local governments. One of the earliest efforts following Proposition 13 was Massachusetts's Proposition 2½, passed in 1980, limiting the overall tax levy to 2.5 percent of the tax base; in addition, yields in the property tax cannot increase by more than 2.5 percent annually unless approved by at least two-thirds of the voters. Idaho (1978) and Arizona (1980) both adopted a combined cap of 1 percent of the tax base.

Thirteen states use some variation of truth in taxation, described more fully in the following chapter, to hold local legislators more accountable for increases in the local property tax burden.[57] Two states, Kentucky and Texas, give voters the power to overrule their local governments should they approve an extraordinary increase in the tax revenue. The advantage of truth in taxation—particularly in states such as Florida and Utah, where a mailed notice is sent to each property owner before a final tax rate is approved—is that it elevates the visibility of the tax rate–setting process while preserving local autonomy from state fiat.

Targeted tax relief measures

In recent years, a number of states have also pursued tax relief measures targeted to specific classes of citizens, particularly senior citizens. For example, Pennsylvania's Act 77 freezes property assessments of senior citizens in counties levying a sales tax. As part of a sweeping tax reform initiative, Michigan adopted a two-tiered rate structure for school property taxes that was designed to reduce the burden on home owners. In lieu of locally set school taxes, the state now imposes a 6 mill tax on all primary residences and a 24 mill tax on secondary homes and businesses that fund schools. Still other states, such as Texas, freeze the school taxes of senior citizens at the amount they pay the year either spouse turns 65. In 2003, Texas voters amended the state constitution to give cities and counties the option to extend the **senior tax freeze** to their levies. City councils and county commissioner courts have been slow to adopt the freeze because of the long-term adverse impact it has on local budgets.

Do tax limitations work?

There are two general answers to this question: First, it depends on the type of tax limitation, and second, tax limitations almost never work as proponents intend and often have unintended and counterproductive consequences. Although no comparative analysis of tax limitation measures has been undertaken, casual observation suggests that those limitations requiring voter approval to change tax (or fee) rates limit increases in the tax burden most effectively, followed by those limitations requiring extraordinary majorities of legislative bodies for changes in the rate or base.

Formal analyses of tax limitations suggest, however, that these measures have consequences frequently unanticipated and even antithetical to the proponents' original intentions. For example, several studies of California's Proposition 13 have found that the amendment has resulted in

- Greater concentration of decision making at the state level

- A significant reduction in the fiscal and political autonomy of local governments, particularly school districts and counties, thereby impeding the home-rule capabilities of local governments and their capacity to shape their local economies

- Less accountability for local governments as they shift dependence to more indirect (hidden) taxes and to property exactions such as impact fees

- Marked increases in horizontal inequities between new buyers of property, whose property is assessed at its purchase price, and long-term residents, whose increases in property assessments are limited to 2 percent per annum (resulting in tax burdens for comparable properties that are as much as five times greater for the recent buyer)

- A significant shift in the property tax burden to home owners and away from business owners because of the more frequent turnover of residential property

- Chronic housing shortages, especially for multifamily units, because of the punitive tax burden for new housing, and thus the lower profit margins for newer developments compared with existing developments

- Competitive disadvantages for newer commercial businesses for the same reasons as cited immediately above, giving a competitive advantage to established retail and service industries. As a result, retail markets in California are less competitive, which means higher prices for consumers.[58]

Accumulated evidence from several tax limitation initiatives suggests that their full impact is often delayed by several years, and in the case of Proposition 13, even decades, but that their effects become cumulative and most apparent in recessions. A 2002 study identified three phases of the post–Proposition 13 era in California: state bailout (1978–1981), institutionalization and transition (1981–1991), and readjustment (1991–present). It then quoted a former Alameda County administrator who observed that "1991 was the beginning of the 'great depression' for California counties."[59] It was during the recession of 2001 that Californians began to experience the cumulative effects and drag on economic growth that Proposition 13 imposed on the state's economy.

Finally, tax limitations, while providing relief to some fortunate taxpayers, result in shifts in the burden to other, often less equitable and economically efficient sources, particularly more narrow based excise taxes. Most disconcerting is their long-term impact on state and local governments' capacity to pursue countercyclical measures. Casual observation suggests that recessions are steeper and more protracted in states with limited tax and spending options. Tax limitations make it more difficult for state and local governments to take preemptive action to restore economic stability and strengthen employment opportunities.

Revenues and disaster management

Today local governments must have plans for dealing with disasters, and those plans should include the effects of emergencies and disasters on local government revenues, not to mention expenditures.

Emergency management involves four different types of actions: mitigation, preparation, response, and recovery.[60] Budget issues, and specifically local tax and nontax issues, should be part of the planning and decision making in each of these phases. No research exists on the impact of disasters and emergencies on local revenue structures, although there is a small but growing body of knowledge on their

Dealing with disasters through information sharing

The key to building understanding and competence in dealing with disasters is for local governments to share their knowledge and experience in this area. Within the following topics are some of the questions that might be answered through sharing.

Mitigation

1. Is our insurance coverage sufficient for large-scale losses of city or county property?

2. What impact would the most likely types of disasters or emergencies have on the property tax base? Sales tax base? Water and wastewater service charges? Other major revenue sources?

3. What level of budget reserves is appropriate given a community's vulnerability to particular types of disasters or emergencies?

4. What protection should be available to cover debt service costs in the event of a disaster?

Preparedness

1. What role should state government have in ensuring the continuity of operations in disaster-prone local governments?

2. What is the cost and what procedures should be followed to restore revenue administration (collections and enforcement) in the event of a disaster?

3. Do mutual aid agreements include assistance with revenue-related needs in the event of a disaster?

Response

1. What surcharges to taxes or service charges would be available to cover short-term revenue needs in the event of a major disaster?

2. Under what conditions can the local government incur short-term debt to cover the operating costs associated with an emergency or disaster?

3. What loans or grants are available from the state or federal government to ensure continuity in operations for the local government?

Recovery

1. What tax relief options should be considered for households and businesses in the event of a disaster?

2. What alternatives should be available for taxpayers unable to pay their liability? For those unable to pay for locally provided utility services? How should penalties and interest on late payments be treated for victims of a disaster?

---

effects on local and state expenditures. The U.S. Department of Homeland Security's color-coded system for terrorism alerts certainly has an impact on state and local operating budgets. Although each community's vulnerability to natural and technological disasters is unique, including budget issues in its comprehensive emergency plan will mitigate the long-term effects of those events on the local economy and its capacity to return to normalcy. Like businesses, a local government needs to have a plan in place for maintaining and financing continuity of operations. In 2002 the parish of Terrebonne, Louisiana, adopted a 0.25 percent sales tax dedicated to hurricane protection, but few other examples exist of such dedicated revenue sources for disaster preparation.

When Moore, Oklahoma, was hit by two devastating tornadoes in 1999 and 2003, the first being a category F-5 tornado, several factors affected the city's revenues. First, because Moore relies on the sales tax for much of its operating budget, revenues actually increased following the 1999 tornado, possibly because households and businesses were buying replacement supplies and building materials. The school district, which relies more heavily on property tax revenues, suffered significant revenue decreases. The state legislature did provide property tax relief to victims. Second, the city's primary sales tax generator, a Wal-Mart Supercenter, was not hit by the tornado. Had it been, and had the company chosen not to rebuild or to delay rebuilding, the impact on city revenues would have been greater. Third, the city maintained a good insurance policy that covered most of the damage to city-owned property. The portion that was not covered, including deductibles, was reimbursed by the Federal Emergency Management Agency (FEMA). Fourth, the total cost of cleaning up after the 1999 storm exceeded $6 million, most of which was reimbursed by FEMA. Finally, the city's bond ratings were not adversely affected by either the 1999 or the 2003 tornado. The city was in the process of refinancing a bond issue when the 1999 tornado hit, but it was able to proceed with the sale after appropriate disclosures of the potential impact of the storm.

While federal and, to a lesser extent, state aid help to offset the cost of responding to and recovering from a disaster, much of that cost goes uncompensated. A major series of disasters, such as the multiple hurricanes that swept through Florida in 2004, impose long-term costs on local governments, which must be absorbed locally through delayed growth and ultimately higher state and local tax burdens.

Summary

Evidence indicates that business opportunities (space availability, cost of land and labor, transportation networks, and education level) are vastly more important than tax opportunities to the location decision. However, the local tax burden does increase in importance as firms narrow their search for a possible site.

Local property taxes are more important to firms that have a greater investment in plant and equipment. Evidence also indicates that local governments with higher-than-average property and income taxes experience a decline in property values over the long term as a result of disinvestment by businesses. There is some evidence that an above-average local tax burden has a slight negative effect on job growth at the county level.

A low tax burden does not necessarily mean a lower cost of doing business in that jurisdiction. If lower taxes mean fewer public services, particularly those used by businesses, then operating costs may be much higher because businesses must absorb the cost of providing those services.

Evidence indicates that tax incentives seldom have an impact on business location, except in marginal cases where firms are otherwise indifferent to the choice between two or more possible sites.

To reduce the spillover effects of tax incentives, local governments should have access to a broad-based tax other than the property tax: preferably the incentive should be provided by a larger geographic jurisdiction, such as the county or even the state.

In designing an economic development policy, local governments should assess their strengths and weaknesses and then target their development efforts toward firms likely to benefit the most from those strengths.

Appendix: Policy statement for tax abatement—Plano, Texas

I. General Purpose and Objectives

The City of Plano is committed to the promotion and retention of high quality development in all parts of the City and to an ongoing improvement in the quality of life for its citizens. Insofar as the enhancement and expansion of the local economy are generally served by these objectives, the City of Plano will, on a case-by-case basis, give consideration to providing tax abatements as a stimulation for economic development in Plano. The City of Plano will consider providing incentives in accordance with the procedures and criteria outlined in this document. Nothing herein shall imply or suggest that the City of Plano is under any obligation to provide tax abatement to any applicant. All applicants shall be considered on a case-by-case basis.

II. Criteria

Any request for tax abatement shall be reviewed by the Joint Committee on Tax Abatement, said Committee being comprised of two elected officials from each of the following entities: City of Plano, Collin County Community College and Collin County. Participation on the Joint Committee on Tax Abatement is elective and determined by each taxing entity. Because of provisions of the Texas Education Code, Plano Independent School District will not be able to participate in tax abatements under this policy.

The Joint Committee on Tax Abatement serves as a recommending body to the taxing units regarding whether economic development incentives should be offered in each individual case. Their recommendation shall be based upon an evaluation of the criteria that each applicant will be requested to address in narrative format.

III. Value of Incentives

Following an assessment of the narrative response, the Joint Committee on Tax Abatement shall determine whether it is in the best interests of the affected participating taxing entities to recommend that an abatement be offered to the applicant. Additional consideration beyond the criteria will include such items as the degree to which the project/applicant furthers the goals and objectives of the community or meets or compliments a special need identified by the community.

Tax abatement shall be offered in two categories: 1) real property and/or 2) business personal property. Real property abatements will be offered to applicants that pursue the construction of new or expanded facilities in which to house the applicable project or modernization of existing facilities. The abatement will apply to the value of improvements made. Business personal property abatements will be offered to applicants that pursue the purchase or long-term lease of existing facilities. The abatement will apply to the value of new personal property brought into the taxing jurisdiction.

Once a determination has been made that a tax abatement should be offered, the value and term of the abatement will be determined based upon information provided in the narrative response.

IV. Procedural Guidelines

Any person, organization or corporation desiring that Plano consider providing tax abatement to encourage location, modernization of existing facilities, or expansion of operations within the city limits of Plano, shall be required to comply with the following procedural guidelines. Nothing within these guidelines shall imply or suggest that Plano is under any obligation to provide tax abatement in any amount or value to any applicant.

Preliminary Application Steps

A. Applicant shall complete the attached "Application for Tax Abatement."

B. Applicant shall address all criteria questions outlined in the application in narrative format.

C. Applicant shall prepare a plat showing the precise location of the property, all roadways within 500 feet of the site, and all existing land uses and zoning within 500 feet of the site.

D. 14 days prior to the public hearing, the applicant must provide a metes & bounds property description and a general address of the property.

E. Applicant shall complete all forms and information detailed in items A through D above and submit them to the Director of Finance, City of Plano, P.O. Box 860358, Plano, Texas, 75086-0358 (email: jmcgrane@plano.Gov). Applicant shall also submit a copy of the application to the Executive Director of the Plano Economic Development Board, 4800 Preston Park Boulevard, Suite A-100, Plano, Texas 75093 (email: sbane@airmail.Net).

Application Review Steps

F. All information in the application package detailed above will be reviewed for completeness and accuracy. Additional information may be requested as needed.

G. The application will be distributed to the appropriate City departments for internal review and comments. Additional information may be requested as needed.

H. Copies of the complete application package and staff comments will be provided to the Joint Committee on Tax Abatement.

Consideration of the Application

I. The Joint Committee on Tax Abatement will consider the application at a regular or called meeting(s). The applicant must submit the tax abatement application to the City of Plano at least fourteen (14) days prior to the meeting of the Committee, scheduled on a monthly basis. Upon review, the Joint Tax Committee will determine whether it will recommend a proposed offer of abatement to the applicant. The proposed offer shall not bind the City of Plano or other taxing entities to grant an abatement.

J. Upon receipt of the proposed offer, the applicant will have ninety (90) days to accept, reject or request an extension of the proposed offer. All responses and requests shall be made to the Joint Committee on Tax Abatement to extend the tax abatement proposal. In certain circumstances, the time frame may be shortened. See S. below.

K. Upon written acceptance by the applicant, the recommendation of the Joint Committee on Tax Abatement, with all relevant materials, will be forwarded by the City of Plano to the chief administrative officer of each taxing unit.

L. The City Council of Plano may consider a resolution calling a public hearing to consider establishment of a tax reinvestment zone.

M. The City Council of Plano may hold the public hearing and determine whether the project is "feasible and practical and would be of benefit to the land to be included in the zone and to the municipality after expiration of the tax abatement agreement."

N. The City Council of Plano may consider adoption of an ordinance designating the area described in the legal description of the proposed project as a commercial/industrial tax abatement zone.

O. The City Council may consider adoption of a resolution approving the terms and conditions of a contract between the City and the applicant governing the provision of the tax abatement.

P. The governing bodies of the Collin County and Collin County Community College may consider ratification of and participation in the tax abatement agreement between the City of Plano and the applicant.

Q. Certain information provided to the Joint Committee on Tax Abatement in connection with an application or request for tax abatement may be confidential and not subject to public disclosure until the tax abatement agreement is executed. The Joint Committee on Tax Abatement, through the City of Plano, will respond to requests for disclosure as required by law and will assert exceptions to disclosure as it deems relevant. Texas Government Code Chapter 552; Texas Tax Code section 312.003.

R. If the abatement agreement is approved by the taxing units, the City of Plano will send copies of the agreement to the Texas Department of Economic Development, Office of the Comptroller, and to the State Property Tax Division each April.

S. Property is assessed on January 1 of each year. It is the obligation of the applicant to ensure that all final approvals for the tax abatement agreement have occurred by December 31st of the year prior to the year the improvements are assessed. No tax abatement can be given for improvements that are on the Tax Assessor's Roll before the tax abatement is effective. The applicant should be aware that because of mandatory publication requirements, compliance with the governing body's calendar, and other matters, the process for obtaining approval for a tax abatement with the governing body is extensive and may take as long as six weeks. It is the applicant's responsibility to ensure the follow up of these items and approvals.

V. Tax Abatement Agreement Terms

At a minimum, all tax abatements shall include the following provisions:

1. No business personality shall be located from any other reinvestment zone;

2. A minimum number of jobs must be maintained at the time real property improvements are completed;

3. Right of inspection to the premises must be provided to ensure compliance with the agreement; and

4. The right of recapture of previously abated taxes if applicant defaults in any provision of the agreement, including meeting the threshold value for both real property and business personalty.

Source: City of Plano, Texas, *Tax Abatement Policy Statement,* Resolution No. 2002-9-9 (R), September 9, 2002.

1 William H. Oakland and William A. Testa, "The Benefit Principle as a Preferred Approach to Taxing Business in the Midwest," *Economic Development Quarterly* 14 (May 2000): 154–164.

2 John E. Anderson and Robert W. Wassmer, "The Decision to 'Bid for Business': Municipal Behavior in Granting Property Tax Abatements," *Regional Science and Urban Economics* 25 (December 1995): 739–757.

3 Bryan D. Jones and Lynn W. Bachelor, "Local Policy Discretion and the Corporate Surplus," in *Urban Economic Development,* ed. Richard D. Bingham and John P. Blair (Beverly Hills, Calif.: Sage, 1984), 249.

4 Robert Tannenwald, "Rating Massachusetts' Tax Competitiveness," *New England Economic Review,* Federal Reserve Bank of Boston (November/December 1987): 33.

5 Alberta Charney, "Intraurban Manufacturing Location Decisions and Local Tax Differentials," *Journal of Urban Economics* 14 (September 1983): 184–205.

6 Cited in Tannenwald, "Rating Massachusetts' Tax Competitiveness," 39.

7 Steven G. Koven and Thomas S. Lyons, *Economic Development: Strategies for State and Local Practice* (Washington, D.C.: International City/County Management Association, 2003): 17.

8 Susan S. Jacobs and Michael Wasylenko, "Government Policy to Stimulate Economic Development: Enterprise Zones," in *Financing State and Local Governments in the 1980s: Issues and Trends,* ed. Norman Walzer and David L. Chicoine (Cambridge, Mass.: Oelgeschlager, Gunn & Hain, 1981), 188.

9 W. Norton Grubb, "The Flight to the Suburbs of Population and Employment, 1960–1970," *Journal of Urban Economics* 11 (May 1982): 348–367.

10 Gerald Carlino and Edwin S. Mills, "Do Public Policies Affect County Growth?" *Business Review,* Federal Reserve Bank of Philadelphia (July/August 1985): 12; Timothy Bartik, "Business Location Decisions in the United States: Estimates of the Effects of Unionization, Taxes, and Other Characteristics of States," *Journal of Business and Economic Statistics* 3 (January 1985): 14–22.

11 Cited in Michael Wasylenko, "Local Tax Policy and Industry Location: A Review of the Evidence," in *Proceedings of the Seventy-Eighth Annual Conference of the National Tax Association–Tax Institute of America* (Denver, Colo., 1985), 223.

12 Bartik, "Business Location Decisions"; Rodney Erickson and Michael Wasylenko, "Firm Relocation and Site Selection in Suburban Municipalities," *Journal of Urban Economics* 8 (July 1980): 69–85.

13 Therese J. McGuire, "Do Taxes Matter? Yes, No, Maybe So," *State Tax Today,* 9 June 2003, 22.

14 Katharine L. Bradbury and Helen F. Ladd, "City Taxes and Property Tax Bases," National Bureau of Economic Research (NBER) Working Paper 2197 (Cambridge, Mass.: NBER, March 1987), 27.

15 Ibid., 28.

16 Wasylenko, "Local Tax Policy and Industry Location," 224–226.

17 Ibid., 226.

18 McGuire, "Do Taxes Matter? Yes, No, Maybe So," 21.

19 Ibid., 15.

20 Andrew F. Haughwout et al., "Local Revenue Hills: Evidence from Four U.S. Cities," NBER Working Paper 9686 (Cambridge, Mass.: NBER, May 2003). Available at www.nber.org/papers/w9686.

21 Michael Wasylenko, "The Effect of Business Climate on Employment Growth," in *Final Report of the Minnesota Tax Study Commission,* vol. 2, *Staff Papers,* ed. Robert D. Ebel and Therese J. McGuire (St. Paul, Minn.: Butterworth Legal Publishers, 1986), 62–65.

22 Robert L. Bland and Phanit Laosirirat, "Tax Limitations to Reduce Municipal Property Taxes: Truth in Taxation in Texas," *Journal of Urban Affairs* 19 (spring 1997): 45–58.

23 Edward L. Glaeser and Albert Saiz, "The Rise of the Skilled City," NBER Working Paper 10191 (Cambridge, Mass.: NBER, December 2003). Available at www.nber.org/papers.

24 George R. Zodrow, "Reflections on the Economic Theory of Local Tax Incentives," *State Tax Today,* 9 June 2003, 36.

25 National Association of State Development Agencies, *Directory of Incentives for Business Investment and Development in the United States: A State-by-State Guide,* 6th ed. (Washington, D.C.: National Association of State Development Agencies, 2002), CD-ROM.

26 Texas Comptroller of Public Accounts, "Property Tax Abatements in Texas," chap. 2 in *Special Report: Texas Economic Development Incentives,* March 2003. Available at www.cpa.state.tx.us/specialrpt/ ecodev03.

27 *Tax Abatement* (Springfield: Illinois Department of Commerce and Community Affairs, Office of Urban Assistance, n.d.), 2.

28 "Tools for Growth: Tax Abatement/Tax Increment Financing," *Statement* (Texas State Property Tax Board, November 1986), 4.

29 Craig L. Johnson and K. Friz, "A Review of State Tax Increment Financing Laws," in *Tax Increment Financing and Economic Development: Uses, Structures, and Impact,* ed. Craig L. Johnson and Joyce Y. Man (Albany: State University of New York Press, 2001), 31–56.

30 Rachel Weber, Saurav Dev Bhatta, and David Merriman, "Does Tax Increment Financing Raise Urban Industrial Property Values?" *Urban Studies* 40 (September 2003): 2003.

31 Mark Vander Schaaf, *Biennial Report on Tax Incremental Financing (TIF)* (Madison: Wisconsin Department of Development, Division of Research and Analysis, January 1987), 56.

32 Weber et al., "Does Tax Increment Financing Raise Urban Industrial Property Values?"

33 Joyce Y. Man and Mark S. Rosentraub, "Tax Increment Financing: Municipal Adoption and Its Effects on Property Value Growth," *Public Finance Review* 26 (November 1998): 523–547.

34 Weber et al., "Does Tax Increment Financing Raise Urban Industrial Property Values?"

35 Ibid., 2018.

36 Joel Michael, "Tax Increment Financing: Local Redevelopment Finance after Tax Reform," *Government Finance Review* 3 (October 1987): 18.

37 Vander Schaaf, *Biennial Report,* 4.

38 Michael, "Tax Increment Financing," 18.

39 Vander Schaaf, *Biennial Report,* 7.

40 *Tax Increment Financing* (Springfield: Illinois Department of Commerce and Community Affairs, Office of Urban Assistance, November 1986), 6.

41 "Tools for Growth," 6.

42 *Tax Increment Financing* (Springfield, Ill.), 6.

43 "Tools for Growth," 6.

44 Michael, "Tax Increment Financing," 19.

45 Mary Alice Davis, "Tax Increment Financing: Texas Tries a New Urban Development Tool," Special Legislative Report no. 82 (Austin: Texas House of Representatives, House Study Group, June 11, 1982), 23–24.

46 Andrew Zimbalist, *May the Best Team Win: Baseball Economics and Public Policy* (Washington, D.C.: Brookings Institution Press, 2003), 123.

47 David Swindell and Mark S. Rosentraub, "Who Benefits from the Presence of Professional Sports Teams? The Implications for Public Funding of Stadiums and Arenas," *Public Administration Review* 58 (January/February 1998): 16.

48 Ibid.

49 Gerald A. Carlino and N. Edward Coulson, "Should Cities Be Ready for Some Football? Assessing the Social Benefits of Hosting an NFL Team," *Business Review,* Federal Reserve Bank of Philadelphia (2nd quarter 2004): 7–17.

50 Ibid., 13.

51 Zimbalist, *May the Best Team Win,* 125.

52 Ibid., 126.

53 Edward J. Blakely and Ted K. Bradshaw, *Planning Local Economic Development,* 3rd ed. (Thousand Oaks, Calif.: Sage, 2002), 138.

54 Carlino and Coulson, "Should Cities Be Ready for Some Football?" 9.

55 City Manager's Economic Development Plan Committee, *An Economic Development and Marketing Plan for Arlington, Texas* (Arlington, Tex., November 1986).

56 Robert Agranoff and Michael McGuire, *Collaborative Public Management: New Strategies for Local Governments* (Washington, D.C.: Georgetown University Press, 2003).

57 Bland and Laosirirat, "Tax Limitations to Reduce Municipal Property Taxes," 47.

58 Gregory D. Saxton, Christopher W. Hoene, and Steven P. Erie, "Fiscal Constraints and the Loss of Home Rule: The Long-Term Impacts of California's Post–Proposition 13 Fiscal Regime," *American Review of Public Administration* 32 (December 2002): 423–454; Carol Douglas, "Proposition 13—25 Years Later," *State Tax Notes* 30 (October 20, 2003): 222–226; Lenny Goldberg and David Kersten, "Huge Disparities Found in California Commercial Property Taxes," *State Tax Notes* 31 (May 10, 2004): 437–457; Randall G. Holcombe, "Tax and Expenditure Limitations: Issues for Florida," Policy Report no. 932 (April 2001); Terri A. Sexton, Steve M. Sheffrin, and Arthur O'Sullivan, "Proposition 13: Unintended Effects and Feasible Reforms," *National Tax Journal* 52 (March 1999): 99–111.

59 Saxton, Hoene, and Erie, "Fiscal Constraints and the Loss of Home Rule," 425.

60 For a discussion of competing paradigms in disaster management, see David A. McEntire et al., "A Comparison of Disaster Paradigms: The Search for a Holistic Policy Guide," *Public Administration Review* 62 (May/June 2002): 267–281.

The property tax

The changing role of the property tax
Changes in the property tax base
Economic growth and the property tax base
Balancing residential and nonresidential property taxes

Advantages of the property tax
Provides a stable source of revenue
Reaches nonresident property owners
Finances property-related services
Is difficult to evade
Promotes local autonomy

The property tax cycle
Appraisal
Assessment
Collection

Politics and the property tax
Tax relief
Payment methods
Reappraisal
Equity

Summary

Everyone dislikes the property tax until the alternatives are considered.

—Diane Paul

The property tax

Probably no other task tests the communication skills and patience of managers more than explaining to citizens the mechanics of the property tax. Unlike the sales or income tax, both of which are levied at convenient points in a transaction, the property tax is based on wealth and therefore requires that the legal ownership and taxable value of that wealth be established before tax liability can be determined. The periodic reappraisal of property values inevitably creates consternation among owners, who assume that an increase in their property's appraised value means an increase in their tax burden. In addition, the fact that several overlapping local governments tax the same property confuses taxpayers about the source of changes in their tax bill.

local govt
school districts
park districts

Yet the property tax remains the mainstay of most municipal and county revenue structures. Clearly, the taxpayer revolt, which has continued unabated since the late 1970s, has reduced the tax's importance in local government budgets. However, as is noted further on, municipalities still derive an average of about 23 percent of their general fund revenues from the property tax, and counties, about 38 percent. It is the only major tax common to all fifty states, and it is the oldest tax levied in the United States.

This chapter examines issues associated with the property tax and is designed to help city and county managers answer the questions posed by citizen groups, business leaders, and elected representatives.

The changing role of the property tax

Although the property tax is largely the domain of local governments, especially for funding public education, fifteen states still levy a property tax for their operating and debt service purposes.[1] Heaviest users at this level include Michigan, Minnesota, and New Hampshire, all of whom have assumed greater or complete responsibility for funding public education. In 2001, for example, Minnesota adopted a statewide tax on business property dedicated to public schools as part of a measure designed to bring tax relief to home owners. Nevada's statewide tax of 15 cents per $100 assessed value is dedicated to servicing the state's debt.

One result of the taxpayer uprising during the past three decades has been that state legislators have realized the urgency of reducing local government dependence on the property tax. On the average, property taxes are a declining source of revenue for both municipalities and counties (Tables 4–1 and 4–2). While this is true for all population categories, municipalities under 250,000 population generally derive a greater share of their general revenues from the property tax—about 25 percent—than do their larger, more populous counterparts: the share for municipalities over 300,000 is less than 17 percent. Larger cities usually have greater access than smaller jurisdictions to other broad-based taxes, such as the sales or income tax.

Table 4–1
Municipal government dependence on the property tax: Property tax revenue as a percentage of general revenues.

Revenue source	1991–92	1996–97	2001–02
Property taxes	25.1	22.7	22.8
All other taxes	22.3	23.9	24.2
Service charges	18.7	20.9	20.4
Utility charges	22.1	21.4	21.5
Other non taxes	11.9	11.1	11.1
	100.1	100.0	100.0
Total general revenue (in millions)[a]	$161,293	$202,674	$255,220

Source: U.S. Bureau of the Census, *Finances of Municipal and Township Governments,* 1997 Census of Governments 4, no. 4 (September 2000), table 1 (http://www.census.gov/prod/gc97/gc974-4.pdf); and U.S. Bureau of the Census, *Local Summary Tables by Type of Government: 2001–02,* table 2 (http://ftp2.census.gov/govs/estimate/02slsstab2a.xls).

Note: Percentages may not total 100% because of rounding.
[a] Total general revenue includes utility charges but excludes intergovernmental aid, liquor store income, and insurance trust revenue.

Table 4–2
County government dependence on the property tax: Property tax revenue as a percentage of general revenues.

Revenue source	1991–92	1996–97	2001–02
Property taxes	43.5	38.6	38.4
All other taxes	15.0	17.0	17.1
Service charges	25.6	29.1	29.1
Utility charges	1.8	2.2	2.1
Other non taxes	14.1	13.1	13.2
	100.0	100.0	99.9
Total general revenue (in millions)[a]	$ 94,808	$122,161	$161,483

Source: U.S. Bureau of the Census, *Finances of County Governments,* 1997 Census of Governments 4, no. 3 (September 2000), table 1 (http://www.census.gov/prod/gc97/gc974-3.pdf); and U.S. Bureau of the Census, *Local Summary Tables by Type of Government: 2001–02,* table 2 (http://ftp2.census.gov/govs/estimate/02slsstab2a.xls).

Note: Percentages may not total 100% because of rounding.
[a] Total general revenue includes utility charges but excludes intergovernmental aid, liquor store income, and insurance trust revenue.

Historically, county governments have depended much more heavily than cities on the property tax because counties generally have less access to alternative taxes. Large and small counties depend about equally on the property tax, deriving on average about 30–35 percent of their general revenue from it.

Whether the property tax continues to decline in importance depends on a number of factors. If federal and state aid continues its precipitous decline, then local governments will probably increase their use of the property tax. Alternatively, if state legislatures continue their pattern of allowing municipalities and counties greater access to sales and, to a lesser extent, income taxes, then local governments will use this revenue to replace lost federal and state aid and to reduce their dependence on the property tax.

Do local governments rely too heavily on the property tax? The evidence in Tables 4–1 and 4–2 indicates that taxpayers' remaining resentment against the tax is probably motivated by factors other than overreliance on the tax by counties and municipalities. Although school districts depend even more heavily on the tax, their dependence has moderated in recent years, too.

Changes in the property tax base

The property tax is really a collection of taxes on several different types of property that can be grouped into two broad categories: real property and personal property (Figure 4–1). **Real property** is immobile and includes land, natural resources, and fixed improvements to the land. **Personal property** is mobile and includes **tangible property** (furniture, equipment, inventory, and vehicles) and **intangible property** (stocks, taxable bonds, and bank accounts). Because of the difficulty of establishing ownership, only a few states still include intangible property in the tax base. A third, smaller category is state-assessed property (railroad and other public utilities), which spans several local jurisdictions and whose specialized use makes appraisal by state government more cost-effective and equitable.

The property tax base (TB) comprises the assessed (or taxable) value of all types of property. Tax liability (TL) is then the product of assessed value and the locally determined tax rate (TB × TR = TL). The **effective property tax burden** is measured by the ratio of property tax liability to the market value of a property or, in the aggregate, as the ratio of total property tax revenue to the sum of the market values of all taxable property in a taxing jurisdiction.

Shift from personal to real property   During the past four decades, the property tax base has shifted away from personal property and toward real property. This shift is attributable to the complexity of discovering and valuing personal property and to the much greater growth in the value of real property. Although the exact proportion is difficult to know, at least 85 percent of the tax base is now real property.

Eight states (Delaware, Hawaii, Illinois, New Hampshire, New York, North Dakota, Pennsylvania, and South Dakota) exempt all personal property from state or local taxation.[2] Commercial and industrial personal property remains taxable in forty-two states, but thirty-five exempt business inventories from the property tax (the freeport exemption discussed in the previous chapter).[3] A number of states set the taxable value of inventory at less than 100 percent of its true value: West Virginia assesses inventory items at 60 percent of value; Georgia at 40 percent; Indiana and Oklahoma at 35 percent; Arkansas at 20 percent, and Louisiana and Mississippi at only 15 percent. In some cases, the exemption applies only to fin-

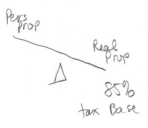

Figure 4–1

Types of property.

Real property	Personal property
Land	Tangible
Farmland	Inventory
Open spaces	Equipment
Timberland	Vehicles
Minerals	Jewelry
	Artwork
Improvements	Furniture
Buildings (residential, commercial, industrial)	Intangible
Infrastructure	Stocks
Underground improvements	Taxable bonds and notes
	Insurance policies
	Bank deposits
	Patents and copyrights
	Trademarks
	Accounts receivable

ished goods destined for out-of-state markets. Georgia authorizes counties and cities, with voter approval, to exempt from 20 to 100 percent of the value on goods in transit.

Agricultural personal property (farm equipment and inventories) is exempt in sixteen states, mostly in the Midwest. In general, the trend toward state exemption of personal property has benefited the business sector far more than the residential sector because a far greater proportion of business fixed assets are in equipment, vehicles, and inventory.

Shift from business to residential real property Significant shifts have also occurred within the real property component of the tax base. Residential real property, especially single-family homes, represents a rapidly growing share of the tax base, while business real property continues to decline in importance. Although nationally aggregated data are not available, the trend in Texas is likely indicative of what is happening across the nation. In 1981, real residential property (single and multifamily) represented 31.5 percent of the tax base in the state, increasing to 44.4 percent in 1991 and to an alarming 57.1 percent in 2001.[4] In other words, in this thirty-year span, real residential property increased from one-third to almost three-fifths of the state's tax base. By contrast, real commercial and industrial property (including utilities) declined from 41.5 percent in 1981 to 37.9 percent of the tax base in 1991 and to 33.2 percent in 2001. The principal cause of this change is the rapid appreciation in residential property values relative to business real property that has occurred during the past thirty years in addition to the above-mentioned shift from personal to real property, especially residential.

During the next decade, the property tax base will continue its shift to real property, and the percentage of property tax revenues obtained from residential property will continue to grow, although probably not at the same rate as in the past. On the other hand, commercial and industrial property, notably tangible personal property, will continue to decline in importance in the tax base—especially as the economy continues its shift toward more services—but again not at the same rate as in the past. In short, the property tax is no longer a general tax on all types of property but is increasingly limited to property that is easiest to discover and appraise and has the greatest potential for appreciation in value.

Economic growth and the property tax base

The important factor in sustaining real property values, according to one study, is the level of economic activity.[5] Per capita property values are highest where residential incomes are higher, where population has increased, and where private employment per capita is higher.

Changes in population in a community have profound effects on property tax revenues. A population increase usually creates higher property values as households and businesses bid for the limited supply of desirable land and buildings. Similarly, property values usually drop with declines in population as demand for property, especially residential property, declines. Other things being equal, remaining property owners incur a higher property tax burden to sustain public services. Of the three types of tax bases—property (wealth), consumption (sales), and income—the property tax base is the most sensitive to population changes.

For communities that rely heavily on the property tax, population losses can have highly destabilizing effects on local budgets if appraisals are kept current with property values. Specific strategies for responding to population losses were outlined in Figure 1–1. To avoid population loss, local governments may choose some of the strategies discussed in Chapter 3 to attract business investment and bring jobs to their jurisdictions.

Balancing residential and nonresidential property taxes

Governments have considerable discretion in distributing the property tax burden. Using such devices as homestead exemptions, circuitbreaker programs, classification of property, use-value appraisals, tax abatements, freezing tax liability for certain classes of property owners, and preferential assessment practices, a local government allocates its property tax between residential and nonresidential sectors. Three questions arise:

1. How does the proportion of commercial and industrial property to residential property affect the tax burden of home owners?
2. Do local governments tend to shift the tax burden to business property?
3. Does the shift from manufacturing to a service-based economy affect the property taxes borne by the business sector?

Taxing commercial and industrial property   A widely held assumption is that the revenue from property taxes on the business sector generally exceeds the cost of providing public services to it. Other things being equal, the expectation is that expanding the commercial and industrial share of the tax base reduces the property tax burden on the residential sector.

A corollary is that jurisdictions experiencing rapid increases in business activity, as measured by the number of private sector jobs per capita, will generally tax business property more heavily than residential property. Studies support this conclusion, too. A 1987 study of the seventy-eight largest U.S. cities showed that those with higher levels of employment per capita generally taxed business property more heavily by providing more tax relief to residential property owners.[6] Conversely, where job growth was slow, property tax relief favored business owners over residential owners. Apparently, cities that wish to attract business investment tend to impose a relatively lower property tax burden on that sector.

Another study, which examined the ninety-three largest cities in Texas, found that those with greater concentrations of industrial property had higher per capita property tax burdens, specifically for operating purposes, than households in other cities in the study, apparently in recognition of industry's greater ability to export its tax burden forward to nonresident consumers or backward to stock owners.[7] By contrast, cities with higher concentrations of commercial property (shopping malls, retail stores, business offices) had relatively lower property tax burdens than other cities in the study, controlling for all other effects. These cities relied on a local option sales tax, which provides a mechanism for tax exportation, especially in the case of regional shopping centers.

Allocating the property tax burden   In many communities, the relative political strength of home owners compared with owners of business property, many of whom are absentee, creates pressure that effectively shifts the tax burden to business. However, the 1987 study of the seventy-eight largest U.S. cities noted above found that the average effective property tax burden on residential property is 98 percent of that on business, suggesting that these cities allocate the tax burden roughly equally between the two sectors. This study also revealed the following patterns:

- Cities that rely more heavily on the property tax impose a relatively lower burden on business property than on residential property.

- Cities where residential property represents a greater share of the tax base tend to impose a lower property tax burden on residential than on nonresidential property.
- Cities appear more willing to increase the property tax burden on business when the local economy is strong than when it is weak.[8]

These findings suggest that local governments use discretionary measures to strategically allocate the property tax burden between the residential and nonresidential sectors to maximize the competitive position of the jurisdiction.

What are some of the measures jurisdictions use to favor either the business or the residential sector? Exemptions, such as those for inventory or equipment, benefit the business sector by lowering its effective tax burden. Tax abatement and tax increment financing (discussed in detail in Chapter 3) provide preferential tax treatment for new or expanding businesses.

To provide tax relief for residential property, one of the most commonly used measures is the homestead exemption available in forty-eight states. This partial exemption reduces the taxable value of the primary residence of property owners, thereby lowering the effective tax burden on this type of property. Some states permit local governments to classify property by use and then apply a different tax rate or level of assessment to each class; this practice is commonly known as a **split tax roll.** Such classification schemes generally favor residential property over income-producing property, although Nebraska assesses all nonagricultural property at 100 percent of value but agricultural property at 80 percent.[9]

Local governments may also use the frequency and methods of appraisal to shift the tax burden. Studies repeatedly document the tendency for local governments to underassess residential property and overassess commercial and industrial property. The 1987 study noted above found that all but ten of the seventy-eight largest cities assessed residential property at a lower fraction of market value than nonresidential property, although only nine cities were legally permitted to classify property for tax purposes.[10]

Impact of growth in the service sector   According to the 1987 study, "the mix of employment by industry has no apparent systematic relationship with property values, contrary to the hypothesis that cities with more nonmanufacturing jobs have lower property values."[11] For city and county managers, then, the loss of manufacturing jobs should not be overly disconcerting—as long as these jobs are replaced with jobs in other sectors, including the service sector. (Unfortunately, communities experiencing the greatest loss in manufacturing jobs tend to be the least able to generate new jobs.) However, this same study found that although relative growth in service employment does not reduce the nonresidential share of the gross tax base, it does decrease the share of property taxes borne by the business sector.[12] This is because service firms have a lower investment in property-intensive facilities for manufacturing, warehousing, and transporting finished goods. Service industries may also receive favorable tax treatment because they are generally more mobile than manufacturing firms and so local governments must make efforts to stem their emigration to jurisdictions with lower taxes.

Summary   In sum, the tax burden on residential owners does decline significantly as the per capita amount of commercial and industrial property increases. However, tremendous diversity exists among local governments in how they allocate the burden between the residential and business sectors. Local governments seem to allocate this burden so as to maximize their competitive position relative to other governments.

Getting to value

One of the most confusing aspects of the property tax is the process for establishing taxable value. The following terms should be understood:

Market value The price that a knowledgeable and prudent buyer would agree to pay a willing seller in a competitive and open market. True market value is unknown and can only be estimated.

Sales price The amount of money (or other goods or services) exchanged for a property. In legal parlance, sales price is often referred to as the **consideration** given for a property.

Appraised value An estimate of market value made by a knowledgeable person using appropriate methods. Appraisers rely on three basic methods to estimate market value: (1) the **sales comparison method** uses data from recent sales as an indicator of what buyers are asking and sellers are negotiating for settlement prices; (2) the **cost method** determines property values, especially for unique properties or intermediary facilities like warehouses, by using the cost of materials and labor, less depreciation, for replicating the structure plus the value of the land associated with the structure; and (3) the income method uses the capitalization formula [value = (revenues–expenses) / rate of return] to determine the value of income-producing property such as a retail or wholesale outlet or industrial plant.

Use (or production) value An alternative basis for establishing appraised value that considers the property's worth given its *current* use (such as a farm) rather than its highest and best use (such as a housing development).

Mass appraisal A variation of the sales comparison method. Sometimes referred to as computer-assisted mass appraisal, this method uses statistical modeling to replicate the market and provide a basis for estimating market value, especially for single-family residential properties.

Assessed value The taxable value (tax base) of the property. The appraised value is adjusted for partial exemptions (such as a homestead exemption) and/or fractional assessment to establish a property's taxable value. This value is then multiplied by the tax rate to determine tax liability (TB × TR = TL). In order to protect property owners from excessive increases in their taxable values, six states cap annual increases in assessed value: California at 2 percent; Florida, New Mexico, and Oregon at 3 percent; and Michigan and Oklahoma at 5 percent.[13]

Acquisition value Proposition 13 introduced this new valuation standard in which appraised and assessed value are recalibrated only when a real property sells. Florida and New Mexico limit use of this valuation standard to single-family residences; the standard sets appraised value at a property's selling price and then benchmarks the capped annual increases in assessed value to this new appraised value.

Equalized value An adjustment to assessed value, often made by a state agency, to bring assessments into closer conformance with a common statewide assessment ratio. In states where the formula for allocating funding for public education includes a factor for the taxable value of property in the school district, equalized values assures equity in the allocation of that aid.

Advantages of the property tax

Given the lengthy list of its disadvantages, the survival and continued use of the property tax is remarkable. Although experts have often predicted its demise, the tax continues as a mainstay in the revenue structures of most local governments, probably because of its capacity to adapt to the preferences and needs of different interest groups. For example, local governments can target tax relief to groups considered deserving while they shift more of the tax burden to sectors with a greater ability to bear it. On the other hand, abating the property tax provides a discretionary incentive that local governments can use to attract business investment.

From a strictly fiscal perspective, the property tax has many advantages that also make it a likely permanent fixture in local revenue structures. Among these advantages, it

- Provides a stable source of revenue
- Taxes nonresident property owners who benefit from local services
- Finances property-related services, such as police and fire protection, and the construction of publicly owned infrastructure, such as streets, curbs and sidewalks, and storm drainage systems
- Is difficult to evade, making collection and enforcement easier for local governments
- Enables local governments in the United States to achieve their unique form of autonomy from state and federal control, thereby forestalling centralization of power at higher levels of government.

The next five sections consider these advantages in detail.

Provides a stable source of revenue

The primary reason for the property tax's continued importance to local governments is the reliable flow of revenue it provides during the budget period (although revenue from the tax does vary from one budget period to another, depending on the frequency of revaluation and on the local real estate market). Other taxes, such as the sales and income taxes and even nontax revenues, fluctuate with changes in the local and national economies. Governments that depend more heavily on the property tax are less vulnerable to midyear revenue shortfalls precipitated by changing economic conditions. On the whole, local governments should have access to either a general sales tax or an income tax, but they should also continue to rely on the property tax for most of their general fund revenue because of the tax's stability through the budget year. Ideally, local governments should raise no more than $1.00 in sales taxes and $1.50 in income taxes for every $1.00 in property taxes.

Reaches nonresident property owners

Another advantage of the property tax is that it reaches nonresident property owners who benefit from local services yet escape the local sales or income tax.

A related merit of the property tax, from a local government perspective, is its exportability. Exportability depends primarily on the nature of the demand for a product or service. The tax burden shifts forward when there are few substitutes for a good or service and consumers' purchases are relatively unaffected by price fluctuations. The more sensitive consumers are to price changes, or the more available substitutes are that are not subject to the tax, the more the burden shifts backward to owners. The property tax can shift the tax burden (especially on income-producing property) forward to nonresident consumers through higher prices or backward to nonresident owners, such as stockholders, through lower profits. In a 2003 study, the Texas state comptroller estimated that 21.1 percent of the property taxes levied by that state's school districts was exported to out-of-state consumers and owners, with the remainder borne by in-state property owners.[14]

Finances property-related services

The property tax recaptures for the community some of the increase in property value created by government-provided services. For example, assume that two towns have exactly the same population characteristics and spending levels, but one spends twice as much on police protection and has half the crime rate of the other. Other things being equal, property values will be higher in the town with the lower crime rate. Through the property tax, property owners return to the local government some of the value its services have created, giving the tax a benefits-received component. A familiar example of this phenomenon occurs in the variations in housing values created by the differences in the quality of public schools. The property tax is unique in its capacity to recoup government-created increases in property value.

Is difficult to evade

Tax levies on real property, which now make up 85 percent of the property tax base, are secured in most states by an automatic tax lien on the property. If the owner fails to make timely payment, the local government can seek a court judgment foreclosing on the lien and then sell the property for back taxes, penalties, and interest. Compared with those for other taxes, collection rates for the tax on real property remain high, usually 92–96 percent of the current levy. Although collection is still legally complex, the automatic lien and the impossibility of obtaining a mortgage without the lien's removal greatly simplifies the eventual recovery of the 4–8 percent of the levy that is delinquent.

Promotes local autonomy

The property tax is the only tax levied in all fifty states. (Five states levy no sales tax, and seven states have no personal income tax.) At the local level, the fact that the tax is on relatively immobile assets enables more than one government to tax the same property while maintaining political autonomy from overlapping local governments. More important, the property tax has effectively become the domain of local governments, which strengthens their autonomy from state control. Glenn Fisher, one of the foremost authorities on the property tax, observed that

> It is clear that the tax had one feature that was of great importance in explaining its development and growth: it was ideally suited to financing local government in a large, developing, diverse country populated by people with a very strong sense of independence and a very great distrust of centralized bureaucracy. . . . Local government, as it developed in the United States, could not survive without the property tax.[15]

In summary, the property tax has proven remarkably resilient and capable of being tailored to local interests, and it survives as the most prominent source of revenue in local government primarily because of its stability and the ease with which it can be enforced.

The property tax cycle

Because the property tax, unlike most other taxes, falls on the value of wealth, the government must determine the taxable value of that wealth—a task that greatly complicates administration of the tax. Figure 4–2 depicts the three phases of the property tax cycle: appraisal, assessment, and collection.

Figure 4–2
Phases of the
property tax cycle.

Appraisal determines the value of property for tax purposes, using legally specified standards of valuation.

1. Taxable and tax-exempt property are discovered.
2. Legal owners and taxable site of property are identified.
3. Property is appraised on the basis of use and estimated value as of the appraisal date.
4. Property owners are notified of changes in appraised value.
5. Appeals from property owners are heard by independent board of review.
6. Adjustments to appraisals are reviewed and approved by board and appraiser.
7. Final certified appraisal roll is prepared.

Assessment adjusts appraised value to determine the taxable value of property.

1. Appraised value is multiplied by assessment rate (or ratio) to determine assessed value.[a]
2. Assessments are equalized by state agency to the same percentage of full value across jurisdictions.[a]
3. Assessed value is adjusted for partial exemptions, such as homesteads.[a]
4. Truth-in-taxation notices are prepared and published.[a]

5. Public hearing is held on proposed tax rate and/or budget.
6. Tax rate(s) is(are) set by governing board.
7. Rate(s) is(are) certified as being within legal limits.[a]
8. Tax roll is prepared and certified.

Collection involves the preparation and distribution of tax notices to both current and delinquent taxpayers.

1. Tax bills are prepared and mailed to owners of record.
2. Lien is attached to property to secure payment of taxes, penalties, and interest.
3. Current tax payments are received, credited, and distributed.
4. Unpaid taxes become delinquent after due date.
5. Delinquent-tax roll is prepared.
6. Delinquent-tax notices are prepared and property owners are notified.
7. Court order is sought to foreclose on lien on outstanding delinquencies.
8. Property is sold at a public auction for payment of back taxes, penalties, and interest.

[a] An activity that is not performed in all states.

Appraisal

The appraisal phase begins with the identification and valuation of all taxable property in a jurisdiction and ends with the preparation of an **appraisal roll,** which lists the owner of each property, gives the property's legal description, and lists its appraised value. State law typically specifies a particular date, such as January 1, as the date to which all appraisals are pegged and on which legal ownership is established. The owner of the property on the appraisal date is legally liable for the tax, regardless of whether the property is subsequently sold.

State law usually defines the basis for appraising property for tax purposes. In most states the basis is an estimate of the property's fair market value. However, there are significant deviations from this standard. For example, in California, the post–Proposition 13 basis is the selling price of the property or its 1975–1976 appraised value if the property has not sold since ratification of the amendment. Starting with this basis, California county assessors may annually increase real property appraisals by no more than 2 percent or the consumer price index, whichever is less. Whenever a property sells, the purchase price becomes its new appraised (and assessed) value, creating a higher tax liability for home buyers, including first-time buyers, and businesses moving into or relocating within the state. Curiously, property transferred within a family across generations retains its original value plus, of course, the annual 2 percent adjustment. As noted in Chapter 3, a number of studies have documented the significant inequities and adverse economic effects over the long term that such a valuation scheme introduces.

Both Florida and Michigan have adopted this acquisition basis of appraised value, capping annual increases in assessments at the rate of inflation or at 3 percent in Florida and 5 percent in Michigan, whichever is less. Unlike California, however, the Florida and Michigan caps apply only to the principal residences of home owners.

Because it directly affects the allocation of the tax burden in a jurisdiction, property appraisal is a politically charged task, but it is a matter of expert judgment that should be removed from the political arena. As might be expected, state laws vary considerably in defining how appraisals are done; variations include (1) the level of local government responsible for appraisal administration, (2) the frequency of reappraisal, and (3) the state's role in ensuring professional standards of appraisal.

Administration of appraisals   County governments are most frequently assigned the task of administering appraisals, although New England states tend to give the task to cities and towns. Maryland is the only state that places responsibility for appraisal administration in a state department of assessments and taxation. In Montana, the county assessor is a state employee, and the state provides all the funding for the assessor's office.

Texas has made the greatest effort to remove appraisal from the political arena by creating 253 countywide appraisal districts charged with the responsibility for valuing property in the district. While their boundaries are coterminous with counties, central appraisal districts (or CADs) are politically and administratively self-governing. Each CAD is governed by a board of directors appointed by local governments levying a property tax in the district, and each annually prepares an appraisal roll for its taxing jurisdictions. Local governments in the appraisal district then use this roll to develop their certified **tax roll.** Appraisal districts receive their funding through service charges on the local governments they serve.

Property tax experts recommend that appraisal administration be centralized at the county level at a minimum.[16] Centralization provides greater economies of scale and more efficient use of limited professional staff.[17] Only one appraisal for tax purposes should be done for each property. A few states still permit overlapping taxing jurisdictions to do separate appraisals, which confuses taxpayers and is an inefficient use of administrative resources.

Frequency of reappraisal   Reappraisal poses a major political problem for state and local legislators because taxpayers anticipate that their tax burden will increase. However, frequent reappraisal prevents large shifts in the tax burden across classes of property and, depending on the frequency, also prevents large increases in individual appraisals. The result is increased equity in the allocation of the property tax burden.

Out-of-date appraisal records, such as land maps and property descriptions, increase the cost of reappraisal, so more frequent reappraisals are generally less costly to administer. Local governments are advised to reappraise all property at regular intervals and real property at least once every three years.

Most states require that property owners be notified by mail of any changes in appraised and assessed values and be given an opportunity to appeal the revaluation. Figure 4–3 is a sample reappraisal notice used by the Denton (Texas) Central Appraisal District. States usually assign the task of hearing appeals to an independent board of review. North Carolina assigns this task to the county board of commissioners; Illinois creates a separate board of review in each county. It is also important that taxpayers have access to appraisal information on comparable prop-

Figure 4–3   Sample reappraisal notice, Denton (Texas) Central Appraisal District.

DENTON APPRAISAL DISTRICT
PO BOX 2816   3911 MORSE ST
DENTON, TX 76202-2816
940-349-3800 FAX 940-349-3801
METRO 972-434-2602

NOTICE OF APPRAISED VALUE
This is NOT a Tax Bill

Date: 05/12/2004

Account # (Refer to this # when inquiring about your property)
R22560
Street Address:
1234 BLISSFUL LANE
Property Description:
AVONDALE 3, BLOCK H, LOT 25,
25/1001-H\\\H. CARTER AB 281

Overlapping County Information:

DOE, JOHN AND JANE
1234 BLISSFUL LANE
DENTON, TX 76201-1234

Dear Property Owner:

We have appraised the property listed above for the **2004** tax year. Based on the appraisal date of January 1 of this year, the appraisal is as follows:

Appraisal Information	Last Year	Proposed This Year[a]
Land's Market Value	24,652	24,652
Agricultural or Timber Market Value	0	0
Agricultural or Timber Productivity Value	0	0
Improvements (Building) Appraised Value	113,615	116,870
Personal Property Appraised Value	0	0
Mineral Interest Appraised Value	0	0
Total Market Value of this Property	138,267	141,522
Total Appraised Value (with Homestead Limit)	138,267	141,522
Exemptions	HS	HS

Last Year's Taxable	Taxing Units[b]	Proposed Appraised	Proposed[c] Exemptions	Proposed Taxable[d] (Less Exemptions)	Last Year's Tax Rate[e]	Proposed Tax Estimate[f]
138,267	DENTON COUNTY	141,522	0	141,522	0.247170	349.80
123,267	DENTON ISD	141,522	15,000	126,522	1.864000	2,358.37
133,267	CITY OF DENTON	141,522	5,000	136,522	0.548150	748.35
	TOTAL					3,456.52

The above tax estimates use last year's tax rates for the taxing units. The governing body of each unit – school board, county commissioners, and so on – decides whether property taxes increase. The appraisal district only determines your property's value. The taxing units will set tax rates later this year. *The Texas Legislature does not set the amount of your local taxes. Your property tax burden is decided by your locally elected officials, and all inquiries concerning your taxes should be directed to those officials.*

If you are 65 or older and received the $10,000 school tax exemption on your home last year from the school listed above, your school taxes for this year will not be higher than when you first received the exemption on this home. If you improved your property (by adding rooms or buildings), your school tax ceiling may increase for improvements. If you are a surviving spouse age 55 or older, you may retain the school tax ceiling.

Contact the appraisal office if you disagree with this year's proposed value for your property or if you have any problems with the property description or address information. If the problem cannot be resolved, you have a right to schedule a hearing with the appraisal review board (ARB) by filing a WRITTEN protest with the Board. You may either use the provided form or prepare a letter (including your name, your property description, and what appraisal office action you disagree with). Your protest must be delivered by mail to the above address or in person at the appraisal district office before the protest deadline.

Normal office hours are 8:00 AM to 5:00 PM Monday through Friday. In addition, the Denton CAD office will be open 8:00 AM to 7:00 PM Tuesdays starting May 18, 2004 through June 8, 2004. If you have any questions or need assistance, contact our office at the phone numbers or address listed above.

Sincerely
Denton Appraisal District
www.dentoncad.com

Enclosures

Protest Deadline: **June 11, 2004**
ARB Hearings Begin: **June 16, 2004**

Location of ARB Hearings:
3911 Morse St
Denton, TX 76208

Notes are author's explanation:
[a] Detail on appraised value
[b] Overlapping taxing jurisdictions
[c] Homestead exemptions
[d] Assessed value (no fractional assessments)
[e] Tax rate per $100 assessed value
[f] Tax liability if tax rate from last year were applied to this year's tax base

EXPLANATION OF APPRAISAL INFORMATION FROM FRONT OF APPRAISAL NOTICE

AGRICULTURAL OR TIMBER MARKET VALUE:
The market value of agricultural land approved for ag land-use.

AGRICULTURAL OR TIMBER PRODUCTIVITY VALUE:
The value of the agricultural land based on the agricultural productivity value. This value is used in the calculation of the total taxable value.

IMPROVEMENTS (Buildings) APPRAISED VALUE:
The appraised value of any structures included on your land. For example: your home, barns, office buildings, pools, etc.

PERSONAL PROPERTY APPRAISED VALUE:
Value of property such as machinery, office equipment, furniture and fixtures or inventory used to conduct your business.

MINERAL INTEREST APPRAISED VALUE:
Value of interest in a mineral that may be removed by surface mining, or real property interest in oil or gas.

EXEMPTIONS:
A whole or partial exemption from taxation of all, or a portion of the property's value. If you have applied for, and been granted tax exemptions, the amounts would appear here.

PROPOSED TAX ESTIMATE:
Estimate of taxes based on proposed notice values less exemptions. Actual tax bills are usually mailed in October.

APPRAISED VALUE WITH HOMESTEAD LIMIT: *The appraised value of a residence homestead is limited to an increase of no more than 10 percent per year since it was last appraised unless new improvements, excluding ordinary maintenance, have been made. This limitation takes effect on January 1 of the tax year **following** the first year the property owner qualified for any homestead exemption and expires on January 1 of the first tax year that neither the property owner nor the owner's spouse qualifies for a homestead exemption. Your property will now carry two values: (1) the limited appraised value which is the value, less exemptions, that your taxes will be based on, and (2) the total appraised value which is the true value of the property. Should you sell your property or no longer qualify for any homestead exemption, the limitation on the appraised value of your property will be removed and the tax base will increase to the total appraised value. THIS LIMITATION ONLY APPLIES TO PROPERTY RECEIVING A HOMESTEAD EXEMPTION.*

TAXING UNITS:
A list of the taxing entities that are authorized to impose taxes on your property. Should you wish to object to an increased tax rate or government spending, please contact the governing body of your local taxing unit.

PROPOSED TAXABLE:
The proposed taxable amount calculated by deducting the amount of the current year exemptions from the proposed appraised value.

ATTENTION: PROPERTY OWNER
Advisory notice issued by the State Comptroller of Public Accounts as required by Texas Property Tax Code Section 6.025.

If the description of your property on the reverse side of this notice indicates your property overlaps into an adjoining appraisal district, more than one county appraisal district appraises your property. This situation occurs if your property is located in a taxing unit with boundaries extending into a neighboring county or counties. When filing any papers with the appraisal districts, you must file the information with each district. The names and addresses of the appraisal districts are listed below:

Denton Central Appraisal District
3911 Morse Street
P O Box 2816
Denton, TX 76202-2816

Wise County Appraisal District
400 E Business 380
Decatur, TX 76234
(940) 627-3081

Dallas Central Appraisal District
2949 N. Stemmons Frwy.
Dallas, TX 75247-6116
(214) 631-0520

Cooke County Appraisal District
201 N. Dixon
Gainesville, TX 76240
(940) 665-7651

Tarrant County Appraisal District
2500 Handley-Ederville Rd.
Fort Worth, TX 76118
(817) 284-0024

Grayson County Appraisal District
205 N. Travis St.
Sherman, TX 75090-5922
(903) 893-9673

Collin Central Appraisal District
2404 K Ave
Plano, TX 75074
(972) 578-5200

The law requires chief appraisers to have a written understanding that each appraiser has use of information, including an exemption application, rendition, or other property owner report. The chief appraisers will eliminate differences in their appraisal records data, including the property's ownership, description, and physical characteristics. To the extent coordination is feasible, they will work together to appraise property at the same value.

The law requires chief appraisers to agree on the appraised or market value of your property by May 1. If they do not agree, then appraisers must use the lowest appraised or market value on your property as determined by those appraisers. If a CAD's appraisal review board or a court later reduces your property's value, then the CAD's chief appraiser will notify the other chief appraisers who must reduce your value on all other appraisal rolls.

Below are some types of information that, when filing, you must file with each appraisal district office.

1. **Current mailing address** and any changes in property ownership,
2. **Homestead Exemption** application to qualify for lower taxes,
3. **Agricultural or timber appraisal application** for special land appraisal based on productivity use,
4. **Property rendition**, if required, to list your property and to give your opinion of its value,
5. **Property protest** to the appraisal review board (ARB) if you disagree with any appraisal district action on your property, and
6. **Any other information or reports** that may help the appraisal district office list and appraise your property.

Texas Property Taxes: Taxpayers' Rights, Remedies & Responsibilities, published by the Texas Comptroller of Public Accounts, has more information about filing reports and their deadlines. For a copy, please call or visit any of the appraisal district offices listed or call the Texas Comptroller's property tax assistance at 1-800-252-9121.

You also will find the booklet and other property tax information on the Texas Comptroller's webpage at:
www.window.state.tx.us/taxinfo/proptax/proptax.html.

\\DENTON\wp\04notices\bknotice1.doc

erties. Illinois requires the county assessor to list in a newspaper the appraised value of each property in the county.[18]

State involvement in appraisal   With the exception of Delaware and Hawaii, all state governments assume some role in overseeing local appraisal practices. State involvement, which is critical to the long-term improvement of appraisal quality, must begin with state-provided in-service training and certification of local appraisers. At least twenty-eight states require certification of appraisers, and six others offer voluntary certification programs.[19] States should also provide to local tax offices technical assistance such as manuals on appraisal law and practice, maps, computer software, forms, and readily accessible technical or legal advice. For railroad and utility properties, which are difficult to appraise, the task of valuation is almost always assigned to a state agency, with the taxable value then allocated among local governments.

State government must enforce a professional standard of quality, either indirectly through interjurisdictional equalization or more directly through challenging valuations, adjusting local appraisals, or assuming responsibility when inequities exceed acceptable limits. (For the appraisal standards prescribed by the International Association of Assessing Officers, see the section "Equity" near the end of this chapter.) State involvement in promoting more professional appraisal practices is critical to improving the quality and equity of local appraisals.

Assessment

Variations among state practices are greatest in the assessment phase. Assessment involves making adjustments, such as partial exemptions or fractional assessments, to a property's appraised value to determine its taxable value. A property's assessed value provides the basis on which the tax levy is distributed among property owners.

The assessment phase begins with the appraised value of each property being multiplied by the statutory assessment ratio, which is the principal adjustment in this phase. At least twenty states and the District of Columbia nominally require full-value assessments; that is, assessments cannot be at a fraction of appraised value.[20] The remaining thirty states generally sanction fractional assessment. For example, if property is assessed at 33⅓ percent of its value, a property with an appraised value of $100,000 has an assessed (or taxable) value of $33,333. Additional adjustments, such as a homestead exemption, are usually applied after the adjustment for fractional assessment and lower the taxable value even further.

Fractional assessment is generally introduced when a long-delayed reappraisal would otherwise result in a sudden jump in appraised values and when a shift to full-value assessments would prompt considerable anger among taxpayers. However, evidence and experience show that appraisal equity improves significantly when governments use the full-value standard. In their review of assessment practices, John Bowman and John Mikesell concluded that property tax administration is most uniform when assessment ratios are high—that is, at or near 100 percent—and done with regularity.[21]

Texas's experience is instructive. In 1981, the state implemented a previously ratified constitutional amendment abolishing fractional assessments and empowering the State Property Tax Board to monitor the progress of CADs toward achieving full-value and more uniform assessments. In 1985, the 253 CADs achieved a statewide median assessment ratio of 0.90, with an overall **coefficient of dispersion** of 18.49. (The greater the coefficient of dispersion, the less uniform the assessments are relative to value.) That is, on average the reported taxable value of property was at 90 percent of its estimated (appraised) value. By 2003, these statewide measures had improved to 0.99 and 11.55, respectively—a remarkable administrative accomplishment and a testament that quality assessment practices can be achieved even in volatile real estate markets.[22] Additionally, state law requires CADs to reappraise real property at least once every three years and personal property annually.

In addition to Texas, North Carolina and Kentucky, among other states, provide evidence that full-value assessment can be achieved without creating a taxpayer uprising. The keys to success include preventing local governments from reaping revenue windfalls from reappraisal (through either full disclosure or a tax levy freeze), keeping taxpayers fully informed of the reappraisal process, sustaining a regular cycle of reappraisal, and state intervention to compel local governments to move toward a full-value standard.

Collection

Collection involves two activities: the collection of current taxes and the collection of delinquent taxes. The more successful a government is at the first task, the less the need for the second. As a general rule, local governments responsible for collecting property taxes should achieve at least a 95 percent collection rate on the current levy. That is, no more than 5 percent of the current levy should become delinquent.

Level of compliance depends primarily on local economic conditions, especially the unemployment level, and on the aggressiveness of the collection effort. The role of the tax collector requires professionalism and a balance of fairness and firmness. The accompanying sidebar lists strategies for improving current and delinquent tax collections.

Collecting current taxes   The design of the tax statement is a key factor in improving the current collection rate. A well-designed statement clearly identifies the amount due, the basis for determining tax liability, and the penalties and interest charges for late payment. A return envelope should be enclosed with the statement. Some governments are also sending tax invoices electronically to reduce printing and mailing costs and provide more timely notice to taxpayers. State laws usually define the information that must be provided on the statement, but within those guidelines governments can exercise discretion in bringing taxpayers' attention to the amount due and the due date.

Some governments offer discounts for early payment, but the effectiveness of this approach is doubtful given the unattractive discount rates local governments are able to offer. A more effective measure is to mail or e-mail a reminder notice to taxpayers two to three weeks before the due date. While this increases collection costs, governments generally find the improved collection rates well worth the effort.

Strategies for improving property tax collection

Current taxes	Delinquent taxes
Use well-designed tax statements	Pursue delinquencies immediately and aggressively
Mail reminder notices two to three weeks before taxes are due	Increase the intensity and urgency of each successive notice to delinquent taxpayers
Keep taxpayer records current, especially mailing addresses	Use discretionary powers, such as setoff provisions
Build taxpayer goodwill through more convenient collection points and office hours	Contract out delinquent collections to a law firm or collection agency
Apply penalties and interest rates that discourage delinquent payment	Publish in a newspaper names of delinquent taxpayers and the amount owed
	Use small-claims court for minor delinquency cases

The primary cause of delinquent payment is undeliverable tax bills, which are returned to the local government because the addressee has moved or because the address is unknown. Maintaining a current mailing address for all property owners is one of the tax collector's greatest challenges. Several measures can remedy this problem: At a minimum, local governments should request a notification of change of address from the postal service. It is also recommended that they maintain a consolidated database for taxpayers and utility users, which eases comparison and referencing of information and economizes on the task of keeping address information current.

Another means of improving current collections is to build taxpayers' goodwill through more convenient collection methods, such as an online payment option and extended office hours during peak collection periods. For example, Fairfax County, Virginia, introduced online payments in 2001 and saw about 16,000 payments, or about 1.6 percent of their accounts, made using e-checks that year. By 2004, usage of online payments, both electronic transfers and credit card payments, had swelled to almost 125,000, or 12.5 percent of the county's tax accounts. This pattern will continue as more citizens become comfortable with this option. If it is legally possible, the tax collector should accept partial payment, with the unpaid balance subject to penalties and interest. Formal provisions should also be developed for hardship cases.

Collecting delinquent taxes   The collection of delinquent taxes begins with the preparation of a delinquent taxpayer roll. Some states, such as Kansas, require the tax collector to publish in a newspaper the names of delinquent taxpayers and the amount owed.

Convincing taxpayers that they will eventually have to pay back taxes is critical to a successful delinquent-tax collection program. Once the due date passes, the tax collector should immediately send delinquent individuals a reminder that taxes are past due. Governments may use the same form as is used for the current tax statement but with penalties and interest added. Each successive contact with the taxpayer should increase in intensity and urgency. For example, if there is no response to a letter asking the taxpayer to contact the tax collection office, a letter should be sent by certified mail specifying the legal measures that will follow to collect overdue taxes. A payment plan can usually be worked out except in cases of bankruptcy, cases in which a taxpayer cannot be located, or cases in which taxable assets have been removed from the jurisdiction.

Increasingly, local governments are including a **setoff provision** in their contracts that withholds payment from contractors who owe delinquent property taxes or utility service charges. In addition, a growing number of local governments contract out the collection of delinquent taxes to law firms specializing in this service, thereby saving the valuable time of staff attorneys for other work. A law firm has the expertise to prepare the legal documents and undertake the necessary title search in those cases where foreclosure on the lien is necessary. Contracting out to a law firm also sends a message to taxpayers that the government intends to collect all taxes it is owed. Some states permit an additional collection fee to be added to delinquent taxes as compensation for the law firm. And contracting out protects local government staff from appearing to strong-arm delinquent taxpayers.

Politics and the property tax

The property tax ranks along with the federal income tax as one of the taxes most unpopular with taxpayers (Table 4–3). This pattern has continued even after the passage of Propositions $2\frac{1}{2}$ and 13; the nearly universal approval by state legislatures

Table 4–3 Public attitudes toward taxes: Percentages of respondents identifying tax as the least fair.

Type of tax	2001	1994	1990
Property tax	22	28	28
Federal income tax	30	27	26
State income tax	13	7	10
State sales tax	13	14	12
Don't know	10	11	9

Source: John Kincaid and Richard L. Cole, "Changing Public Attitudes on Power and Taxation in the American Federal System,"*Publius* (summer 2001): 209.

88   *87*   *85*

Taxpayer dissatisfaction

Reasons for dissatisfaction	Measures to reduce dissatisfaction (number of states, if known)
Tax falls on unrealized capital gains, making it punitive for those who are property rich but cash poor	Circuitbreaker program (33) Tax liability freeze (12) Tax rate limits or freeze (38) Homestead exemption (48) Tax deferral program (24) Split tax roll
Tax is collected in large lump-sum payments	Installment option
Anxiety about reappraisal	Full disclosure or truth-in-taxation (13) Fractional assessments (29) Cap on increase in assessments (19) Classification of property values (24) Use-value appraisals (50) Acquisition-based appraisals (3)
Inequitable assessments and appraisals	Full-value assessments (20) More frequent reappraisal Full-time appraiser State oversight of local appraisal practices

of targeted relief, particularly to home owners; and the nearly universal reduction in local dependence on the tax. Why, then, is there still dissatisfaction with the tax, and what can local governments do to alleviate it? The accompanying sidebar summarizes the sources of irritation with the tax and some of the remedies for reducing taxpayer dissatisfaction.

Tax relief

Because it is a tax on wealth rather than on income or consumption, the property tax is particularly onerous for those who are *property rich but cash poor,* such as elderly residents. And because it falls on capital assets (property) that have not been realized (sold in the market), the property tax is a prime candidate for relief under the "everybody is a special case" principle discussed in Chapter 2. Many state-initiated measures of the past decade have been aimed at giving local governments the ability to provide relief in one of the following ways.

Circuitbreaker programs   Circuitbreaker programs provide property tax relief to low-income home owners, or renters or both, through a state income tax credit or rebate. The amount of relief varies inversely with household income up to a maximum income level, after which point relief ceases. Most programs limit tax relief to under $1,000 per household although Minnesota and Vermont have maximum ceilings of $1,500 per household. With a circuitbreaker, states can target relief to the most needy groups, and the state rather than local governments bear the financial cost of the tax expenditure, which is not the case for most other tax relief programs. The drawback of these programs is their relatively high cost of administration, the adverse impact on state budgets through lost income tax revenue especially during economic downturns, and the need for beneficiaries to file a state income tax return even if they have no taxable income.

To limit the cost of this subsidy, nineteen states target their circuitbreaker benefits to only senior citizens, usually defined as home owners over age sixty-five.[23] Kansas limits its program to home owners over fifty-five who have children under eighteen. Six states—Maryland, Michigan, Minnesota, Vermont, Wisconsin, and Wyoming—extend benefits to all home owners, regardless of age. Four other states—Maine, Montana, New Jersey, and New York—use a two-tiered benefit system, with more generous benefits to seniors than to their younger counterparts. Of the twenty-eight states that extend the circuitbreaker credit to renters, all but seven limit tax relief to senior citizens.[24]

Tax freeze   As noted in the typology of tax incentives in Chapter 3, a **tax freeze** is another approach to tax relief. States can freeze the tax base, tax rate, or tax liability. For example, Indiana freezes tax levies in counties that adopt a local income tax, but in other counties it freezes only the tax rate.[25] As noted earlier in this chapter, several states freeze property assessments, or at least severely limit annual increases in those values, which limits the effects of appreciation in property value on tax liability. Twelve states freeze the tax liability, usually when home owners reach age sixty-five.[26] Rhode Island and Tennessee make it a local option. State law in Texas automatically freezes the tax liability for school purposes once one spouse in the household reaches sixty-five, but it gives cities and counties the option of extending the benefit to their senior home owners.

As noted in the previous chapter, several states now require voter approval to increase property tax rates. Other limits restrict the amount of revenue to a percentage of the property tax base, such as the 1 percent cap in California (Proposition 13) and the 1.5 percent cap in Oregon. The most common form of limitation among the thirty-eight states with rate limits is a statutorily or constitutionally set maximum tax rate for different types (cities, towns, counties, schools) or population groupings of local government.[27]

Homestead exemptions   Homestead exemptions target tax relief to some or all home owners by exempting from taxation a fixed dollar amount or percentage of a property's assessed value. Partial exemptions have the important advantage of being easily understood by taxpayers and easily administered by local governments. After a property's appraised value has been determined, its assessed (or taxable) value is determined by deducting any partial exemptions, such as the homestead. For example, a $5,000 homestead exemption means that a house with an appraised value of $100,000 has an assessed value of $95,000. The owner's tax liability is then determined by multiplying the tax rate (usually in mills or dollars) by the property's assessed value.

Among the forty-eight states with homestead provisions (only Missouri and North Dakota offer none), all grant this partial exemption to elderly as well as disabled home owners, especially disabled veterans.[28] However, among the twenty-

four states that extend an exemption to home owners of all ages, the common practice is to grant elderly and disabled home owners higher levels of exemptions than
other groups. The amount of exemption varies from the first $1,000 of value in
Oklahoma to $150,000 in Alaska. Homestead programs are often instituted concur-
rently with statewide reappraisal programs to soften the effects of the reappraisal on
home owners' tax liability. For example, Florida increased its homestead exemption
for all owner-occupied residences to $25,000 at the same time that the state ordered
county assessors to revalue all property.

The economic value of the homestead exemption depends on the level at which
property is assessed. In states where property is assessed at less than its appraised
value (i.e., where taxable value is set at some legally specified fraction of appraised
value), the homestead exemption's economic value increases. For example, New
Mexico assesses property at 33.3 percent of value and applies the homestead
exemption after application of the assessment ratio. Thus, for a house with an
appraisal value of $100,000 and a $5,000 homestead exemption, the following com-
putation applies:

Appraised value	$100,000
× Assessment ratio	0.333
	33,300
− Homestead exemption	5,000
Taxable value	$28,300

Organizations of veterans and the elderly are often the most vocal opponents
of **full-value assessments** because they reduce the value of the homestead
exemption.[29]

Tax deferral A fourth approach to relieving the tax burden on lower-income
households is a **tax deferral,** which, when opted for by the home owner, delays
tax payments until the property is sold or the estate is settled. The deferred portion
of the tax is essentially a loan from the local government, rather than a state or
local subsidy, to the property owner. Deferred taxes usually incur an interest
charge but less frequently a penalty. Because deferred taxes become a lien on the
estate, they are used infrequently by home owners. Currently, twenty-four states
and the District of Columbia offer a tax deferral program, and in all but three
states—Florida, Iowa, and Pennsylvania—it is limited to elderly home owners.[30]
Most states also impose a limit on the amount of taxes eligible for deferral that is
usually pegged to a percentage of the value of the home. The value of the property
serves as collateral for the deferred taxes.

Split tax roll A growing practice is the use of a split tax roll: taxing single-family
residential property at one rate and all other property at a higher rate. Michigan, as
part of its sweeping education finance reform initiative, basically eliminated tax
rates set by school districts and in their place introduced a two-tiered rate structure
levied statewide: 6 mills on all primary residences and 24 mills on secondary homes
and businesses.[31] Municipalities and counties continue to levy their own taxes.
While such a plan reduces interjurisdictional inequities, creating two classes of
taxpayers has a high likelihood of opening Pandora's box to the creation of more
classes as taxpayer groups jockey for preferential treatment under the state tax code.
It also shifts control over school governance from locally elected boards to a more
distant and centralized state authority.

In an older version of the split tax roll idea, the nineteenth-century economist
Henry George advocated imposing a higher property tax on land values than on

improvements as a way to encourage more efficient urban development.[32] Economists contend that the tax discourages landowners from making improvements on their property, a clarification that is particularly damaging to declining areas. For example, an absentee landlord has little incentive to improve an apartment complex if the result will be a higher tax liability and no increase in rental income. Vacant lots in developed urban areas go undeveloped because the expected increase in the land's value exceeds the cost of the property tax on the undeveloped land. Several local governments in Pennsylvania, including Pittsburgh and Scranton, have at various times implemented George's theories. Typically, tax rates on land values are twice those on improvements, which penalizes speculators for leaving vacant land undeveloped. Because of their heavy reliance on wage taxes, local governments in Pennsylvania make relatively moderate use of the property tax, and thus the use of split rates on land development patterns in Pennsylvania has probably had a moderate impact.

Payment methods

The general practice among local governments has been to collect the property tax annually in one lump-sum payment. This increases the tax's visibility and may partially explain its unpopularity with taxpayers relative to other taxes.

Depending on the turnover rate in a jurisdiction's housing market, anywhere from 40 percent to 80 percent of the property tax payments from residential owners are collected from mortgage lenders. Usually these lenders establish an escrow account into which each home owner makes monthly payments against property tax liability. This reduces the visibility of the property tax for these owners, while at the same time effectively making tax liability payable in installments. The problem of lump-sum payments is greatest for owners who must pay their tax directly, either because they have no mortgage obligation or because the mortgagor does not require an escrow account.

Most states now permit local governments to collect the tax in smaller, more frequent installments. For example, Pennsylvania gives local governments the option of collecting the tax in quarterly installments. Some states, such as Arizona and recently Maryland, require semiannual payment of the tax. Local governments in Texas may, at their discretion, adopt the split payment plan. The province of Ontario provides no statutory limits on the number or timing of tax due dates, but local governments must give taxpayers at least fourteen days' notice before taxes are due.

One disadvantage of more frequent payments is that local governments lose interest income during the additional time that tax receivables remain outstanding. Other problems are the increased administrative cost of notifying taxpayers of payment dates and the additional accounting required for partial payments. Increasingly, local governments are giving taxpayers the option of paying via the Internet and with a credit card. Such payment options give taxpayers choices that they are accustomed to having in the retail market and give local governments opportunities for creating goodwill and enhancing taxpayer compliance.

Reappraisal

In general, taxpayer concern about property reappraisal will be the greatest where reappraisal is done infrequently or at irregular intervals. The longer the intervals between revaluations, the greater the inequities that will develop during the intervals and the louder the complaints from property owners who had benefited from undervaluation. Most states have no statutory requirements on the frequency with which reappraisals must be performed. In those states requiring regular reappraisal of real property, frequencies range from every two years in Colorado, Iowa, Missouri, and Virginia to every ten years in Rhode Island.[33]

However, frequent reappraisal increases the cost of administering the tax. Moreover, in a period of rapid appreciation in property values created by inflation or population increase, frequent reappraisal may not reduce taxpayer concern, as was the case in California prior to Proposition 13.

Full disclosure Reappraisal usually leads to increases in taxable value. If the tax rate remains unchanged, taxpayers will incur higher tax liabilities. To protect taxpayers and prevent the local government from reaping a windfall that taxpayers have not approved, some states require a **full-disclosure** procedure, sometimes known as **truth in taxation** or **truth in millage.** Essentially, full disclosure does for the property tax what indexing of the marginal tax rates does for state and federal income taxes. Full disclosure shifts responsibility for increases in the tax levy away from reappraisal (and the appraiser) and onto the tax rate (and the legislative body responsible for setting it).

Full disclosure originated in Florida in 1971 and is now used in thirteen states.[34] Although state statutes vary widely in the specifics, full disclosure involves three steps:

1. Each taxing jurisdiction determines a tax rate that will yield the same tax levy produced in the preceding year. In a jurisdiction where taxable property values are increasing, this rate, called an **effective** or **constant yield rate,** will be lower than the preceding year's rate. (All states exclude voter-approved debt from the computations.)

2. The effective rate is then published in a local newspaper. (In Florida and Utah, individual notices are mailed to property owners along with an estimate of the owner's tax liability.)

3. The taxing jurisdiction then adopts a tax rate that will generate sufficient tax revenues to balance the current operating budget, and it advertises or individually notifies property owners of the percentage difference between the final rate (or levy) and the effective rate. Kentucky and Texas authorize citizens to petition for an election to roll back extraordinarily large increases in tax rates. In Texas, local governments that adopt a tax rate that is more than an 8 percent increase over the effective rate are subject to a taxpayer-initiated referendum in which voters may approve a rollback of the tax rate to no more than an 8 percent increase. For increases above 4 percent, Kentucky allows citizens to roll back taxes to the effective rate.

Figure 4–4 is a sample notice used by Florida's local governments to notify citizens of the impact of proposed property tax changes on them and the time and location of the public hearing where the proposed budget will be discussed.

Fractional assessing and assessment caps Two approaches aimed at constraining increases in assessments—**fractional assessing** and **capping increases in assessments**—have provided momentary relief for taxpayers but almost always at the expense of horizontal equity in the property tax burden. Assessing property at less than 100 percent of appraised value now has official sanction in at least twenty-nine states. Assessment ratios in South Carolina have sunk to 4 percent for residential property: that is, a $100,000 home should have an assessed value of $4,000.[35] Capping assessments, as previously noted, takes several forms. For example, local governments in Allegheny County, Pennsylvania, freeze the assessed values of the residences of senior citizens as a way of providing tax relief.[36]

At least nineteen states now limit increases, following reappraisal, in the assessed value of residences as a way of cushioning the impact of rising market

Figure 4–4   Notice of proposed property taxes and public hearings used by local governments in Florida.

NOTICE OF PROPOSED PROPERTY TAXES AND PROPOSED OR ADOPTED NON-AD VALOREM ASSESSMENTS
DO NOT PAY
THIS IS NOT A BILL

The taxing authorities which levy property taxes against your property will soon hold **Public Hearings** to adopt budgets and tax rates for the next year.

The purpose of these **Public Hearings** is to receive opinions from the general public and to answer questions on the proposed tax change and budget **Prior To Taking Final Action.**

Each taxing authority may **Amend or Alter** its proposals at the hearing.

Taxing Authority	Your property taxes last year	Your taxes this year if proposed budget change is made	A public hearing on the proposed taxes and budget will be held:	Your taxes this year if no budget change is made
County				
Public Schools:				
By State Law				
By Local Board				
Water Management District				
Independent Special Districts• Voter Approved• Debt Payments				
Total Property Taxes				
	COLUMN 1*	COLUMN 2*		COLUMN 3*

	Market Value	Assessed Value	Exemptions	Taxable Value
Your property value last year:				
Your property value this year:				

PROPOSED OR ADOPTED NON-AD VALOREM ASSESSMENTS

Levying Authority	Purpose of Assessment	Units	Rate	Assessment
				Total

• SEE REVERSE SIDE FOR EXPLANATIONS

• IF YOU FEEL THE MARKET VALUE OF YOUR PROPERTY IS INACCURATE OR DOES NOT REFLECT FAIR MARKET VALUE, CONTACT YOUR COUNTY PROPERTY APPRAISER AT:

• IF THE PROPERTY APPRAISER'S OFFICE IS UNABLE TO RESOLVE THE MATTER AS TO MARKET VALUE, YOU MAY FILE A PETITION FOR ADJUSTMENT WITH THE VALUE ADJUSTMENT BOARD; PETITION FORMS ARE AVAILABLE FROM THE COUNTY PROPERTY APPRAISER AND MUST BE FILED ON OR BEFORE:

• YOUR FINAL TAX BILL MAY CONTAIN NON-AD VALOREM ASSESSMENTS WHICH MAY NOT BE REFLECTED ON THIS NOTICE SUCH AS ASSESSMENTS FOR ROADS, DRAINAGE, GARBAGE, FIRE, LIGHTING, WATER, SEWER, OR OTHER GOVERNMENTAL SERVICES AND FACILITIES WHICH MAY BE LEVIED BY YOUR COUNTY, CITY, OR ANY SPECIAL DISTRICT.

DR-474N
R. 01/02

EXPLANATION: (s. 200.069, Florida Statutes)

COLUMN 1- -"YOUR PROPERTY TAXES LAST YEAR"
This column shows the taxes that applied last year to your property. These amounts were based on budgets adopted last year and your property's previous taxable value.

COLUMN 2- -"YOUR TAXES IF PROPOSED BUDGET CHANGE IS MADE"
This column shows what your taxes will be this year under the BUDGET ACTUALLY PROPOSED by each local taxing authority. The proposal is NOT final and may be amended at the public hearings shown on the front side of this notice.

COLUMN 3- - "YOUR TAXES IF NO BUDGET CHANGE IS MADE"
This column shows what your taxes will be this year IF EACH TAXING AUTHORITY DOES NOT INCREASE ITS PROPERTY TAX LEVY. These amounts are based on last year's budgets and your current assessment. The difference between columns 2 and 3 is the tax change proposed by each local taxing authority and is NOT the result of higher assessments.

ASSESSED VALUE MEANS:

For homestead property: value as limited by State Constitution;

For agricultural and similarly assessed property: classified use value;

For all other property: market value.

Note: Amounts shown on this form do NOT reflect early payment discounts you may have received or may be eligible to receive. (Discounts are a maximum of 4 percent of the amounts shown on this form.)

Note: Non-ad valorem assessments are placed on this notice at the request of the respective local governing boards. Your tax collector will be including them on the November tax notice. For details on particular non-ad valorem assessments, contact the levying local governing board.

values. Unfortunately, higher-valued properties tend to increase more rapidly in value, and any limit in assessed values differentially favors these property owners over other taxpayers. Not only do assessment caps introduce horizontal inequities, but they also create vertical inequity to the extent that household income (ability to pay) is correlated with property value.

Property classification   Whereas a split tax roll always targets tax relief, often for home owners, through the use of differential tax rates and is a tool for bringing equity to education funding, **classification of property** is more closely associated with providing tax relief on the heels of a reassessment. Classification involves grouping real property by type and then treating each class differently—either by applying a different assessment level to each class, which is the case in nineteen states; or by applying a different tax rate for each class, which is the case in Hawaii, Kentucky, New Hampshire, South Dakota, and West Virginia.[37]

Where revaluation is done infrequently or where enforcement of a uniform assessment level is lax, residential property generally has lower assessment ratios than nonresidential property, and a reappraisal will shift the tax burden back onto owners of single-family homes. Some states use classification to legitimize the favorable level of assessment given de facto to residential property.[38] For example, under a multipart classification scheme adopted as part of a statewide reappraisal effort, Kansas assesses residential property at 11.5 percent of appraised market value; vacant lots at 12 percent; commercial, industrial, and utility properties at 25 percent; and public utilities at 33 percent of value.[39] Agricultural land is assessed at 30 percent of its estimated production value. Most always classification in effect grandfathers a situation created by negligent appraisal practices.

State legislatures must address two issues when considering the adoption of a classification system. The first is the number of classes to create. Of the twenty-four states and the District of Columbia that classify property, most designate from two to four classes. Missouri law specifies three classes of real property, each assessed at a different fraction of appraised market value: residential (19 percent), agricultural (12 percent), and income-producing property (32 percent). Because political rather than economic criteria are the basis of all state classification policies, residential and agricultural property are almost always the most favored classes. Unfortunately, once the practice of classification is introduced, political pressures build to create even more classes. For example, Minnesota began with just four classes in 1913 but now has possibly more than one hundred classes, creating an administrative nightmare for tax assessors and a patchwork of assessments of doubtful fairness to taxpayers.[40]

The second issue concerns the degree of differentiation among the classes. Mississippi assesses residential property at 10 percent, all other real and personal property at 15 percent, and state-appraised utility property at 30 percent of its value.[41] Montana has at least thirteen classes of property, with assessment ratios ranging from 3 percent to 100 percent of market value. (It assesses coal reserves at 100 percent of value as a way to export the tax burden.) No economic criteria guide these decisions, only the relative political power of affected groups.

Use value   Like classification, use value (or production value) treats particular types of property more favorably, especially those that are adversely affected by a reappraisal. Use-value appraisals, first adopted by Maryland in 1960, give preferential treatment to farmland and open spaces by basing the value of the property on its current use rather than on its best possible use or market value.[42] The intent of this approach, now used for some types of agricultural land in all fifty states, is to reduce the adverse impact of reappraisal on farmland surrounding urban areas, where the potential for future development causes land values to appreciate rapidly.

Most states impose penalties if the property's use is changed once it has been classified and valued as farmland. Some states enter into contracts with owners of agricultural property that restrict land use in return for appraising the property at its production value. While the intention is to protect farmers from the adverse effects of urban growth, owners can abuse the approach by holding their land for future development while keeping it in farm production to qualify for the tax break.

Acquisition-based appraisal   As noted earlier in the chapter, Proposition 13 ushered in **acquisition-based appraisal,** a new basis for valuing property now used in California, Oregon, and Georgia (local option).[43] Not only are annual increases in assessments capped in these states (the lesser of 2 percent or the consumer price index in California and 3 percent in Oregon), but property is reappraised only when it sells. As noted in the previous chapter, such skewed valuation standards interject significant and economically destructive inequities and inefficiencies that eventually drag down a state's economic growth and discourage new business investment.

Equity

Appraisal equity within a taxing jurisdiction is measured by the intra-area coefficient of dispersion (CD), which measures the average deviation in assessment levels from the median level of assessment. Higher CDs imply greater dispersion and thus greater levels of inequity in appraisal practices. A CD equal to zero implies perfect appraisal equity; that is, all properties within each appraisal class, if applicable, in a jurisdiction are appraised at the same percentage of market value of that class.

The International Association of Assessing Officers prescribes the following appraisal standards:[44]

- Intra-area CDs for single-family residential property should be less than 10 percent.

- Intra-area CDs for all other types of property should be less than 15 percent.

- Where property is classified and assessed at different fractions of appraised value, the average assessment ratio for each class should be within 10 percent of the legally prescribed level of assessment.

Inequitable tax appraisals most commonly arise from (1) state laws that permit assessments at a fraction of appraised value (less than full-value assessments), (2) infrequent and irregular revaluations, (3) the absence of qualified personnel to perform appraisals, and (4) the absence of state oversight to enforce uniform professional practices. Research confirms that these factors, especially the first three, are associated with poor-quality appraisals. For example, one study using property assessment information from Virginia found that where assessments were closer to full market value (no fractional assessments), CDs declined markedly.[45] Full-value assessments provide assessors with less opportunity to "bury their mistakes." Assessments made at full market value are more easily understood and scrutinized by property owners than those that are permitted by state law to be some fraction of market value.

The same study also found that local governments in Virginia that undertake more frequent reappraisals had lower appraisal errors (CDs) than governments that undertake reappraisals less frequently.[46] Similarly, governments with a full-time appraiser had lower CDs, which implies that a full-time professional staff devoted solely to property valuation contributed significantly to reducing appraisal inequities.

Although not addressed by research, it would seem that state oversight of local valuation practices should lead to greater uniformity in assessment levels.

Summary

Several significant trends are now apparent in the role and character of the property tax:

- Beginning in the 1970s, the property tax has declined in importance as a source of revenue for counties and municipalities with a leveling off in its importance since 1997.
- The property tax base is increasingly dependent on real property, and residential property represents an increasing share of the real tax base. It is increasingly a tax on property that is easiest to discover and appraise and has the greatest potential for appreciating in value.
- Growth in the property tax base has been greatest in cities with higher levels of economic activity.
- The decline in manufacturing and the growth in service industries have not reduced the amount of potential business property subject to taxation. Local governments exercise wide discretion in how they allocate their property tax burden between residential and business property owners. It appears that they allocate the burden so as to maximize their competitive position with respect to other local governments.

The property tax survives despite its unpopularity with taxpayers because (1) it provides a stable source of revenue to local governments; (2) it is exportable to absentee property owners; (3) it is equitable to the extent that the benefits from the public services funded by the tax are rolled into higher property values and thus higher tax liability; (4) it has several administrative advantages, including the difficulty of evading the tax, especially on real property; and (5) it is largely a locally levied tax in the United States, which helps promote the political autonomy of local governments.

The property tax cycle consists of three phases. Appraisal or valuation of property establishes legal liability for the tax and the beginning point for establishing the tax base. Assessment involves adjusting appraised value through the application of fractional assessments and partial exemptions to establish taxable value. The legislatively set tax rate is then applied to the assessed value to determine tax liability. The third phase involves collection of current and delinquent property taxes. To address taxpayer concerns that arise in the pursuit of these phases, states have introduced a number of innovations, ranging from circuitbreaker provisions to homestead exemptions to truth in taxation.

Finally, the chapter discussed a number of sources of taxpayer resentment for the tax and the measures local and state governments have taken to address each. One fact remains clear: the property tax is remarkably adaptive to the political machinations of the day. It is because of that adaptablity that the tax survives—and even thrives in some states.

1 National Conference of State Legislatures (NCSL), *A Guide to Property Taxes: An Overview* (Denver, Colo.: NCSL, May 2002), 14.

2 Ibid., 17–19.

3 National Conference of State Legislatures (NCSL), *A Guide to Property Taxes: Property Tax Relief* (Denver, Colo.: NCSL, November 2002), 25–27.

4 State Property Tax Board, *Statement* 5 (February 1982), 2; Texas Comptroller of Public Accounts, *Statement* 15 (February 1992), 4; Texas Comptroller of Public Accounts, *Statement* 25 (November 2002), 6.

5 Katharine L. Bradbury and Helen F. Ladd, "City Property Taxes: The Effects of Economic Change and Competitive Pressures,"

New England Economic Review, Federal Reserve Bank of Boston, (July/August 1987): 30.

6 Ibid., 30.

7 Robert L. Bland and Phanit Laosirirat, "Tax Limitations to Reduce Municipal Property Taxes: Truth in Taxation in Texas," *Journal of Urban Affairs* 19 (spring 1997): 45–58.

8 Bradbury and Ladd, "City Property Taxes," 30.

9 *NCSL, Guide to Property Taxes: An Overview,* 23.

10 Bradbury and Ladd, "City Property Taxes," 27.

11 Ibid., 25.

12 Ibid., 30.

13 Terri A. Sexton, "The Property Tax Base in the United States: Exemptions, Incentives, and Relief," *Assessment Journal* 10 (fall 2003): 6.

14 Texas Comptroller of Public Accounts, "Tax Exemptions and Tax Incidence" (January 2003), 71.

15 Glenn W. Fisher, "The Changing Role of Property Taxation," in *Financing State and Local Governments in the 1980s: Issues and Trends,* ed. Norman Walzer and David L. Chicoine (Cambridge, Mass.: Oelgeschlager, Gunn & Hain, 1981), 45.

16 Paul V. Corusy, "Improving the Administration of the Property Tax," in *The Property Tax and Local Finance,* ed. C. Lowell Harriss (New York: Academy of Political Science, 1983), 88.

17 David L. Sjoquist and Mary Beth Walker, "Economies of Scale in Property Tax Assessment," *National Tax Journal* 52 (June 1999): 207–220.

18 *The Illinois Property Tax System* (Springfield: Office of Local Government Services, Illinois Department of Revenue, n.d.). Available at www.revenue.state.il.us/Publications/LocalGovernment/PTAX1004.pdf.

19 Robert M. Clatanoff, *Patterns of Property Tax Administration in the United States* (Chicago: International Association of Assessing Officers, June 1986), 104.

20 NCSL, *A Guide to Property Taxes: An Overview,* 20–26.

21 John H. Bowman and John L. Mikesell, "Improving Administration of the Property Tax: A Review of Prescriptions and Their Impact," *Public Budgeting and Financial Management* 2 (November 2, 1990): 151–176.

22 Texas Comptroller of Public Accounts, *Statement* 22 (September 1999): 4; Texas Comptroller of Public Accounts, *Statement* 27 (March/April 2004): 4–5.

23 NCSL, *Property Tax Relief,* 15–21.

24 Ibid, 18–20.

25 John H. Bowman, "Direct Property Tax Relief in Minnesota: An Analysis," in *Final Report of the Minnesota Tax Study Commission,* vol. 2, *Staff Papers,* ed. Robert D. Ebel and Therese J. McGuire (St. Paul, Minn.: Butterworth Legal Publishers, 1986), 285.

26 NCSL, *Property Tax Relief,* 32–34.

27 Ibid., 30–34.

28 Ibid., 7–15.

29 Mark Bertozzi, "Veterans Exemption Reform: The New York State Experience," *Property Tax Journal* 4 (September 1985): 231–243.

30 NCSL, Property Tax Relief, 21–24.

31 Paul D. Ballew, Richard H. Mattoon, and William A. Testa, "School Reform and Tax Reform: A Successful Marriage?" *Government Finance Review* 10 (August 1994): 32–35.

32 Sexton, "The Property Tax Base in the United States," 10.

33 NCSL, *A Guide to Property Taxes: An Overview,* 6–7.

34 Bland and Laosirirat, "Tax Limitations to Reduce Municipal Property Taxes," 47.

35 NCSL, *A Guide to Property Taxes: An Overview,* 24.

36 Brian K. Jensen and James W. Turner, "Act 77: Revenue Sharing in Allegheny County," *Government Finance Review* 16 (December 2000): 17–21.

37 Sexton, "The Property Tax Base in the United States," 7 and 11.

38 Glenn W. Fisher, *The Worst Tax? A History of the Property Tax in America* (Lawrence: University Press of Kansas, 1986), 163–186.

39 NCSL, *A Guide to Property Taxes: An Overview,* 12.

40 John H. Bowman, "Real Property Classification: The States March to Different Drummers," *Proceedings of the Seventy-Ninth Annual Conference of the National Tax Association— Tax Institute of America* (Columbus, Ohio, 1986): 293.

41 NCSL, *A Guide to Property Taxes: An Overview,* 22.

42 Sexton, "The Property Tax Base in the United States," 10.

43 Ibid., 6.

44 *Property Appraisal and Assessment Administration* (Chicago: International Association of Assessing Officers, 1990).

45 John H. Bowman and William A. Butcher, "Institutional Remedies and the Uniform Assessment of Property: An Update and Extension," *National Tax Journal* 39 (June 1986): 162.

46 Ibid.

5

The general sales tax

The evolving role of the local sales tax

Local government access to the general sales tax
Local government dependence on the sales tax
Factors affecting the sales tax base

Issues in the design of a local sales tax

Effects of a sales tax on retail sales
Effects of a sales tax on the property tax and on government spending
Impact of the local sales tax on the distribution of tax burdens
Exportability
Coordination of local sales tax rates
Dedicated sales taxes
Local discretion in sales tax administration

Summary and recommendations

An invasion of armies can be resisted, but not an idea whose time has come.

—Victor Hugo

The general sales tax

Consumption taxes distribute the cost of local government services according to spending levels of individuals and businesses. In most cases, vendors merely collect the tax from consumers on behalf of the state or local government. However, the actual legal relationship is more complex in state law depending on whether the tax is on vendors as a business privilege levy, on consumers as a consumption levy, or on some combination of the two.

This and the following chapter examine the key issues that local governments encounter when considering the adoption of consumption-based taxes. These taxes are of two types: the general sales tax, which is levied on a broad range of goods and services not subject to resale, and excise taxes, which are levied on specific types of transactions, under separate statutory authority, and at separate rates. Often excise tax revenues, such as from motor fuels, are earmarked for purposes that benefit consumers of the good or service being taxed. It is not uncommon for some goods, such as tobacco products, to be subject to both an excise tax and the general sales tax.

Next to the property tax, the general sales tax has become the most important tax source for local governments. Adoption of the tax has been most widespread among cities, particularly in the Midwest. Nearly 6,500 cities across the United States now levy a general sales tax. Counties have also increased their use of the tax, with more than 1,500 jurisdictions now collecting it. The loss of the federal income tax deduction for sales taxes as a result of the Tax Reform Act of 1986, at least until 2004 when it was temporarily reinstated by Congress, did not dampen local governments' enthusiasm for the tax or its popularity with taxpayers relative to other taxes (see Table 4–3). It remains the option of first choice for tax diversification by local governments.

The most important reason for the sales tax's relative popularity is that it is collected in small increments over a large number of transactions. Another factor is that legislative authorization is now almost always couched in terms of providing property tax relief, especially to residential property owners. Some states go to unusual lengths to ensure that revenues from the local sales tax will be used for this purpose. For example, the Texas legislature authorizes counties not served by a public transit district to levy a 0.5 percent optional sales tax, but it specifies that revenue from the tax must be held in escrow by counties and used only to replace revenues lost through a reduction in their property tax levy.

A local sales tax enables governments to tax a broad range of activities and a large number of individuals. For example, the tax reaches nonresidential shoppers who do not pay a property tax. It increases local government autonomy and reduces dependence on federal and state aid, thereby giving local managers added flexibility in financing their operating and capital budgets.

A sales tax is almost always adopted in tandem with a **use tax.** A jurisdiction levies a use tax on items purchased in another jurisdiction but brought back into the taxing jurisdiction. Use taxes protect retailers in the taxing jurisdiction by discouraging consumers from making their purchases outside the jurisdiction simply to avoid its sales tax. Enforcement of use taxes, however, is effective only in cases where governments maintain records of ownership, such as when a vehicle's registration is transferred from one state to another. Enforcement of use taxes has assumed greater attention nationally with the advent of Web-based purchases and the trend toward national and even international marketing by vendors through online sales.

As with the property tax, locally levied general sales taxes assume many forms, particularly in terms of their coordination with a state sales tax (Figure 5–1). This chapter considers only locally adopted general sales taxes and does not treat dedication by states of a portion of their sales tax receipts to municipal or county governments. Five states levy no statewide sales tax: Alaska, Delaware, Montana, New Hampshire, and Oregon. Alaska is unique within this group in permitting its boroughs and cities to levy a local general sales tax.

In most cases, state enabling legislation is required to levy a sales tax, although municipalities in Colorado, Illinois, and North Dakota rely on their home-rule powers, and local governments in Alabama and Arizona derive their authority from business licensing powers.[1] Currently, thirty-three states authorize a local sales tax: twenty-four authorize their municipalities to levy the tax and thirty-two authorize their counties to do so.[2] Ten states authorize their transit authorities to levy the tax and one state, Louisiana, allows school districts to levy the tax, although several states now link their county levies to school funding. Several states give local governments limited control over their tax bases, including the option of including food for home consumption in their tax base while excluding it from the state base. And twenty-two states sanction local discretion over tax rates, a privilege that allows local governments to better match revenue yield to local budget needs but also greatly increases border-city effects. North Dakota gives its municipalities the power to limit tax liability on any one transaction, and most have chosen a cap of $25 per transaction. A few states also allow local governments to abate or remit part of sales tax revenues, particularly for large commercial projects such as regional shopping centers, as a tool for economic development.

The evolving role of the local sales tax

Several characteristics affect the role of the general sales tax in local government revenue structures:

- Once one level of local government gains access to the tax, political pressure builds to extend authority to other levels. Typically cities are the first to receive authorization to levy the tax, followed by counties and then special districts, especially public transit, fire, and hospital districts.

- Over time, states tend to decouple their tax base from that of their local governments, adding to the administrative complexity of the tax base and lessening its neutrality.

- Tax rates tend to migrate upward as local governments face growing expectations for services and limitations on other revenue sources, particularly the property tax.

- Because the sales tax base is more responsive to economic growth than other tax bases, local governments become increasingly dependent on it.

- Revenue yields from the sales tax are procyclical (i.e., they expand and contract with the business cycle), increasing the likelihood of midyear budget shortfalls for local governments whenever the business cycle turns downward. The more dependent a local government is on the tax, the more vulnerable its operating budget to the ups and downs of the business cycle.

Figure 5–1

Variations of local control over the general sales tax.

No local control	Local discretion over base	Local discretion over rates	Local discretion over liability	Local administration
(15)	(4)	(22)	(3)	(7[a])

Note: Numbers in parentheses reflect the number of states in which each variation exists.

[a] Local administration is available in seven states. In Alaska, which has no state sales tax, and Louisiana, local governments must collect their own sales tax. Most smaller local governments in the other five states opt for state administration while the more populous cities and counties prefer to collect and enforce the tax locally.

Since local option sales taxes were introduced in the 1930s, their popularity among the states has spread and their use by local governments has increased. As seen from Tables 5–1 and 5–2, cities now derive 8.4 percent of their revenue from the tax, up from 7.5 percent in 1991, and counties derive 9.7 percent of their revenue from the tax, up from 8.7 percent in 1991. Although several factors may slow this rate of growth in dependence on the tax, particularly sales through the Internet and the significant expansion of the service sector, which generally lies outside the tax base, the general sales tax remains the tax of choice by state and local governments seeking to diversify their revenue sources.

Local government access to the general sales tax

An increasing number of local governments are turning to the general sales tax as the preferred method for tax diversification. States especially in the South, Midwest, and West have given municipalities and counties access to the tax, with rates usually in the 1–3 percent range. Local sales taxes are virtually nonexistent in the Northeast with the notable exception of counties in New York.

In the initial years of local adoption of sales taxes, states tend to authorize only one level of local government, and often that authorization is given only to selected cities or counties. With time, as the tax gains acceptance politically and administratively, states expand authorization to all cities and/or counties; some states even authorize that revenues be shared locally among cities and counties and sometimes special districts. Two states—Nebraska (131 cities) and South Dakota (208 cities)—still give municipalities exclusive access to the tax; six states—Florida, Georgia, North Carolina, Ohio, Wisconsin, and Wyoming—give their counties exclusive access. Most Georgia counties redistribute the revenue to their schools; Iowa also makes extensive use of a voter-approved countywide tax for infrastructure improvements in school districts. North Carolina, which has designed one of the most equitable and economically neutral local sales tax policies, requires that revenue from the 2.5 percent county tax be allocated to cities on a pro rata share of population or assessed value, a formula that greatly reduces intergovernmental competition for the tax base.

Table 5–3 identifies states with significant levels of participation by municipalities, and Table 5–4 lists those states where most counties levy the tax. Adoption of a local option sales tax is more universal in states where voter approval is not required; however, voter approval does not appear to significantly deter its spread. Although not evident from the tables, the more urban cities and counties make the greatest use of the tax. States generally specify the maximum sales tax rate that local governments can levy, or the maximum total sales tax that can be levied in any one jurisdiction by overlapping governments (state, county, city, and special districts).

Local government dependence on the sales tax

Expected revenue yield is of paramount concern to local managers and elected officials considering adoption of a sales tax. Revenue from a sales tax is income

Table 5–1
Municipal
government
dependence on
the general sales
tax: Sales tax
revenue as a
percentage of
general revenues.

Revenue source	1991–92	1996–97	2001–02
Property taxes	25.1	22.7	22.8
General sales tax	7.5	8.1	8.4
Selective sales taxes	5.1	5.3	5.5
Other taxes	9.7	10.5	10.3
Service and utility charges	40.8	42.3	41.9
Other non taxes	11.9	11.1	11.1
	100.1	100.0	100.0
Total general revenue (in millions)[a]	$161,293	$202,674	$255,220

Source: U.S. Bureau of the Census, *Finances of Municipal and Township Governments,* 1997 Census of Governments 4, no. 4 (September 2000), table 1 (http://www.census.gov/prod/gc97/gc974-4.pdf); and U.S. Bureau of the Census, *Local Summary Tables by Type of Government: 2001–02,* table 2 (http://ftp2.census.gov/govs/estimate/02slsstab2a.xls). Disaggregation of general sales from selective sales tax revenues provided by Kheang Hang at the U.S. Census Bureau.

Note: Percentages may not total 100% because of rounding.
[a] Total general revenue includes utility charges but excludes intergovernmental aid, liquor store income, and insurance trust revenue.

Table 5–2
County
government
dependence on
the general sales
tax: Sales tax
revenue as a
percentage of
general revenues.

Revenue source	1991–92	1996–97	2001–02
Property taxes	43.5	38.6	38.4
General sales tax	8.7	10.1	9.7
Selective sales taxes	2.1	2.3	2.5
All other taxes	4.2	4.6	4.9
Service and utility charges	27.4	31.3	31.2
Other non taxes	14.1	13.1	13.2
	100.0	100.0	99.9
Total general revenue (in millions)[a]	$94,808	$122,161	$161,483

Source: U.S. Bureau of the Census, *Finances of County Governments,* 1997 Census of Governments 4, no. 3 (September 2000), table 1 (www.census.gov/prod/gc97/gc974-3.pdf); and U.S. Bureau of the Census, *Local Summary Tables by Type of Government: 2001–02,* table 2 (http://ftp2.census.gov/govs/estimate/02slsstab2a.xls). Disaggregation of general sales from selective sales tax revenues provided by Kheang Hang at the U.S. Census Bureau.

Note: Percentages may not total 100% because of rounding.
[a] Total general revenue includes utility charges but excludes intergovernmental aid, liquor store income, and insurance trust revenue.

elastic—that is, yields grow, or decline, at rates greater than growth or decline in the local economy. If the local economy is growing, revenue from the tax tends to increase in importance in a local government's revenue structure.

The pattern of increasing dependence, however, poses a serious budget risk to local governments. Because the sales tax is procyclical, local governments that depend heavily on it to finance their operating budgets risk incurring revenue shortfalls midyear and greater revenue volatility from year to year. The best way to guard against this risk is to avoid overdependence on the sales tax. As a general rule, municipalities and counties should derive no more than $1.00 in consumption-based tax revenue for every $1.00 in property tax revenue. Governments that draw more revenues from sales taxes than from property taxes should consider increasing their property tax levy to replace more narrowly based, less neutral excise taxes, such as amusement and occupation taxes, in order to increase the overall stability and neutrality of their revenue structures.

Table 5–3
Municipal sales
taxes by state.

State	Range in tax rates (%)	Most frequently used rate (%)	Voter approval	Participation (%)
Nearly all cities levy tax				
Arizona	1.40–3.50	2.00	no	<90
Arkansas	0.50–3.50	1.00	yes	<90
California[a]	1.00	1.00	no	<90
Colorado[b]	1.00–4.50	3.00	yes	<90
Illinois	0.25–1.50	1.00	no	<90
New Mexico[c]	0.50–2.4375	1.4375	optional	<90
Oklahoma	0.50–5.00	3.00	yes	<90
Texas[d]	0.50–2.00	1.00	yes	<90
Utah[e]	1.00–3.10	1.00	yes	100
Virginia	1.00	1.00	no	100
Washington[f]	0.50–2.10	1.10	no	100
Most cities levy tax				
Alabama	1.00–8.00	3.00	no	<75
Alaska	1.00–6.00	4.00	no	<80
Iowa	1.00	1.00	yes	<74
Kansas	0.50–2.75	1.00	yes	<86
Louisiana[g]	1.00–3.00	1.00	yes	<80
Missouri[h]	0.50–2.625	1.00	yes	<55
Nebraska[i]	1.50–1.50	1.00	yes	<34[j]
North Dakota	1.00–2.50	1.00	yes	<85
South Dakota[i]	1.00–2.00	2.00	yes	<68

Sources: Web sites of state revenue departments and telephone interviews with state officials.

[a] City tax rate of 1.0% is a credit against the county rate.
[b] Most larger Colorado cities administer their own sales tax. Rates tend to be the highest in the mountain resort communities. Colorado cities have the discretion to include food for home consumption in the tax base, and several apply a separate tax rate to such transactions.
[c] City sales tax takes precedence over county tax in incorporated areas.
[d] City levies in Texas preempt county sales taxes within their borders. The combined state (6.25%), city (up to 2.0%), county (up to 0.5%), and transit authority (up to 1.0%) rates cannot exceed 8.25%.
[e] A city's rate of 1% takes precedence over the county's in incorporated areas.
[f] City sales taxes in Washington preempt the county tax in incorporated areas. An additional 0.5% sales tax applies to sales in restaurants and bars in King County.
[g] The combined rates for parishes and municipalities generally do not exceed 4% unless approved in a special election. In addition to municipalities, other levels of local governments tapping the sales tax include school districts (1.0–2.5%), law enforcement districts (0.25–1.0%), and police juries (1.0–3.5%).
[h] City rates are levied on top of county taxes. The maximum combined tax rate in Missouri is 8.725% (4.225% state, 2.5% county, and 2.0% city).
[i] Municipalities have exclusive authority to levy a sales tax.
[j] While only 131 of Nebraska's 385 cities levy the tax, all of the state's more populous cities have adopted the tax in a state dominated by small rural communities.

Factors affecting the sales tax base

In most cases the sales tax base consists of purchases of goods or services by households and businesses for final consumption. The tax rate is assessed as a percentage of the retail value of the goods and services purchased. State laws vary as to the types of transactions included in the tax base. Only Hawaii, New Mexico, and South Dakota tax virtually all transactions, including almost all services.[3] By contrast, Connecticut, Massachusetts, Minnesota, and Rhode Island exempt all prescriptions, food purchased for home consumption, consumer utilities, clothing, and services. Minnesota limits its utility exemption to residential use of natural gas and electricity purchased for heating between November and April.

Table 5–4

County sales taxes by state.

State	Range in tax rates (%)	Most frequently used rate (%)	Voter approval	Participation (%)
All counties levy tax				
California[a]	1.25	1.25	no	100
Georgia[b,c]	1.00–3.00	3.00	yes	100
Louisiana[d]	0.50–5.00	4.00	yes	100
Missouri	0.50–2.50	1.00	yes	100
New Mexico[e]	0.125–1.4375	0.375	optional	100
New York[f]	3.00–4.25	4.00	no	100
North Carolina[c]	2.50–3.00	2.50	no	100
Ohio[c]	0.50–2.00	1.00	no	100
Tennessee[g]	1.50–2.75	2.25	yes	100
Utah[h]	1.00–1.25	1.00	yes	100
Virginia	1.00	1.00	no	100
Washington[i]	0.50–2.10	1.10, 1.20	no	100
Most counties levy tax				
Alabama	1.00–3.00	1.00	no	<85
Arkansas	0.50–3.00	1.00	yes	<95
Colorado	0.25–4.00	1.00	yes	<75
Florida[c,j]	0.50–1.50	1.00	yes	<80
Illinois[k]	0.25–1.50	0.25	no	<30
Iowa	1.00	1.00	yes	<75
Kansas	0.25–2.00	1.00	yes	<75
Oklahoma	0.25–2.00	1.00	yes	<85
Texas	0.50	0.50	yes	<50
Wisconsin[c]	0.10–0.60	0.50	no	<85
Wyoming[c]	1.00–2.00	1.00	yes	<90

Sources: Web sites of state revenue departments and telephone interviews with state officials.

[a] City tax rate of 1% is a credit against county rate.

[b] Georgia counties levy up to 3% tax piggybacked onto the state's 4% tax. Depending on the county, each increment in the rate may be divided as follows: the first 1% increment may be divided between cities and the unincorporated area of the county; another 1% increment may be dedicated to schools, which 90% of the counties have opted to do; the last 1% increment in the rate may be dedicated by county voters to capital improvements.

[c] Counties have exclusive authority to levy a sales tax.

[d] Combined rates for parishes normally do not exceed 4% unless approved in a special election.

[e] City sales tax takes precedence over county tax in incorporated areas.

[f] City and county rates cannot exceed 4% except in specifically exempted counties, including Nassau and Suffolk and New York City's five boroughs. Cities and counties usually negotiate a split.

[g] A county tax rate takes precedence over a city's, and the combined rates cannot exceed 2.75%. Only 21 Tennessee cities levy a tax greater than the county rate.

[h] A city's rate of 1% takes precedence over the county's in incorporated areas. Most Utah counties levy an additional 0.25% tax.

[i] City sales taxes in Washington preempt the county tax in incorporated areas. An additional 0.5% sales tax applies to sales in restaurants and bars in King County.

[j] In Florida, the county discretionary surtax applies only to the first $5,000 of a transaction's price.

[k] The state's 6.25% tax is shared with all cities and counties: cities receive the revenue from 1% of the state's tax collected in their borders, and counties receive the revenue from 1% rate collected in unincorporated areas plus that from 0.25% collected countywide. In addition, counties may levy the additional sales taxes reported in Table 5–4.

Inclusion of services   In recent years, state legislatures have expanded their tax bases by adding services—personal, professional, repair, computer, and amusements. This rapidly expanding sector of the economy—58 percent of personal consumption in 2000 compared with 33 percent fifty years earlier—represents a politically tantalizing source of revenue for states and their local governments. In the 1980s Florida and Massachusetts significantly expanded coverage but met with considerable political opposition from affected service providers, and the legislatures in both states rescinded the tax expansion. More recently, states have again turned to services in their search for additional revenues, but this time they have been more selective in bringing services under the tax umbrella. The general conclusion among experts is that adding professional and business services, in particular, to the tax base is ill-advised because of the opportunities for tax avoidance (e.g., consumers can use an out-of-state law firm) and tax pyramiding (as taxing business inputs increases the cost of outputs to the consumer, who in most cases bears the cumulative incidence of the tax).[4]

Internet sales   At the national level, debate over the sales tax has focused on the moratorium on state and local taxation of Internet sales, which Congress first imposed in 1998 and renewed in 2001.

The issue has its origins in the much earlier case of *National Bellas Hess, Inc., v. Department of Revenue of the State of Illinois* (1967), in which the U.S. Supreme Court ruled that states could not compel a mail order firm to collect use taxes if it had no taxable nexus in the state.[5] Such a nexus exists if a firm has any physical presence in the state, such as a warehouse, sales representatives, or a retail outlet. But merely mailing a catalog to potential buyers does not, in the Court's opinion, constitute a taxable nexus. *National Bellas Hess* reduced the effectiveness of use taxes in protecting in-state retailers from unfair competition by nonresident mail order companies. Without a mechanism for collecting taxes from retailers, states are left to compel compliance from consumers, which is impossible except in cases where licensing or title transfer occurs such as with vehicles. With the explosive growth in Web-based marketing and retailing, the loss of use taxes has become much more costly.

Then in 1998 a new and more serious threat to sales tax revenue emerged. In response to growing pressure from Internet-based vendors, Congress imposed a moratorium on both state and local taxes on Internet sales and on the service fee charged for access to the Internet. Part of the justification was to prevent stifling growth of this technology and the capacity of retailers to use this venue. But as Internet retailing has gained in popularity with consumers, it has placed located retailers at a competitive disadvantage to their cyber-based counterparts and eroded the sales tax bases of state and local governments. Short of a congressional resolution, the twin issues of taxing Internet transactions and Internet service providers will remain at the fore of national debate for the foreseeable future.

Exemptions for food   Another issue involves the taxation of food purchased for home consumption. Evidence shows that the general sales tax is regressive with respect to household income. Exempting food purchased for home consumption, which twenty-nine states now do, reduces but does not eliminate the tax's regressivity.[6] Four states—Illinois, Missouri, South Carolina, and Virginia—have a two-tiered tax structure and tax food at a lower rate. Illinois, for example, levies a 1 percent tax on food but a 6.25 percent tax on all other purchases. Colorado, Georgia, Illinois, Louisiana, Missouri, and North Carolina complicate tax equity, neutrality, and administration by giving local governments the option of including food in their tax base. Colorado cities that include food typically impose a different

a credit reduces regressivity more effectively man exemption? How??

rate from their general sales tax and, in a few cases, tax food at higher rates. All states include food consumed in restaurants in their sales tax base.

An alternative to exempting food is to provide an **income tax credit** for lower-income households to offset the tax paid on food purchases. Currently five states—Hawaii, Idaho, Kansas, South Dakota, and Wyoming—provide such a credit.[7] Although this approach reduces the sales tax's regressivity more effectively than a blanket exemption or a two-tiered rate structure, it has not proven politically popular with most state legislatures.

Population changes   Like the property tax base, the sales tax base is sensitive to population changes. According to one study, however, the sales tax base is less sensitive to population changes than the property tax base because it draws on the expenditures of consumers throughout a metropolitan area and thus is not as closely linked to changes in a particular city's population.[8]

State regulation   When states expand their sales tax base, they often grapple with whether and to what extent they should forestall a revenue windfall for local governments. In some cases, as a tradeoff for increases in the sales tax revenues, legislators compel local governments to reduce their dependence on the property tax by capping property tax appraisals, rates, or yields; one trend in recent years has been to couple expansion of the sales tax base with property tax relief to seniors. In other cases, the state may seek to capture the windfalls through reduced state aid or reductions in other shared revenues. Unfortunately, most responses fail to recognize

---

Sales tax holidays

A new development in the past few years has been the introduction of sales tax holidays, now used in nine states and the District of Columbia.[1] First introduced by New York in 1997, a sales tax holiday offers a temporary moratorium on state and usually local sales taxes, usually two to four days long and usually in August. The holiday exempts the sales tax on back-to-school items such as clothing, supplies, and even computer hardware and software. While the specifics vary among the states, the holiday has proven quite popular with legislators and consumers but unpopular with tax experts, who see it as a "gimmick."

Part of the criticism arises because of the obvious inefficiencies that these holidays introduce: a reduction in the tax's neutrality and an increase in its administrative complexity. From a local government's perspective, they represent

further state-mandated erosion of the tax base and an unwelcome reduction in tax revenues. Local governments point out that while state legislatures fret about the revenue windfalls that local governments receive whenever the base is broadened, no such fretting seems to vex their deliberations when the base is narrowed, even temporarily, as in the case of sales tax holidays. One study found that consumers only receive about 80 percent of the tax benefit, with the remaining 20 percent going to vendors as higher profits.[2]

The political reality remains that these temporary exemptions are popular with consumers who see them as a targeted relief for working families, particularly those with school-age children. In fact, it is one of the few tax relief measures targeted to this group, with most other relief measures favoring more politically active groups, such as senior citizens.

[1] Federation of Tax Administrators, "State Tax Holidays: Tax Holidays Continue Despite Criticisms" (June 2002): www.taxadmin.org/fta/rate/sales_holiday.

[2] Richard K. Harper et al., "Price Effects Around a Sales Tax Holiday: An Exploratory Study," *Public Budgeting & Finance* 23 (winter 2003): 108–113.

that local governments face even greater fiscal pressures than those experienced at the state or national levels, particularly from the cumulative impact of unfunded mandates.

Tax base conformance Sales tax experts strongly recommend tax base conformance—that is, that the state and local base be the same. Wherever local bases vary, border-city and border-county effects follow. Consumers have an incentive to shop in areas where particular transactions are exempt or taxed at lower rates, introducing an economic drag on the local economy. As discussed in Chapter 2, a uniform tax base eliminates the net losses to a state's economy created by the time and resources wasted in avoiding the tax. Tax base conformance also simplifies collection of the tax for sellers, since only one set of rules governs the definition of taxable items, as well as the auditing of tax returns and the verification of tax liability by the tax enforcement unit. But despite the advantages of conformance, the trend among states has been to increase local government discretion in the definition of their sales tax base.

Issues in the design of a local sales tax

Once a state legislature grants one or more levels of local government access to the tax, policy makers must then resolve several issues in the design and implementation of the tax. These include the following questions:

- Does a sales tax adversely affect local retail sales?
- Does a sales tax reduce the property tax burden, or does it merely encourage increased local government spending?
- Does a local sales tax shift the overall tax burden away from business and onto households, which purchase most of the taxable items?
- If both cities and counties impose a sales tax, how should the revenue collected within the city limits be allocated to the two levels of local government?
- Should revenue from the tax be dedicated to funding particular services?
- How much discretion should local governments have in administering the tax?

Effects of a sales tax on retail sales

The most frequently expressed concern about a local sales tax is that it will hurt retail sales. This issue becomes especially significant when a local government has a range of rates to choose from and the proposed rate is higher than those in surrounding jurisdictions, creating a border-city effect.

No recent studies have examined the border-city effect. Studies done in the 1970s and 1980s, however, suggest that the impact of a rate differential on local business is moderate where the differences in rates are low (less than 1 percent) but that the impact increases where the differences in rates are high.[9] As discussed in Chapter 2, higher rate differentials make it more economically feasible for shoppers to travel to lower-tax areas. To minimize effects on local businesses, state legislatures should design legislation so that local rates are relatively uniform (varying by no more than 1 percent) and local adoption is widespread or, ideally, universal.

To promote widespread adoption, state law must give local governments an incentive to adopt the tax. Before 1985, Wisconsin had authorized a 0.5 percent tax for counties but stipulated that all of the revenue had to be distributed to villages and cities within the county. No county adopted the tax. In 1985, the legislation was changed to allow counties to retain the revenue from the tax. Currently, sixty of Wisconsin's seventy-one counties have adopted the tax (see Table 5–4).

A related issue concerns the impact of a general sales tax on consumer spending. Does the tax reduce retail sales? Intuitively, the answer is yes. Consumers have a fixed budget and if more of a household's income goes for sales taxes, there is that much less available for purchasing goods and services. A 2004 study of Fort Collins, Colorado, found that an increase in the local sales tax rate reduced economic activity (gross city product) in the city.[10] Furthermore, the rate increase had the greatest negative impact on lower-income households.

A study from 1996, which took a much longer-term view of the impact of the sales tax, concluded that the general sales tax is fully shifted forward to consumers, increasing prices of products commensurate with the tax increase.[11] Yet a more recent and methodologically careful study of twelve common household products (from bananas to shampoo) found that not only was the tax burden shifted forward but in several cases there was overshifting—that is, the price increase was greater than the tax increase and, in a few cases (bread, Crisco, shampoo, soda, and boys' underwear), was twice as large.[12] The researchers attributed this to markets that lack sufficient competition to contain price increases.

In summary, the adoption of a local sales tax does lower retail sales, and the impact is augmented if consumers have a choice of shopping in lower-tax areas. A far greater detrimental impact occurs if states adopt policies that result in significant border-city effects. However, if regional differences in rates are small and there is widespread adoption of the tax (at least countywide), the effect of tax differentials on sales is negligible.

Effects of a sales tax on the property tax and on government spending

Although reducing the property tax is one common justification for adopting a local sales tax, some critics contend that the sales tax only increases local government spending. While a 1979 study of forty-one large U.S. cities found that the sales tax does significantly lower the property tax burden,[13] a more recent study of Texas cities found that dependence on the sales tax had no effect on property tax burdens levied for operating purposes.[14] This later study controlled for more factors, including other taxes and nontaxes, and its conclusions were less likely affected by external factors because it considered cities in only one state. However, a 1991 study found that some Illinois municipalities, particularly those in nonmetropolitan areas, were able to substitute increasing revenue from their sales tax for the property tax.[15]

A 1996 study examined the impact of the sales tax on property values in twenty-one towns in the Phoenix, Arizona, area.[16] The connection between property values and sales taxes is that, other things being equal, higher sales taxes reduce the amount of income a household has to spend on housing and other goods and services, thereby lowering their value. The study found that the reduced purchasing power leads to lower property values in those cities with higher sales taxes. In other words, households are attuned to differences not only in local property tax burdens but also in sales tax burdens.

Impact of the local sales tax on the distribution of tax burdens

Another concern about the imposition of a local sales tax is that it shifts a greater share of the local tax burden onto households, especially renters, and reduces the burden borne by the business sector. But while consumers perceive that they bear a major portion of state and local sales taxes, in fact most states impose the tax on a wide range of business purchases. A frequently cited 1999 study on this issue found that, nationally, consumers' share of the sales tax is 59 percent, although state-by-state variations range from 28 percent in Hawaii to 89 percent in West Virginia, depending on the composition of a state's tax base and exemptions.[17] The remainder of the sales tax falls on business purchases. However, the recent trend toward narrowing the sales tax base, especially by removing machinery, tools, and building materials, undoubtedly shifts a greater proportion of the sales tax to households. (Even the portion of the sales tax paid by business may be shifted forward to consumers in the form of higher prices for finished goods and services. Firms in the same industry that incur the same tax burden can more easily shift that burden forward to the final buyer as a price increase.) The concern that a local sales tax will increase the overall tax burden of households thus has some justification.

Exportability

Exporting the sales tax to nonresident consumers—commuters, tourists, and nonlocal businesses—is one means of reducing the burden on local households. For example, local governments whose economies are based on recreational services or tourism can export a significant portion of their sales tax burden because consumer demand for their goods and services is inelastic; in other words, because tourists lack information on where to find the lowest prices, they typically incur higher prices than local residents. For this reason, Colorado resort cities such as Vail, Crested Butte, Steamboat Springs, Telluride, and Estes Park levy the highest rates in the state: 4–4.5 percent. Utah authorizes an additional 1 percent levy for its resort cities, and Idaho limits local sales taxes to specific resort communities. The study cited earlier of Fort Collins, Colorado, found that 30 percent of the sales tax revenue came from purchases by nonresident households and businesses.[18]

Where state law does not allow local governments to share sales tax revenue with each other, jurisdictions with sales tax authority have a strong incentive to pursue regional shopping centers that attract nonresident buyers. If they can export the tax burden to nonresident shopping center patrons, they can provide better public services without raising the cost to residents. Local governments in some states try to lure mall developers by devoting a portion of the sales tax revenue to tax abatement incentives. But these "beggar thy neighbor" measures create sales tax winners and losers among local governments. The North Carolina approach, described in the next section, minimizes these economically costly maneuvers while preserving local autonomy and promoting interjurisdictional equity.

A 2004 study of county sales taxes in six states—Florida, Georgia, Indiana, Ohio, South Carolina, and Tennessee—offers particularly useful insights into the implications of local sales tax policies for economic development.[19] First, the largest benefit in increased sales taxes for this sample of counties came from the relocation of construction firms. The addition of jobs in the service, agricultural, and public utilities sectors also had a favorable impact on sales tax yields. However, virtually no tax benefits were derived from the relocation of manufacturing firms or the preservation of military bases, which, the study's authors speculate, was because of the extensive exemptions and abatements afforded manufacturers and their finished goods generally being sold in markets outside the local community.

Second, in terms of tax yield, the addition of hotel/motel facilities has a significant impact on local sales tax receipts for this sample of counties. This impact is enhanced if the community has the amenities and tourist attractions to support leisure and business travelers. Finally, the study found that commuters—both those working in the county but living outside (in-commuters) and those living in the county but working outside (out-commuters)—had significant but inverse effects on sales tax yields. For this sample of counties, in-commuters add an average of $2 to county sales tax receipts for every $1 lost by out-commuters. Urban counties experience this impact more than rural ones.

Coordination of local sales tax rates

As can be seen from Tables 5–3 and 5–4, most state legislatures give local governments the option of adopting a sales tax, and many provide a range of rates from which the local governments may choose; this creates the potential for significant disparities in interjurisdictional revenue capacities. A further complication occurs when more than one level of local government levies a sales tax. Within a city's borders, if the city, county (or parish), and transit authority all collect a sales tax, the three overlapping tax rates can have a significant impact on consumer behavior. States have resolved interlocal rate disparities and overlapping tax rates in a number of different ways (Figure 5–2).

At one extreme is the approach used by North Carolina, where all one hundred counties levy the full 2.5 percent optional tax but fifty-eight counties share revenues from it with cities on a per capita basis and the other forty-two do so on the basis of a pro rata share of the property taxes levied. North Carolina's approach reduces intercity competition for retail business because the sales tax benefits are distributed countywide rather than to a particular city where the sale occurred—a **tax base–sharing** plan at the county level. Some New York counties also negotiate revenue-sharing formulae with their villages, towns, and cities. However, not all counties in New York use this approach, and local rates vary considerably within the 4.25 percent maximum rate allowed by state law.

Several states resolve the problem of overlap by restricting the tax to only county or municipal governments. In Nebraska and South Dakota, the two states where only cities levy the tax, households and businesses have an incentive to shop in or relocate to unincorporated areas. However, this is not a serious problem where rates are kept low.

California uses still another approach to overcoming overlap while promoting uniformity in local rates. Cities may adopt a rate of up to 1 percent, which is credited against the county's rate of 1.25 percent. Revenue from the unused portion of the county rate within the city limits and all of the 1.25 percent rate in unincorporated areas goes to the county's general fund. All counties and most of the cities in California have adopted the tax, making the local rate nearly uniform statewide. The exception occurs in areas served by a transit district, which may levy an additional 0.5 percent rate. Tennessee uses a similar approach, but the county rate takes precedence over the municipal rate within city corporate limits, and the county redistributes a portion of the revenue back to cities according to the point of sale.

The least coordination occurs in states such as Texas and Louisiana, where local rates are stacked on top of each other, with a maximum combined rate usually imposed by state law. For example, Louisiana municipalities may generally levy a rate of up to 2.5 percent. Parishes and school districts may levy a combined tax of 6 percent within city borders, but the city rate takes precedence. When the state's 4 percent rate is included, combined state and local rates range as high as 10 percent, as in the city of Newellton in Tensas Parish: 4 percent state, 0.75 percent city, 0.25 percent law enforcement district, 1.5 percent school, and 3.5 percent for the parish (police jury). The problem with this approach is that it creates border-city effects that skew business development, and it complicates tax compliance for vendors with multiple outlets who must keep records on the various tax rates levied in each jurisdiction.

Figure 5–2
Strategies for interlocal coordination of sales tax rates.

Minimum overlap ◄———————————————► Maximum overlap

Only counties levy tax but cities receive a share of revenue:	Only one level is given access, with no sharing of revenue:	City rate takes precedence over county rate within city's boundaries:	County rate takes precedence over city rate:	Local rates are stacked on top of each other:
North Carolina	South Dakota (cities) Wisconsin (counties)	California	Tennessee	Louisiana Texas

Considerable variation exists in the way that states resolve the problem of tax rate overlap. North Carolina's approach offers the most benefits, including universal participation by local governments, more equitable redistribution of sales tax revenue, and reduced interlocal rivalry for retail business.

Dedicated sales taxes

The proliferation of local sales tax authority has been accompanied by more widespread dedicating of tax revenues to particular purposes. The chronology of Ohio's county sales tax is illustrative. As is typical, the initial authorization in 1987 imposed no restrictions on the use of the revenue. Then in 1993, the legislature expanded county powers to levy an additional incremental tax with revenues earmarked for detention facilities. In 1995 sports facilities were added, and then in 2001 acquisition of agricultural easements was added.[20] The use of dedicated sales taxes for law enforcement/crime control is particularly popular among local governments in Illinois, Louisiana, Missouri, Ohio, and Texas.

In 1994, Allegheny County and Philadelphia were granted authority to become the first local governments in Pennsylvania to levy a local 1 percent sales tax, piggybacked onto the state's sales tax. Allegheny County's revenue is dedicated to the preservation of regional assets: libraries, parks, zoos, sports arenas, museums, and performing arts facilities.[21] Although cities in Texas have had access to the general sales tax for unrestricted purposes since 1967, increases in the rates in recent years have been accompanied by legislative restrictions on the use of the revenue. Among the approved uses are economic development and crime control. The tax dedicated to crime control requires renewed voter approval at least every twenty years.

While legislative dedication of revenue increases political support for rate increases, it complicates local budgeting. Because of the volatility of the tax, services benefiting from the dedication experience fluctuations in funding that rarely match their expenditure needs.

Local discretion in sales tax administration

In granting local governments access to a sales tax, state legislatures must address four issues concerning the adoption and collection of the tax:

1. Should voter approval be required for local adoption of the tax?
2. How much discretion should local governments be given in choosing a tax rate?
3. Should tax liability be based on the point of sale or the point of delivery?
4. Should the state collect and enforce the local tax?

Voter approval Whether voter approval is required generally depends on precedent in each state. If a state requires voter approval on tax and debt issues, it will more than likely require voter approval for adoption of a local sales tax.

As noted earlier, requiring voter approval reduces the level of participation by local governments. (Yet some states, such as Texas, have achieved widespread adoption of the tax even though voter approval is required.) States not requiring a referendum have more universal adoption of a local sales tax and thus fewer opportunities for the development of border-city effects. On the other hand, requiring taxpayers to approve the sales tax adds to its legitimacy and shifts political responsibility for imposing it from public officials to the electorate.

Local discretion in tax rates Most states give their local governments a range of tax rates from which they may choose and then limit the combined overlapping rate of all local governments. For example, Nebraska limits the total state-city rate to 7 percent, with 5.5 percent claimed by the state and the remainder available to cities in 0.5 percent increments: 6 percent (two cities), 6.5 percent (eighty-eight cities), and 7 percent (forty-one cities). Arkansas imposes a somewhat different cap. It limits city and county levies to $25 per transaction per 1 percent rate. But local governments define what constitutes a single transaction and that definition varies by jurisdiction. Florida limits the 1 percent county tax to the first $5,000 of a single sale.

Alabama has the highest combined state-local rate of up to 11 percent. When only local rates are considered, combined *local* tax rates generally cluster around 2–3 percent, although there are several notable exceptions. For example, combined local rates in Alabama and Colorado range as high as 7 percent. Local governments in Alaska, Louisiana, and Oklahoma follow with maximum combined rates of 6 percent. In the remaining states, maximum local rates are substantially less.

Another trend has been the tendency among state legislatures to increase the maximum rates that local governments may impose, especially as additional levels of local government are given access to the tax and greater discretion to deviate from the state's tax base. For example, the original 1967 enabling legislation gave Texas cities a voter-approved 1 percent sales tax that was piggybacked onto the state tax base. Amendments to that original act have increased the city levy to as much as 2 percent, with some of the additional revenue dedicated to particular purposes, as noted above.

Allowing local governments discretion in setting tax rates enables them to meet revenue needs and gives those local governments in a position to benefit from exportation of the tax burden an opportunity to do so. On the other hand, too much discretion creates an incentive for local governments to try to attract business by removing or reducing the sales tax and leads to the inequities and inefficiencies from border-city effects. The greatest amount of discretion exists for local governments in Alabama, Alaska, Louisiana, and Oklahoma.

Tax liability If sales tax revenue is not redistributed countywide on a basis like that used by North Carolina, then the state legislature must determine whether sales tax receipts are credited to the jurisdiction where the sale occurred or to the jurisdiction where delivery is made. Seventeen states use the latter approach,[22] the benefits of which are that (1) taxpayers have no incentive to shop in lower-tax jurisdictions and (2) communities that have little or no commercial activity receive a share of the revenue. However, this approach greatly complicates tax compliance for retailers, who must maintain records on taxpayer residency, and it provides significant opportunities for tax evasion by taxpayers who claim residency in lower-tax areas. Furthermore, it complicates auditing of tax returns and increases the chances of allocating revenue to the wrong jurisdiction. Because of these disadvantages, sales tax experts recommend that tax liability be based on the point of sale and not on the buyer's jurisdiction of residence.

State administration and enforcement A final set of issues concerns the collection, distribution, and enforcement of the local tax. Only seven states still permit some local administration of the tax.[23] In four of these states—Alabama, Arizona, Colorado, and Minnesota—local governments may choose state collection or administer the tax themselves. Most smaller governments opt for state administration by piggybacking their tax onto the state's. Larger governments still administer their own tax. Arizona and Colorado encourage state collection and enforcement by providing their services free to local governments.

The consensus among sales tax experts is that piggybacking collection and enforcement of the local tax onto the state's is more cost-efficient and effective than local administration. State collection makes it unnecessary for local governments to staff their own collection office. It also simplifies compliance for vendors, who need complete only one tax return. If the state collects the tax, two issues must be resolved. The first concerns the charge for collecting the local tax. State charges vary from no charge in six states (Arizona, Colorado, Florida, Illinois, Iowa, and Kansas) to 3 percent of collected revenues in three state (Arkansas, Mississippi, and Nebraska).[24] The second issue concerns the frequency with which revenues are returned to local governments. Most states provide for a monthly remittance cycle, although a few states distribute quarterly.[25] Arizona distributes revenue back to local governments on a weekly basis.

A related concern is whether the state should compensate local governments for the interest earned on the local share of revenue while it is in state custody. Most states retain these earnings, but eight states reimburse local governments for interest earnings.[26] California, Florida, Iowa, and New York provide their local governments with advance remittances each month based on past revenue receipts. Most all states now provide for wire transfers of reimbursements to further expedite remittances.

One final problem occasionally associated with state administration is incorrect information on vendor location, which causes revenues to be credited to the wrong local government. This is especially likely in metropolitan areas, where businesses identify the major central city as their location rather than the less well-known suburban community where their facilities are actually located. One simple solution is for state law to require local government certification of the vendor's location as part of the process for obtaining a sales tax permit.

Summary and recommendations

The following summary and recommendations are based on the discussion in this chapter:

Adoption of a local option sales tax is more common in states where voter approval is not required. If state legislatures want to encourage universal adoption at the local government level and thereby reduce the inefficiencies that result from border-city/county effects, then legislatures should require adoption of the tax—preferably at the county level, with revenue sharing between the county and its cities. The North Carolina model offers the best example of a well-designed local sales tax policy that preserves local autonomy, reduces costly interlocal competition for the tax base, and promotes economic growth.

The base for the sales tax is procyclical, meaning that tax revenue rises and falls with the business cycle, creating the potential for midyear revenue shortfalls whenever the local economy turns downward. Therefore, local governments should avoid becoming too dependent on the sales tax by deriving no more than $1.00 in sales tax revenue for every $1.00 in property taxes.

The trend among states has been to narrow the sales tax base by exempting food purchased for home consumption and business purchases of machinery and building materials. This reduces the tax's regressivity (a gain on equity).

A fundamental requirement for a neutral local sales tax structure is that state and local bases must be the same. However, states have granted more discretion to local governments in defining their tax base, resulting in greater divergence in the definition of taxable transactions at the state and local levels. This has produced considerable economic inefficiency by giving individuals and businesses an incentive to make purchases in jurisdictions that exempt particular types of transactions.

Studies indicate that a local sales tax lowers retail business activity somewhat, but the effect is insignificant when differences in local rates are minimal and adoption of the tax is widespread among local governments.

Studies appear to conflict on the impact of the local sales tax on the property tax. Evidence indicates that the tax does not increase spending by local governments, but it appears that the burden of the sales tax is being borne increasingly by households and less by businesses.

When more than one level of local government levies the sales tax, one problem is how to divide the revenue (or rate) between the levels of government. The most equitable and administratively simple approach is to levy the tax at the county level, then distribute the revenue to cities and the county on a per capita basis or on the basis of a pro rata share of the property taxes levied. This approach also reduces intercity rivalry for retail business.

The consensus among sales tax experts is that piggybacking collection and enforcement of the local tax onto the state's is more efficient and cost-effective than local administration because of the economies of scale that come with centralization.

1 John H. Bowman and John L. Mikesell, *Local Government Tax Authority and Use* (Washington, D.C.: National League of Cities, 1987), 51–53.

2 National Conference of State Legislatures (NCSL), *Critical Issues in State-Local Fiscal Policy: A Guide to Local Option Taxes* (Denver, Colo.: NCSL, November 1997), 20.

3 Federation of Tax Administrators, *Sales Taxation of Services. 1996 Update,* Research Report no. 147 (Washington, D.C.: Federation of Tax Administrators, April 1997), 1.

4 Kirk J. Stark, "The Uneasy Case for Extending the Sales Tax to Services," *State Tax Notes* 29 (July 21, 2003): 211–232.

5 Gary C. Cornia, David L. Sjoquist, and Lawrence C. Walters, "Sales and Use Tax Simplification and Voluntary Compliance," *Public Budgeting & Finance* 24 (spring 2004): 2.

6 Federation of Tax Administrators Web site: www.taxadmin.org/fta/rate/sl_sales.

7 Ibid.

8 George E. Peterson and Thomas Muller, *The Economic and Fiscal Accompaniments of Population Change* (Washington, D.C.: The Urban Institute Press, 1980), 102.

9 John L. Mikesell, "Central Cities and Sales Tax Rate Differentials: The Border City Problem," *National Tax Journal* 23 (June 1970): 211; John L. Mikesell and C. Kurt Zorn, "Impact of the Sales Tax Rate on Its Base: Evidence From a Small Town," *Public Finance Quarterly* 14 (July 1986): 335; Ronald C. Fisher, "The Sales Tax in the District of Columbia Revenue System," in *Technical Aspects of the District's Tax System,* as submitted to the Committee on the District of Columbia, U.S. House of Representatives, S-11 (Washington, D.C.: Government Printing Office, 1978), 37–66.

10 Harvey Cutler and Irina Strelnikova, "The Impact of the U.S. Sales Tax Rate on City Size and Economic Activity: A CGE Approach," *Urban Studies* 41 (April 2004): 875–885.

11 James M. Poterba, "Retail Price Reactions to Changes in State and Local Sales Taxes," *National Tax Journal* 49 (June 1996): 165–176.

12 Timothy J. Besley and Harvey S. Rosen, "Sales Taxes and Prices: An Empirical Analysis," *National Tax Journal* 52 (June 1999): 157–178.

13 Robert P. Inman, "Subsidies, Regulations, and the Taxation of Property in Large U.S. Cities," *National Tax Journal* 32 (June 1979 Suppl.): 163.

14 Robert L. Bland and Phanit Laosirirat, "Tax Limitations to Reduce Municipal Property Taxes: Truth in Taxation in Texas," *Journal of Urban Affairs* 19 (spring 1997): 45–58.

15 Andrew J. Krmenec, "Sales Tax as Property Tax Relief? The Shifting Onus of Local Revenue Generation," *Professional Geographer* 43 (February 1991): 60–67.

16 Joyce Y. Man and Michael E. Bell, "The Impact of Local Sales Tax on the Value of Owner-Occupied Housing," *Journal of Urban Economics* 39 (January 1996): 114–130.

17 Raymond J. Ring, "Consumers' Share and Producers' Share of the General Sales Tax," *National Tax Journal* 52 (March 1999): 81–92.

18 Cutler and Strelnikova, "The Impact of the U.S. Sales Tax Rate," 881.

19 Richard Hawkins and Matthew N. Murray, "Explaining Interjurisdictional Variations in Local Sales Tax Yield," *Public Finance Review* 32 (January 2004): 82–104.

20 State of Ohio, Department of Taxation, "Sales and Use Tax," www.ohio.gov/tax: 141–143.

21 Brian K. Jensen and James W. Turner, "Act 77: Revenue Sharing in Allegheny County," *Government Finance Review* 16 (December 2000): 17–21.

22 John F. Due and John L. Mikesell, *Sales Taxation: State and Local Structure and Administration,* 2nd ed. (Washington, D.C.: The Urban Institute Press, 1994), 293.

23 Ibid., 299.

24 R. Gregory Michel, "Local Sales Taxes: State Practices for Collection, Distribution, and Auditing," *GFOA Research Bulletin* (March 1997): 6.

25 Ibid., 3.

26 Ibid., 4.

6

Excise taxes

Role of excise taxes in local revenue structures

Classifying excise taxes
Revenue potential of excise taxes

Gross receipts taxes on utilities

Defining the gross receipts tax base
Determining the tax rate
Administering the gross receipts tax

Hotel and motel occupancy taxes

Effects of an occupancy tax on local business
Effects of an occupancy tax on local government budgets
Administering an occupancy tax

Motor fuels taxes

Effects of a motor fuels tax on sales
Coordinating motor fuels tax rates
Administering a motor fuels tax

Other sumptuary taxes

Privilege and other excise taxes

Summary and recommendations

One may solve one's problems not only by getting what one wants but also by wanting what one gets.

—Ralph Burton Perry

Excise taxes

Excise, or **selective sales,** taxes are levies on specific products or services at rates specific to each type of taxable transaction. Although revenue yields from excise taxes trail those of the general sales tax, the use of excise taxes is more widespread. Counties and cities in forty-eight states derive revenue from at least one type of excise tax; only Connecticut and New Hampshire report no revenue from excise taxes. Unlike the general sales tax, excise taxes are usually locally administered.

The legal authority for each local excise tax is usually state enabling legislation separate from that for the general sales tax. In some cases, however, home-rule powers provide the legal basis for an excise tax, especially in states such as Colorado and Illinois, where local governments have broad discretion under their home-rule statute. Local governments in Alabama and South Carolina derive their authority to levy utility taxes from their business licensing powers, and municipalities in Oklahoma rely on their general taxing powers to levy certain excise taxes.[1] Rarely do local governments obtain voter approval before adopting an excise tax. Among the notable exceptions are the utility taxes levied by Arizona's cities and towns and the optional motor fuels tax levied by Florida's counties.

As discussed in Chapter 2, excise taxes lack the equity and neutrality features that characterize good tax policy. Except for those targeted to luxury goods, excise taxes are usually regressive, falling more heavily on those less able to pay. On the other hand, a number of benefits-based excise taxes work like service charges (i.e., the more one consumes, the more one pays), which makes them more equitable to the extent that users of the public service bear the cost. Moreover, because they are controlled locally, excise taxes are more likely than general sales taxes to create border-city/county effects. However, since they tend to fall on products and services with few substitutes or with inelastic demand, excise taxes have less adverse impact on the local economy. As a rule, these taxes persist because of their political appeal and their relative ease to administer locally, and not because of their economic benefits.

Role of excise taxes in local revenue structures

Like the discussion of the general sales tax in Chapter 5, this discussion is limited to locally levied excise taxes and excludes dedication of a portion of state excise tax receipts to local governments. Many of the questions discussed in the preceding chapter on the general sales tax resurface with excise taxes, including

- What are the most common types of excise taxes used by local governments?
- What is the revenue potential of each?
- What effect do excise taxes have on the local economy?
- Which types of excise taxes are best for local governments?

The following section examines the first two questions in detail. The remaining sections of the chapter consider specific excise taxes, giving particular attention to their desirability as revenue sources and to the effect of each on the local economy.

Classifying excise taxes

Excise taxes are of three types: benefits based, sumptuary, and privilege (see Figure 6–1). **Benefits-based taxes** recover at least part of the cost of a public service from those who benefit from it. These taxes include room taxes on hotel/motel occupancy, levies on gasoline and other motor fuels, and to some extent **gross receipts taxes** (or street rental fees) on utilities. Occupancy or lodging taxes compensate local governments for the additional capacity needed to serve the increased demands that come from tourists and participants in conventions. Many state laws require that at least a portion of the revenue be used for promoting tourism, convention business, and historic preservation, thereby strengthening the connection between these taxes and the benefits received. Motor fuels taxes are usually dedicated for street and road maintenance, which benefits those who bear the tax. Utility taxes are levied against private utility companies for their use of city or county rights-of-way.

Sumptuary taxes, also known as **sin taxes,** are levied, in part, to discourage consumption of certain classes of goods, such as alcohol or cigarettes, by rendering their cost prohibitive for many consumers. Recent evidence suggests that sumptuary taxes do reduce consumption of these products, especially cigarette consumption by adolescents. Taxes on gasoline and diesel fuel, although benefits based, also qualify as sumptuary taxes because they effectively raise the price of these fuels and thus reduce consumption over the long term.

Privilege taxes are levied on the privilege of conducting a particular type of business or transaction. Examples include occupational privilege taxes levied on particular professions or on individual employees, such as Pittsburgh's annual $10 occupation privilege tax levied on every person employed in the city. Other privilege taxes include levies on admissions, restaurant meals, deed transfers, and bank franchises. Even taxes on utilities constitute a levy on the privilege of having an exclusive franchise to provide service to local residents.

Sumptuary taxes, such as tobacco taxes, are usually levied on a per unit (in rem) basis, although mixed drinks taxes are based on the selling price. Some benefits-based taxes, such as those on hotel/motel occupancy, are levied as a percentage of the value (ad valorem) of the service, whereas gasoline taxes are levied on a per gallon basis. Finally, the tax base for excise taxes on privileges, such as those on utility franchises and entertainment, tend to be levied on gross receipts, such as total charges for cable service; however, occupation privilege taxes are a head tax, meaning that they are levied on each person.

Revenue potential of excise taxes

Because of the variety of excise taxes levied by local governments and the difficulty in obtaining information on their use, few studies have been undertaken of their role in local government. However, some trends can be discerned from the data produced by the Census Bureau:

- Large urban cities and resort communities make the greatest use of excise taxes. Both use excise taxes selectively to export their tax burden.

- Use of locally levied excise taxes varies widely among the states. Two states— Connecticut and New Hampshire—levy no local excise taxes, but cities in three states—Arkansas, Missouri, and Oklahoma—derive more revenue from their excise taxes than from the property tax, a dependence that has existed for at least twenty years.

- The largest source of excise tax revenue for municipalities is the gross receipts tax on utilities. Counties make comparatively greater use of sumptuary taxes, although revenue from these taxes has declined in importance for both cities and counties.

- Both cities and counties have moderately increased their dependence on the revenue from excise taxes, although these taxes represent a relatively modest source of revenue in the aggregate.

- Local governments making greater use of excise taxes with broader bases, such as gross receipts taxes on utilities, depend more heavily on excise tax revenue.

Currently, forty-eight states give one or more levels of local government access to at least one selective sales tax. Tables 6–1 and 6–2 provide an indication of the importance of revenue from selected excise taxes for municipalities and counties. Cities and towns generally rely more on excise tax revenue than do counties—particularly on revenue from broader-based excise taxes such as gross receipts taxes on utilities, which yield larger amounts of revenue as the local economy grows. Counties are more likely to levy sumptuary excise taxes, such as those on motor fuels, alcoholic beverages, and tobacco. Since they are levied on a per unit basis, revenue yields from these taxes are much less responsive to economic growth. Consumption of these products does not keep pace with the growth of other revenue sources, such as sales and property taxes.

Figure 6–1
Types of excise tax bases.

Type of tax	Examples (basis for determining liability)
Benefits-based	Hotel/motel occupancy (ad valorem); motor fuels (in rem)
Sumptuary	Tobacco (in rem); alcoholic beverages (in rem); mixed drinks (ad valorem)
Privilege	Utility franchise tax (ad valorem); occupation privilege tax (in rem)

Table 6–1
Municipal government dependence on excise taxes.

Type of excise tax	Percentage of total excise tax revenue, 2001–02	Number of states where municipalities levy tax, 2002[a]
Public utilities	61.6	40
Hotel/motel occupancy	15.0[b]	37
Restaurant	4.0[b]	14
Motor fuels	2.2	9
Alcoholic beverages	1.7	8
Tobacco products	0.9	19
Other excise	14.6	
Total excise revenue (in millions)	$13,964.85	

Source: U.S. Bureau of the Census, *Local Summary Tables by Type of Government: 2001–02,* table 2 (www.census.gov/govs/estimate/02slsstab2a.xls) and industry sources.

[a] The counts are taken from the National Conference of State Legislatures, *Critical Issues in State-Local Fiscal Policy: A Guide to Local Option Taxes* (November 1997), except for alcoholic beverages and public utilities excise taxes, which are taken from the U.S. Bureau of the Census, *Local Summary Tables by Type of Government: 2001–02.*

[b] Estimated from industry sources.

Table 6–2
County government dependence on excise taxes.

Type of excise tax	Percentage of total excise tax revenue, 2001–02	Number of states where counties levy tax, 2002[a]
Hotel/motel occupancy	20.0[b]	38
Public utilities	28.5	27
Motor fuels	19.0	12
Alcoholic beverages	3.0	13
Tobacco products	1.7	8
Restaurant	3.0[a]	14
Other excise	25.0	
Total excise revenue (in millions)	$4,034.67	

Source: U.S. Bureau of the Census, *Local Summary Tables by Type of Government: 2001–02*, table 2 (www.census.gov/govs/estimate/02slsstab2a.xls) and industry sources.

[a] The counts are taken from the National Conference of State Legislatures, *Critical Issues in State-Local Fiscal Policy: A Guide to Local Option Taxes* (November 1997), except for alcoholic beverages and public utilities excise taxes, which are taken from the U.S. Bureau of the Census, *Local Summary Tables by Type of Government: 2001–02*.
[b] Estimated from industry sources.

Chicago, like most large cities in the United States, makes extensive use of excise taxes. The twenty-eight excise taxes it levies, listed on the city's Web page under "Licenses, Permits and Taxes" for businesses, include a 7 percent amusement tax on ticketed events (3 percent on live performances), a payroll tax on employers of $4.00 per employee per month, and a 9 percent tax on soft drink syrup sales.[2] Also included on the list are an airport departure tax, an automatic amusement device tax, a foreign fire insurance tax, and an electricity use tax, among others. Collectively, these taxes account for more than 45 percent of the city's total revenue, although some of the smaller nuisance levies have high administrative costs and low yields.

Gross receipts taxes on utilities

Because they have a much broader base than other excise taxes, gross receipts taxes on utility companies offer the greatest revenue potential for cities and towns and are very commonly used. Many of these taxes trace their origins to the nineteenth century, when utilities were regulated by city governments, before consolidation of regulatory oversight at the state level in public utility commissions.

Most states give cities the power to regulate the use of their streets, including access to public rights-of-way. Local governments impose a gross receipts tax on utilities as compensation for the utilities using those rights-of-way to locate their service lines. Often the tax is part of a broader contractual agreement granting a utility company an exclusive franchise to provide service to consumers in the jurisdiction, and it represents compensation for the cost of administering the franchise. Taxes are usually fixed at a percentage of the utility's gross receipts, although charges are sometimes based on a fixed annual fee, a percentage of the utility's net earnings or dividends declared, the number of miles (or feet) of street used, the number of utility poles erected, or the number of units of service sold.

Except in Arizona and North Dakota, voter approval is not required for adoption of these taxes.[3] Missouri law requires that cities seek voter approval on any increases in the tax rate, and Oklahoma requires voter approval only on city and county gross receipts taxes on telephone companies. In New Mexico, citizens may petition for a referendum to approve a proposed utility tax, but cities are not required to conduct the election unless petitioned to do so.

For municipalities in the forty states where these taxes are levied, revenue averaged about 26 cents for every $1.00 in property taxes in 2001. As seen from Table 6–3, cities in Arkansas, Missouri, and Oklahoma rely most heavily on these taxes, deriving about as much revenue from them as from the property tax.

Dependence on utility taxes also varies widely among local governments within a state. For example, Chicago's taxes on natural gas and electric utilities are 8 and 7 percent of gross receipts, respectively; utility-related taxes provide about 18 percent of the city's general operating revenue. All other cities in Illinois are limited by state law to a maximum of 5 percent on the gross receipts of these utilities and derive relatively less revenue for operating purposes.

In addition to the more conventional taxes on such utility providers as natural gas, electricity, telephone, water, and cable television, gross receipts taxes are occasionally imposed on taxicab companies, private solid-waste collection services, and, most recently, fiber-optic telephone service. Several municipalities have agreements with fiber-optic firms for access to the city's rights-of-way. Usually the fee is specified on a per foot basis, ranging from less than a dollar to significantly higher rates in more congested urban centers. Where permitted by state law, local governments should charge all telecommunications providers for the use of public rights-of-way or for the privilege of holding an exclusive franchise to provide service to local consumers.

The gross receipts tax is similar to the general sales tax in several ways. First, state and local regulatory bodies usually permit utility companies to pass forward the cost of such taxes to consumers. Thus, the tax is regressive, falling more heavily on lower-income households because they spend a greater proportion of their income on utility services. Second, revenue from the tax is quite responsive to cycles in the local economy, which makes local governments that depend heavily on the tax vulnerable to midyear budget crises as a result of revenue shortfalls. As is the case with the general sales tax, the stability of revenue yields depends on the composition of the gross receipts tax base; yields for local governments with a larger proportion of residential utility customers tend to be more stable.

Table 6–3 Municipal government dependence on gross receipts taxes on utilities, 2001.	States	Utility gross receipts tax as a percentage of property tax
	Significant use of tax	
	Arkansas	100.5[a]
	Missouri	91.7
	Oklahoma	95.8
	Moderate use of tax	
	Arizona	33.4
	California	33.3
	Florida	54.7
	Illinois	38.2
	Kansas	53.1
	Nebraska	33.4
	Nevada	37.4
	Washington	47.6
	West Virginia	38.9
	Wyoming	59.1

Source: U.S. Bureau of the Census, *Local Summary Tables by Type of Government: 2001–02*, table 2 (www.census.gov/govs/estimate/02slsstab2a.xls).

[a] Percentage exceeds 100% because Arkansas derives almost a dollar in property taxes for every dollar in utility taxes.

Three issues are of greatest concern to managers and legislators in local government whenever utility taxes are reviewed:

- Which gross receipts of the utility company are included in the tax base?
- What tax levy fairly compensates the local government for the utility's use of public rights-of-way or the privilege of holding an exclusive franchise?
- What conditions should be included in the contract or ordinance to ensure more effective administration of the tax?

Defining the gross receipts tax base

Local managers encounter at least four issues when defining the gross receipts tax base. First, if gross receipts of the utility company constitute the tax base, then the base is minimally defined to include retail utility services to consumers or to include wholesale services as well. With deregulation of telecommunications and the growth of cellular technology, franchise taxes on the gross receipts of telecommunications utilities have become increasingly ensnarled in litigation. From the perspective of the local exchange services provider, the key is fair treatment of all telecommunications providers, including those that skim the high-revenue/low-cost accounts. Given the increasing variety of services provided by telephone companies and the expansion of deregulation, particular attention should be given to carefully specifying the services included in that utility's tax base.

Second, if the tax is legally characterized as a fee for the use of public rights-of-way, then state and federal laws usually permit utility sales to governments and other organizations otherwise exempt from local taxes to be included in the gross receipts tax base. Whether a tax or fee, gross receipts levies provide an important means for local governments to broaden their revenue base to include otherwise tax-exempt property owners. For example, Washington, D.C., includes utility sales to federal agencies and foreign embassies in its gross receipts tax base.

A third issue is whether wholesale transactions—such as the sale of water or electricity to a distributor for resale to final consumers in another jurisdiction—will be included in the tax base. Overland Park, Kansas, includes gross receipts for wholesale electricity transactions in its tax base, but many governments specifically exclude receipts from such sales.

Last, franchise agreements and the ordinances imposing the tax should make clear whether connection fees, tap fees, and revenue from advertising in the yellow or white pages of a telephone directory are included in the tax base.

Determining the tax rate

In most cases, state law gives local governments some latitude in setting the tax rates levied on public utilities. As a result, rates vary widely among governments within a state and even among utilities being taxed by the same government. Texas cities levy rates ranging from 2 percent to 4 percent of gross receipts. The lower rates generally prevail for electric and natural gas utilities, and the higher rates prevail for telephone and cable television services. Little Rock, Arkansas, levies a 5.2 percent rate on all utility providers. Fairfax County, Virginia, levies an 8 percent tax on the first $50 of a residential customer's monthly bill and the first $1,600 of a commercial customer's bill. Overland Park, Kansas, levies only a 1 percent tax on the receipts from governmental users of natural gas but a 3.5 percent tax on all other users. Although no standards exist on what constitutes a fair rate of taxation, the rate should produce revenue that approximates the rental value of the right-of-way used by the utility. In addition, the levy should compensate a local government for the cost of administering the franchise it has granted to the utility company.

In 1984, the federal Cable Communications Policy Act limited municipal taxes on cable television suppliers to 5 percent of their gross receipts. Considerable variation exists among local governments in their tax treatment of these franchises. Amarillo, Texas, uses an innovative approach, staggering its tax rate according to the percentage of the households in the city subscribing to any one cable television provider.[4] The rate ranges from a low of 4 percent of gross receipts if less than 35 percent of the households subscribe, to a maximum of 5 percent if more than 50 percent subscribe. This policy reduces the provider's tax burden during its start-up period, when fixed costs are highest.

Administering the gross receipts tax

One of the greatest advantages of the utility tax is the low cost of collection and administration. Utility companies collect the tax, sometimes identifying it as a separate item on users' statements, and then remit the tax periodically to the local government. The exclusive nature of utility service lowers the cost of collection to local governments because there are only a few collection points. Compliance costs for utility providers are also low because the tax is paid as a lump sum based on gross receipts or collected incrementally as a separate charge on the customer's invoice.

Administratively, franchise agreements should specify the following:

- The length of the contract period. Historically, franchise agreements extend for long periods of time, as much as thirty years. More recent contracts, especially for cable television providers, specify shorter contract periods.

- The frequency with which the tax is remitted to the local government. Usually the tax is remitted annually. Given the lost interest income from yearlong intervals between payments, local governments should specify more frequent collection periods—either monthly or quarterly. The agreement should also specify the documentation to be included by the utilities with the tax payment, including a certified statement by the chief financial officer of the amount of taxes owed.

- The authority of the local government to verify compliance with the franchise agreement. One survey found that most local governments do not audit utilities for compliance.[5] As a result of an audit of its utility companies, Houston, Texas, recovered more than $1 million in additional taxes. This indicates the importance of auditing tax returns.

The audit should focus on two aspects. First, it should verify that customers are properly classified if different rates apply to different classes of users, and that customers residing near the border of the local government's jurisdiction are properly categorized. Utility companies should receive prompt notification of any annexations or disannexations, and their records should be examined to verify that each utility has properly made those changes. Second, the audit should verify that all the receipts specified in the franchise agreement are being included in the tax base and that the tax is being properly computed by the company.

Hotel and motel occupancy taxes

Although revenue from the occupancy tax on hotel and motel rooms is considerably less than that produced by gross receipts taxes on public utilities (Tables 6–1 and 6–2), over the past decade lodging taxes have been the excise taxes most often adopted by local governments. Virtually all states levy the tax, and local governments in forty-four states are also authorized to use it. Most states give local governments the option of adopting the tax.[6] As many as eleven states require voter approval for adoption; the rest require only local legislative action. According to hotel and motel industry sources, more than 90 percent of the largest U.S. cities now levy the tax.[7]

The general sales tax base often includes the consideration paid for a hotel or motel room. An occupancy or room tax, however, is an *additional* levy imposed on that consideration, in part to compensate the local government for expanded services, such as police and fire protection and highway and public transit capacity, needed to meet weekend or peak convention demand. Hotel and motel taxes also compensate communities for such indirect costs as the additional pollution and congestion created by the presence of visitors; in this sense occupancy taxes are benefits based. In addition to the room price, some states permit restaurant meals and other hotel or motel services to be included in the tax base.

The occupancy excise tax, which is borne almost entirely by nonresidents, exports the local tax burden. As noted in Chapter 1, the portion of the tax that is exported should ideally be limited to the cost of providing services to nonresidents. In fact, intergovernmental competition compels local governments to maximize the amount of exported taxes to reduce the tax burden on residents.

State law usually specifies the maximum rate that local governments can impose. According to industry sources, combined state and local rates typically fall between 8 percent and 15 percent, with the local share usually at least half of the levy.[8] Local rates tend to be highest in California, Ohio, and Washington and in communities with strong tourist appeal.[9] Some communities impose a complex array of overlapping taxes. For example, Las Vegas, Nevada, levies a 9 percent combined local tax rate, which is composed of the Convention and Visitors Bureau, 4–5 percent (lower for smaller hotels); the city of Las Vegas, 1–2 percent (higher for smaller hotels); Clark County transit, 1 percent; and Clark County schools, 1 percent. There is also a state-mandated 1 percent tax, and to complicate tax administration even further, the Fremont Street area of the city incurs an additional 1–2 percent tax on hotel rooms located in the area.

If both counties and municipalities levy the tax, then either the rate or the revenue must be allocated between the two levels, along the lines of the alternatives described in Figure 5–2 for the general sales tax. For example, the city room tax in Georgia precludes collection of the county tax inside city limits. In Oregon several charter counties share revenue from the tax with their cities.

When considering adopting or changing the tax, local government managers and legislators invariably encounter the following questions:

- Does the occupancy tax adversely affect businesses dependent on tourism, especially hotels and motels?
- What effect does the tax have on local government budgets?
- Who should administer the tax?

These issues are addressed in the following sections.

Effects of an occupancy tax on local business

The principal source of opposition to a proposed occupancy tax naturally comes from the convention and tourism industries, especially hotel and motel operators, who are concerned that the tax will discourage tourism and limit the amount of money visitors spend while in the area. However, most experts believe that a modest occupancy tax has virtually no effect on the demand for resort lodging, because studies indicate that spending by tourists for lodging is insensitive to price increases—that is, **price inelastic.**[10] Although these studies do not distinguish between tourists and conventioneers, demand will be even more price inelastic for large conventions given the limited number of cities that can accommodate a large influx of delegates. This means that hotels and motels can pass the cost of the occupancy tax forward to hotel and motel occupants with little or no effect on demand. This is especially true in resort communities where a substantial portion of the local economy caters to the tourist industry and in large cities that draw convention business.

The inelasticity of the tax also limits the border-city effect described in Chapter 5. In other words, because tourists are insensitive to tax-induced price increases, they will not seek out lower-tax areas surrounding the jurisdiction. Thus, hotel and motel business will not be lost to surrounding communities simply because an occupancy tax is levied.

Effects of an occupancy tax on local government budgets

Industry sources estimate that from 60 percent to 80 percent of the revenue from occupancy taxes is earmarked for tourist-related services, including promotion of tourism and the development and operation of convention centers and visitors bureaus. A common practice is for a local government to enter into an agreement with the local chamber of commerce or visitors and convention bureau whereby the chamber or bureau agrees to use part of the revenue from the tax to promote tourism or economic development.

Some states allow other community activities, such as historic preservation, parks, and the performing and visual arts, to receive revenue from the occupancy tax. However, retaining a portion of the revenue for general operations is entirely justified because of the additional public service capacity that local governments need to meet peak tourist and convention demands.

As with most consumption taxes levied on an ad valorem basis, revenue from the occupancy tax is income elastic. If revenue from the tax grows relative to that from other, less elastic revenue sources and becomes more significant to local governments over time, the local government will be more vulnerable to midyear revenue shortfalls during economic downturns. Given the volatility of the travel and tourism industry, especially following the attacks of September 11, 2001, occupancy tax yields are particularly unstable. Earmarking the revenue for tourism promotion and convention development buffers operating budgets somewhat from that volatility. To ensure that contractors, such as chambers of commerce and convention and visitors bureaus, bear the risk of a revenue shortfall, agreements with such organizations should specify a percentage of the revenue from the tax that is for their use rather than a fixed sum. A maximum level of funding may also be specified to prevent extraordinarily large windfalls from going to such organizations. Alternatively, local governments may create an escrow account to deposit tax revenues and then award grants to contractors on the basis of actual collections from the preceding year.

Administering an occupancy tax

The issues involved in administering an occupancy tax parallel those for the gross receipts utility tax. A majority of states permit local administration of the tax, although a few require state collection. Generally, state administration of the tax is preferred for the same reasons offered for the general sales tax in Chapter 5. Centralization increases efficiency and lowers the cost of administering the tax, and it reduces the compliance cost for taxpayers, who must complete only one tax return for both the state and local governments. Yet local administration remains the norm, probably because the relatively few collection points for the tax make local enforcement more feasible.

If the local government assumes responsibility for collection, three issues must be resolved in either state law or local policy:

- How frequently the tax is remitted by operators
- What enforcement powers the local government has to collect delinquent taxes
- What auditing authority the local government has.

As with utility taxes, remittance should be at least quarterly for small and midsized hotels and motels and monthly for larger operators. More frequent collection of taxes means less lost interest income for local governments. The unit responsible for tax collection should mail a notice and tax form to each operator prior to the due date to facilitate tax compliance. State or local law should also specify the documentation taxpayers should include with their local tax returns, such as a copy of their state return. Local government policy should also ensure operators of the absolute confidentiality of their tax returns to protect owners from disclosure of information to competitors.

Although delinquency is seldom a problem with the occupancy tax, state law usually gives local governments the power to revoke a hotel or motel operator's permit in the event of delinquency. However, such action is often counterproductive because a firm unable to operate is certainly unable to pay back taxes. Most instances of delinquency occur when a hotel or motel is sold. Some local governments require a bond or other security as a condition for receiving a permit. In some states, local governments can attach a personal lien to the delinquent operator. Probably the most effective tool is a provision for successor liability, which legally extends liability for delinquent taxes to the buyer. Local governments should explore the legality under state statutes of including such a provision in their occupancy tax ordinance.

Finally, the law imposing the tax should clearly specify the local government's authority to audit the records of operators to verify the accuracy of tax returns. Equally important, the local government should establish an ongoing audit program to ensure taxpayers' compliance with the law.

Motor fuels taxes

Local taxes on gasoline and other petroleum products are authorized in at least fifteen states but are levied in only nine: Alabama, Florida, Hawaii, Illinois (Chicago and Cook County only), Mississippi, Missouri, Nevada, Ohio, and Oregon.[11] In all these states, the per gallon tax is levied at the county level with some formula for sharing revenue or the tax rate with cities as a way to minimize border-city effects. In addition, Virginia requires a 2 percent excise tax in counties and cities that participate in a regional transit district, one of the few cases of a local ad valorem tax on motor fuels.

Not only do counties make more widespread use of the tax but, as Tables 6–1 and 6–2 indicate, they also generally depend more heavily on the tax than do municipalities. According to the 2001–02 Census of Government Finances, counties derived about $764 million from motor fuels taxes compared with $312 million for cities, with Cook County, Illinois, and counties in Florida and Nevada deriving the most.[12] Because these taxes are levied on a per gallon basis, their revenue yields generally decline in relative importance because they fail to keep pace with growth in the local economy. As a result, legislatures must adjust the tax rate frequently to maintain revenue yield from the tax.

Local motor fuels taxes are earmarked either for street and bridge maintenance or for public transit.[13] In the case of street maintenance, the benefits-received aspect is obvious: vehicle operators who purchase the fuel benefit from the locally maintained streets and highways. When revenues are used for public transit, drivers also benefit from the reduced congestion on highways during rush hour and from the reduced need to expand highway capacity to meet peak demand. Chicago levies a motor fuels tax of $0.05 per gallon in its jurisdiction and Cook County levies a $0.06 tax per gallon in its jurisdiction, and both use the revenue for streets and bridges.

Florida counties are the nation's greatest local users of the tax, deriving almost $450 million annually from it. They may, with voter approval, impose a tax of 1 cent per gallon on all fuel to be dedicated for street improvements or public transit; this tax is now levied in two-thirds of the counties. They may also levy an additional tax of up to 6 cents per gallon of gasoline or diesel fuel without voter approval, a practice that is universal among Florida's sixty-seven counties. An additional optional excise tax on just gasoline is available to Florida counties as well. Florida law also requires counties to establish interlocal agreements to share fuel taxes with their cities. The state's revenue department remits these revenues directly to cities per the terms of the agreements.

The primary deterrent to greater use of a local option fuels tax is the heavy use of the tax by state and federal governments. For example, some legislators contend that granting local governments access to the tax will preempt state efforts to impose future rate increases. Furthermore, because most states already share a portion of their fuels tax revenue with municipalities and counties, some state legislators believe that a local option fuels tax is unnecessary. Nevertheless, the tax remains an equitable source of new revenue for cities and counties because it is benefits based and because the level of state funding is rarely sufficient to fully compensate local governments for the cost of maintaining streets, roads, and bridges. A local option motor fuels tax can generate sufficient revenue to pay for the full cost of maintaining city streets and county roads and make it unnecessary to use revenue from other taxes, such as the property or sales tax. In the case of public transit subsidies, a motor fuels tax makes more sense on a benefits basis than a general sales tax, although the revenue yield is not comparable.

If a local fuels tax is under consideration, the following issues must be resolved by managers and state and local lawmakers:

- Will the tax adversely affect motor fuels sales in the jurisdiction?

- If both city and county governments levy the tax, how should the revenue collected within the city be allocated to the two levels of government?

- If the tax is adopted, should the state administer the local portion of the tax?

Effects of a motor fuels tax on sales

Like the general sales tax, a motor fuels tax creates the potential for border-city effects. The smaller the jurisdiction levying the tax, the easier it is for motorists to avoid the tax by going outside the jurisdiction to buy fuel. Furthermore, the higher the tax rate, the greater its effect on fuel-buying patterns. If a local fuels tax is levied, it should be imposed throughout a metropolitan area at the county or even the regional level (e.g., within public transit authority boundaries) and at a modest rate.

A related concern is whether a local fuels tax will reduce gasoline consumption as drivers purchase more fuel-efficient vehicles or take other measures to reduce their demand for fuel. Evidence indicates that at least in the short run, drivers' demand for fuel remains insensitive to price increases. Over the longer term, however, consumption does decline in response to higher prices, a desirable outcome given the nation's dependence on imported oil and vulnerability to supply interruptions.[14]

One final issue concerns the distribution of the tax burden. All evidence indicates that the tax is regressive, taking a greater share of a low-income household's budget than of a middle- or upper-income household's budget.[15] However, from a benefits-received perspective, the tax is equitable if it is dedicated to streets and bridges and public transit, because users bear the construction and maintenance costs.

Coordinating motor fuels tax rates

The high potential for border-city effects necessitates that the tax be imposed at least countywide. In metropolitan areas covering more than one county, regional adoption should be encouraged in the legislation authorizing the tax. Because cities and towns also have streets and bridges to maintain, they must be given access to revenue from the tax, without creating an incentive for tax avoidance by fuel buyers.

Each of Hawaii's four island-counties, including Honolulu, levies a motor fuels tax ranging from 8.8 to 18.0 cents per gallon. In Alabama, various coordination solutions are used, including crediting the municipal tax against the 2-cent county tax in Mobile. Florida's approach of requiring interlocal revenue-sharing agreements between cities and the county merits consideration. The alternatives for coordinating the general sales tax, as described in Figure 5–2, are also applicable to motor fuels taxes.

The preferred solution, like that recommended for the general sales tax, is that the county levy the tax and share the revenue with cities and towns on a pro rata basis, perhaps according to the number of miles of streets each government maintains. The allocation formula might include a factor to provide additional compensation to communities whose terrain requires more bridges or higher maintenance costs. A countywide levy would have little effect on where drivers purchase gasoline. Allocating the revenue according to each municipality's share of the number of locally maintained miles of roads in the county would ensure a more equitable distribution of the revenue from the tax than if it were simply granted to the city where the sale occurred. It would also eliminate intercity competition for service stations because the tax benefits would accrue countywide.

Administering a motor fuels tax

The issues in administering a local fuels tax are analogous to those of the general sales tax discussed in Chapter 5, and the recommended solutions are basically the same. In order to reduce border-city/county effects when implementing a motor fuels tax, state law should encourage universal adoption at relatively uniform rates. Some discretion should be given to local governments to set the rate to produce the desired amount of revenue. The greatest discretion exists for counties in Florida, where rates range from 9.7 to 17.7 cents per gallon, with most of the state's sixty-seven counties levying rates of 11.7 or 12.7 cents.

During the 1980s, federal and state investigators discovered elaborate schemes to evade motor fuels taxes.[16] In 1993, federal legislation was approved moving the collection of the federal tax further back in the production process to the terminal (or rack) just after the fuel leaves the refinery. A number of states followed suit in the administration of their excise taxes. This has the effect of reducing the number of points where the tax is collected and enabling more uniform enforcement. In the case of locally levied motor fuels taxes, the proper crediting of the tax is difficult because wholesalers may deliver the fuel to retailers anywhere in the state, and local adoption and tax rates may vary across the state. One possible solution is for the state to allocate revenue according to estimated fuel consumption levels in each county. Estimates could be updated annually to reflect changes in population and driving patterns. The pattern appears to be that the local tax tends to be collected at the same point as the state tax, with the producer responsible for properly allocating tax revenue to the appropriate local government.

In summary, a locally levied motor fuels tax represents an attractive alternative revenue source for municipalities and counties because it is benefits based. If revenue from the tax is dedicated primarily to locally maintained streets or public transit, those who benefit from these services bear a portion of the cost, which means that the tax burden is allocated more equitably. Although only a few states give local governments access to the tax, it has the potential for much more widespread use. To reduce possible border-city effects, the tax should be levied county- or region-wide, with allocation of revenue to cities and the county according to their share of the number of miles of locally maintained highways. State collection is also recommended to lower the cost of administration and compliance.

Other sumptuary taxes

Eight states permit a local levy on cigarette and tobacco sales, and twelve states permit local taxes on alcoholic beverage sales, piggybacked onto the state's tax. Of these two sumptuary taxes, alcoholic beverage taxes produce more revenue, as indicated in Tables 6–1 and 6–2. Heavier use of tobacco taxes is made by Chicago (16 cents per pack) and Cook County along with Evanston and Rosemont, which are the only Illinois local governments authorized to levy the tax. Other users of the tax include cities and counties in Alabama, Alaska (Anchorage and Juneau), Missouri, and Virginia. The highest local rate is levied by New York City: $1.50 per pack. Local levies are in addition to state (average of 60 cents per pack)[17] and federal (39 cents per pack) excise taxes. Most all governments still use tax stamps to certify payment and to prevent bootlegging of tobacco products from tax-exempt sources, such as Indian reservations. One study found that commercial smuggling accounts for 3–4 percent of sales, a percentage that will likely increase as tobacco taxes increase and Web-based sales become more common.[18]

Of the twelve states with local taxes on alcohol products, the heaviest use is by cities and counties in southern states—Alabama, Georgia, North Carolina, and Tennessee. Chicago, Cook County, and New York City also generate worthwhile amounts of revenue from their alcoholic beverage taxes. As with tobacco, excise taxes on packaged alcohol create significant border-city and border-state effects.[19] For example, New Hampshire, which sells its wine and spirits through state-owned liquor stores, has long benefited from selling to consumers in bordering states and Canada; New Hampshire has no general sales tax or excise tax on alcohol, although it generates a handsome profit through its state stores.

A variation on the more traditional beverage tax, which is levied on a per unit or liquid volume basis, is an ad valorem **mixed drinks tax** levied on the retail value of drinks. For example, cities and counties in Texas each levy a tax equivalent to 1.5 percent of the retail value of the drink. The tax is piggybacked onto the state's effective rate of 11 percent of the retail price. Tennessee also gives local governments access to a mixed drinks tax. Because alcohol consumption generally grows faster than the economy, revenue from the tax increases at a rate exceeding the growth in the economy, providing local governments with a small but significant source of revenue.

Privilege and other excise taxes

Local governments levy a host of other excise taxes, many of which are holdovers from the eighteenth and nineteenth centuries. Some of the more frequently used taxes include an admissions (or ticket) tax, business gross receipts tax, occupation privilege tax, bank franchise tax, parking tax, deed transfer tax, and bingo tax. For most local governments, these taxes represent minor sources of revenue with comparatively high administrative costs. The bank franchise tax is usually levied in lieu of a property tax on banks' intangible assets—including federal securities, which are exempt from state and local taxation.

Deed transfer, or real estate, taxes are levied by local governments in at least eleven states, usually at a fixed percentage of the property's sale price.[20] Pennsylvania cities, townships, and boroughs levy a 0.5 percent tax; school districts and the state also levy the tax. New York City, Baltimore, and Wilmington (Delaware) all have specific legislative authority to levy a tax on real estate transactions. Both cities and counties in California and Virginia levy a deed transfer tax, but California effectively restricts the tax to the buyer's down payment; any mortgage or other encumbrance remaining on the property is not included in the tax base. In California, the city rate is one half the county tax rate of $0.55 per $500 of the net sale price. Counties in Maryland, Ohio, South Carolina, Washington, and West Virginia also levy the tax.

Although admission taxes are in fairly wide use by older cities, their revenue significance is negligible in most cases. Many central cities in metropolitan areas levy the tax as a way of exporting their tax burden to nonresidents, especially suburbanites. However, one study found that these taxes, especially those on sport franchises, are borne by owners and labor as lower profits and wages rather than being shifted forward to fans as higher ticket prices.[21] Some shifting forward to ticket buyers may occur for taxes on concerts and movie theaters, although the study concludes that these are highly imperfect methods of taxing suburbanites for the services they receive from the central city. Another study of the 5 percent tax in Boulder, Colorado, on all public events, including movies, concerts, and theatrical performances, concluded that the tax was almost certainly shifted forward to consumers as a higher ticket price.[22] The actual shifting depends on the availability of substitutes that are not taxed and on consumers elasticity of demand for the event.

Local governments in northern and midwestern cities levy a wheel tax or motor vehicle registration tax. In some cases, such as in cities in Massachusetts, the tax is based on the value of the vehicle—$25 per thousand dollars of taxable value, with a generous depreciation schedule; value is the manufacturer's suggested retail price, not the selling price. In other cases, the tax is a fixed amount per vehicle or per axles on the vehicle, giving rise to its name.

Summary and recommendations

The following recommendations are made to guide lawmakers and managers in the use of excise taxes:

The utility gross receipts tax accounts for about 61 percent of the revenues from excise taxes produced at the municipal level but for only 28 percent in counties. Local governments should carefully specify in franchise agreements with utility providers the types of receipts included in the tax base and the tax rate. It is also recommended that utility companies remit the tax at least quarterly, preferably monthly.

The hotel and motel occupancy tax is benefits based in that it compensates local governments for the expanded capacity in public services (police, fire, highways) and indirect costs (congestion, pollution) incurred by serving tourists and conventioneers. Studies indicate that a modest tax has virtually no effect on businesses serving tourists, especially hotels and motels. Occupancy taxes are usually locally administered, although state administration probably offers a somewhat more cost-effective alternative. As with the utility gross receipts tax, remittance of the tax should be at least quarterly and possibly even monthly by larger operators.

Local option motor fuels taxes provide a means of shifting to vehicle owners the full cost of constructing and maintaining streets. If the tax replaces property or sales taxes used for this purpose, it will result in a more equitable distribution of the tax burden by shifting the burden to those using roads and bridges. As a way to reduce the inefficiencies created by the border-city effect, it is recommended that the tax be levied at least countywide and the revenue distributed to cities and the county on a pro rata basis. State administration of the tax is also recommended.

Sumptuary and other non-benefits-based excise taxes are generally unattractive revenue sources for local governments because of their high administrative costs and low revenue yield. Taxpayers see them as nuisance taxes and complain about their high rates; however, no mass opposition has developed, because relatively few taxpayers are affected. Local governments should avoid using such taxes and rely more heavily on broader-based sales, income, and property taxes, as well as on benefits-based excise taxes, such as levies on utility gross receipts, hotel/motel occupancy, and motor fuels.

1 John H. Bowman and John L. Mikesell, *Local Government Tax Authority and Use* (Washington, D.C.: National League of Cities, 1987), 95.

2 See http://egov.cityofchicago.org/city/webportal/home.do.

3 Bowman and Mikesell, *Local Government Tax Authority,* 98–100.

4 Robert L. Bland, *Financing City Government in Texas: A Revenue Manual for City Officials* (Austin: Texas Municipal League, 1986), 90.

5 Susan Hodge, "How Well Is It Monitored? Special Report on Fiber Optics—A Boon or Burden for Cities?" *Nation's Cities Weekly,* 6 July 1987, 8.

6 Bowman and Mikesell, *Local Government Tax Authority,* 127–131.

7 International Association of Convention and Visitors Bureaus, "2003 CVB Organizational and Financial Profile Report," IACVB Foundation (www.iacvb.org/web_images/resource_center/hotel_check_out_tax_rates_2003.pdf); American Economics Group, Inc. *Update 2003: Room Taxes and Economic Impact of the Lodging Industry* (Washington, D.C.: American Hotel and Lodging Education Foundation, January 2004).

8 International Association of Convention and Visitors Bureaus, "2003 CVB Organizational and Financial Profile Report."

9 National Conference of State Legislatures (NCSL), *Critical Issues in State-Local Fiscal Policy: A Guide to Local Option Taxes* (Denver, Colo.: NCSL, November 1997): 29.

10 Carl Bonham et al., "The Impact of the Hotel Room Tax: An Interrupted Time Series Approach," *National Tax Journal* 45 (December 1992): 433–441.

11 U.S. Bureau of the Census, *Local Summary Tables by Type of Government: 2001–02,* table 2 (www.census.gov/govs/estimate/02slsstab2a.xls).

12 Ibid.

13 Todd Goldman and Martin Wachs, "A Quiet Revolution in Transportation Finance: The Rise of Local Option Transportation Taxes," *Transportation Quarterly* 57 (winter 2003): 19–32.

14 Congressional Budget Office, "The Economic Costs of Fuel Economy Standards Versus a Gasoline Tax" (December 2003).

15 Howard Chernick and Andrew Reschovsky, "Who Pays the Gasoline Tax?" *National Tax Journal* 50 (June 1997): 233–259.

16 Dwight V. Denison and Robert J. Eger, "Tax Evasion from a Policy Perspective: The Case of the Motor Fuels Tax," *Public Administration Review* 60 (March/April 2000): 163–172.

17 Federation of Tax Administrators, "The Excise Tax Rates on Cigarettes" (January 1, 2004) (www.taxadmin.org/fta/rate/cigarett.html).

18 Jerry G. Thursby and Marie C. Thursby, "Interstate Cigarette Bootlegging: Extent, Revenue Losses, and Effects of Federal Intervention," *National Tax Journal* 53 (March 2000): 59–77.

19 Patrick Fleenor, "How Excise Tax Differentials Affect Cross-Border Sales of Beer in the United States," Background Paper no. 31 (Washington, D.C.: Tax Foundation, 1999).

20 David Brunori, *Local Tax Policy: A Federalist Perspective* (Washington, D.C.: The Urban Institute Press, 2003), 84.

21 Andrew R. Blair, Frank Giarratani, and Michael H. Spiro, "Incidence of the Amusement Tax," *National Tax Journal* 40 (March 1987): 61–69.

22 James Alm and William H. Kaempfer, "Who Pays the Ticket Tax?" *Public Finance Review* 30 (January 2002): 27–40.

7 The income tax

The income tax's role in local government

Local government dependence on the income tax
The local income tax base
The special case of payroll taxes
Local taxation of corporate income
Summary

Issues in the design of a local income tax

Effects of an income tax on the local economy
Effects of an income tax on local government budgets
Taxing commuters

Administering a local income tax

Summary and recommendations

The basic political and economic reasons for diversification of tax systems lie in the fact that there is no such thing as a perfect tax.

—John Shannon
Former Executive Director
U.S. Advisory Commission on Intergovernmental Relations

The income tax

As with sales and excise taxes, local income taxes come in many varieties, the variations largely emanating from how the tax base is defined and the tax rates applied. Unlike sales taxes, which are in widespread use among local governments, local income taxes are largely concentrated in a few states.

For present purposes, **payroll taxes** are considered income taxes although they possess many of the attributes of an excise tax. The distinction between payroll and income taxes comes down to legal liability: employers are liable for the payroll tax (although employees, especially lower-wage earners, bear the economic burden through lower salaries and wages) while employees are liable for the income tax. Whatever their form, local income taxes have never achieved the same political acceptance as general sales and excise taxes.

The Tax Reform Act of 1986 removed state and local sales taxes from the list of allowable deductions for individual federal income tax returns but maintained the deductibility of state and local income and property taxes. The act thereby increased the attractiveness of the income tax as an alternative revenue source for local governments. In essence, the deduction for income and property taxes represents a federal subsidy to local governments. Moreover, the higher the individual's tax bracket, the greater the benefit of the income **tax deduction.** Then in 2004, Congress passed the American Jobs Creation Act, which restored the federal deduction for state and local sales taxes, with one new twist. Federal tax itemizers must choose between deducting either their state and local sales tax liability or their income tax liability—but not both, as was the case prior to 1986. The deduction expires in 2005 unless renewed by Congress.

Between 1986 and 2004 when income taxes—whether on earnings, personal income (i.e., income from earned and unearned sources), or payrolls—were treated more favorably under the federal tax code, they never gained much appeal politically relative to local sales taxes.

In fact, in 1973 Indiana became the last state to authorize a local income tax; the state gave counties the option to levy the tax in exchange for freezing their property tax *levies* (not to be confused with their property tax *rates*). Since 1976 most new adoptions of an income tax by local governments have occurred in Kentucky and Ohio.

This chapter examines some of the issues that local government managers and elected officials encounter when considering the adoption of an income tax. The next section examines the role of income taxes in local government, including the extent to which the tax is currently in use, the relative importance of the tax in local government revenue structures, the special case of payroll taxes, and the issues involved in taxing corporate income.

The income tax's role in local government

Many of the same policy issues that local government leaders encounter with a sales tax reappear with an income tax. Yet the income tax has much less public support,

142 *A Revenue Guide for Local Government*

as evidenced in Table 7–1. Broad use of the tax is made by local governments in only six states: Indiana, Kentucky, Maryland, Michigan, Ohio, and Pennsylvania. With the exception of California, Iowa, Missouri, and Oregon, variations of the local income tax are used only by states east of the Mississippi River. Iowa authorizes school districts to levy a supplemental tax on the state income tax.

Table 7–1 does not include local governments levying a payroll tax, which functions much like an income tax but is not nearly as visible to taxpayers. Los Angeles and San Francisco levy a payroll tax on employers. Four urban counties in the Portland, Oregon, area levy a payroll tax dedicated to supporting public transit.

Table 7–1

States in which most local governments levy an income tax.

State	Range in tax rates (%)	Most common rate (%)	Nonresident/ commuter rate	Tax base	Administration
Indiana[a]					
Counties	0.10–1.73	1.00	¼ residential	PI, NP	state
Kentucky					
Counties	0.008–2.25	1.00	same	varies[b]	local
Cities	0.075–2.50	1.00	same	varies	local
Maryland[a]					
Counties	1.25–3.15	2.80	none	PI, NP	state
Baltimore[c]	3.05		none	PI, NP	state
Michigan					
Municipalities	1.00–2.00	1.00	½ residential	PI, NP, CI	local
Detroit	2.50		½ residential	PI, NP, CI[d]	local
Ohio					
Municipalities[e]	0.25–2.85	1.00	same	EI, NP, CI	local
Cincinnati	2.10		2.10	EI, NP, CI	local
Cleveland	2.00		2.00	EI, NP, CI	local
Pennsylvania					
Municipalities[f]	0.50–1.25	0.50	none	EI, NP	local
Pittsburgh	1.00[g]		none	EI, NP	local
Philadelphia	4.4625[h]		3.8801	EI, NP, CI[i]	local

Sources: Web sites of state revenue departments and telephone interviews with state officials.

Notes: EI—earned income; PI—personal income; NP—net profits; CI—corporate income.

[a] Counties have exclusive authority to levy an income tax.

[b] Kentucky cities and counties, at their choosing, tax wages, net profits, gross profits, or some combination. A few choose to tax wages at a separate rate from net profits, and one city, Caneyville, levies its occupational tax at the rate of $1 per week worked (www.kyola.org).

[c] Baltimore is an independent city; Baltimore County has no jurisdiction within the city.

[d] Detroit levies a tax of 1.0% on all corporate net income apportionable to the city, regardless of whether it has an office or place of business in the city. Financial institutions and insurance companies are exempt from the tax.

[e] Voter approval is required on any tax over 1%.

[f] Currently, 50 cities, 833 boroughs, and 1,262 townships levy a tax on wages and on net profits of unincorporated businesses. School districts levy a separate tax on this income.

[g] Pittsburgh also levies a 2% wage tax for its school district.

[h] This rate includes funding for the city of Philadelphia schools and, for school purposes, extends to residents' unearned income. Philadelphia is the only city in Pennsylvania authorized to tax nonresident income under current law although efforts are under way to extend this privilege to Pittsburgh as part of its financial bailout plan.

[i] The city of Philadelphia also levies a 6.5% business privilege tax on the net income of all business activity in the city.

Philadelphia holds the distinction of having adopted the first modern version of a local income tax; in 1939 it began taxing employee wages and self-employment income.[1] Cities in Ohio began levying the tax during the 1940s and pioneered the use of a local tax on corporate income. Later in that decade, cities in Kentucky began levying an "occupational license tax" on the income of individuals and corporations. In the 1950s, cities in Alabama also began levying an occupational license tax for the privilege of working in a city. The 1960s saw the greatest expansion in the use of a local income tax: Michigan cities, Maryland counties, Baltimore, and New York City all gained access to the tax. The expansion culminated in 1973 with Indiana's authorization of a county levy.

The most extensive use of local income taxes is in Pennsylvania, where most cities, boroughs, and townships levy a flat-rate tax on gross income from wages and the net profits of unincorporated businesses. In addition, school districts in the commonwealth levy a separate tax on earnings. Most municipalities in Ohio also levy the tax. Income taxes are much less common among county governments, levied by approximately 170 counties in only three states: Indiana, Kentucky, and Maryland. Universal adoption exists only in Maryland, where counties and the independent city of Baltimore are required by state statute to levy the tax.

A few other states make limited use of wage or personal income taxes, all of which are locally administered. In Missouri, only Kansas City and St. Louis levy an earned-income tax. Kansas City received specific statutory authority to levy the tax, subject to voter approval. St. Louis levies the tax under its home-rule powers; voter approval is not required. In New York State, only New York City and Yonkers levy an earned-income tax. New York City levies a moderately graduated tax ranging from 2.55 percent to 3.2 percent on residents' personal income; Yonkers levies a tax of 5 percent of state liability and a 0.25 percent tax on commuters. Both taxes are collected by the state, a unique feature among those states giving income-taxing powers to selected cities. Wilmington, Delaware, levies a wage and net profits tax of 1.25 percent on income earned within its borders.

Arkansas and Georgia both authorize a local income tax, but no local governments in either state have chosen to levy it. Furthermore, cities and counties in Georgia may adopt either an income tax or a general sales tax but not both; since virtually all counties in Georgia levy the sales tax and share the revenue with cities, it is unlikely that a local income tax will ever be levied in that state.

One of the strengths of an income tax is its capacity to extend the tax reach of a city to commuters who work in the city but otherwise bear no cost for financing city services. In other words, an income tax provides cities that serve as the economic hub of an area with the means to reach those who benefit from its role in the regional economy. As discussed later, state laws vary on how they treat nonresident and commuter income. The sidebar on page 144 discusses the special case of professional athletes' earnings.

Local government dependence on the income tax

Of paramount interest to local government leaders is the revenue potential of a new tax or fee. Unlike revenue from the sales tax, revenue from local income taxes has not shown a steady increase for municipalities (Tables 7–2 and 7–3). The 2001 downturn in relative yield for the income tax probably results from the slow growth if not decline in wages experienced during this period by cities in Ohio and Pennsylvania, which primarily depend on the income tax on wages.

The modest level of revenue from the tax for counties, as shown in Table 7–3, reflects the relatively small number of counties levying the tax. In those few states where counties do levy the tax, however, it represents a substantial portion of their revenue. For example, the income tax revenues for Maryland counties in 2001 was

Local taxation of nonresident professional athletes' earnings

In recent years, state and local governments have begun extending their wage and personal income taxes to nonresident professional athletes. These so-called jock taxes occur because athletes earn a pro rata share of their income when they play in the taxing jurisdiction. Philadelphia, for example, extends its nonresident wage tax of 3.8801 percent to football, basketball, baseball, and hockey players for the portion of time they work in one of the city's stadiums or arenas. Players have a *taxable nexus* for the time they are playing and earning income in the city. At least a half dozen cities now impose their income tax on athletes, and twenty states extend their *state* income tax to professional athletes.

Several intergovernmental issues arise because of the jock tax, which is usually extended to other high-dollar wage earners including musicians and actors. Not all states or local governments give a credit for taxes already paid on that income, creating a double tax on those earnings. The jock tax also imposes significant compliance expenses on nonresident athletes, who must complete a tax return for each city and state in which they play. And it gives rise to the potential for discriminatory taxation. For example, Alberta, Canada, imposes an extra 2.5 percent income tax on top of its 10 percent tax on all resident players of its two hockey teams, but it does not tax visiting players.

Source: Most of this information is from David K. Hoffman, "State and Local Income Taxation of Nonresident Athletes Spreads to Other Professions," Special Report no. 123 (Washington, D.C.: Tax Foundation, Inc., July 2003).

27 percent of their general revenues and 35 percent of their tax revenues, second only to revenues from the property tax.

The significance of the income tax in a local government's revenue structure depends on the tax rates levied and the breadth of the tax base. For example, local governments in Indiana, Maryland, and Michigan tax the personal income of individuals and the net profits of unincorporated businesses. In general, these governments experience more rapid growth in income tax revenue than do those with more narrowly based taxes, such as in Ohio and Pennsylvania. This is primarily because components of the tax base change in value at different rates, and data from the Internal Revenue Service (IRS) indicate that the greatest rate of growth occurs with unearned income (interest, dividends, and realized capital gains), which is a component of the Indiana, Maryland, and Michigan tax bases.

The elasticity of the income tax poses a potentially serious problem for local government budgets. For example, a 10 percent decline in personal income in the local economy may result in a 15 percent decline in income tax revenues. The more dependent a local government is on the revenue from the income tax, the more vulnerable it is to midyear revenue shortfalls and budget instability. For this reason, local governments should avoid overdependence on the income tax. As a general rule, cities, towns, and counties should derive no more than $1.50 in income tax revenue for every $1.00 in the more stable property tax.

This recommendation permits greater dependence on the income tax than was recommended in Chapter 5 for the general sales tax (a maximum of $1.00 in sales tax for every $1.00 in property tax). Greater dependence on the income tax is allowable in part because central cities, which are the most dependent on the tax, have experienced greater declines in their property tax bases relative to those of surrounding suburban jurisdictions. The income tax provides these cities with a means for reducing their dependency on the property tax and thereby remaining competitive with suburban jurisdictions in their ability to attract and retain business investment in the city. However, central cities that have become too dependent on the

Table 7–2
Municipal government dependence on income taxes: Income tax revenue as a percentage of general revenues.

Revenue source	1991–92	1996–97	2001–02
Property taxes	25.1	22.7	22.8
General and selective sales tax	12.6	13.4	13.9
Income taxes	6.3	6.8	5.9
Other taxes	3.4	3.7	4.4
Service and utility charges	40.8	42.3	41.9
Other non taxes	11.9	11.1	11.1
	100.1	100.0	100.0
Total general revenue (in millions)[a]	$161,293	$202,674	$255,220

Source: U.S. Bureau of the Census, *Finances of Municipal and Township Governments,* 1997 Census of Governments 4, no. 4 (September 2000), table 1 (http://www.census.gov/prod/gc97/gc974-4.pdf); and U.S. Bureau of the Census, *Local Summary Tables by Type of Government: 2001–02,* table 2 (http://ftp2.census.gov/govs/estimate/02slsstab2a.xls).

Note: Percentages may not total 100% because of rounding.
[a] Total general revenue includes utility charges but excludes intergovernmental aid, liquor store income, and insurance trust revenue.

Table 7–3
County government dependence on income taxes: Income tax revenue as a percentage of general revenues.

Revenue source	1991–92	1996–97	2001–02
Property taxes	43.5	38.6	38.4
Income taxes	1.6	1.8	2.0
All other taxes	13.4	15.2	15.1
Service charges	25.6	29.1	29.1
Utility charges	1.8	2.2	2.1
Other non taxes	14.1	13.1	13.2
	100.0	100.0	99.9
Total general revenue (in millions)[a]	$94,808	$122,161	$161,483

Source: U.S. Bureau of the Census, *Finances of County Governments,* 1997 Census of Governments 4, no. 3 (September 2000), table 1 (http://www.census.gov/prod/gc97/gc974-3.pdf); and U.S. Bureau of the Census, U.S. Bureau of the Census, *Local Summary Tables by Type of Government: 2001–02,* table 2 (http://ftp2.census.gov/govs/estimate/02slsstab2a.xls).

Note: Percentages may not total 100% because of rounding.
[a] Total general revenue includes utility charges but excludes intergovernmental aid, liquor store income, and insurance trust revenue.

income tax should explore ways to better balance their revenue structures, including increasing the role of the property tax.

The local income tax base

The local income tax is most easily distinguished from its state and federal counterparts by its generally narrower tax base. Figure 7–1 shows the different types of income potentially subject to taxation, and Table 7–1 shows the tax bases actually used by local governments in the six states where municipalities and counties levy the tax. As with other taxes, the legal definition of the income tax base affects its revenue yield:

$$\text{Tax rate} \times \text{tax base} = \text{revenue yield}.$$

The broader the tax base, the lower the tax rate needed to produce a given level of revenue.

Figure 7–1
Types of income.

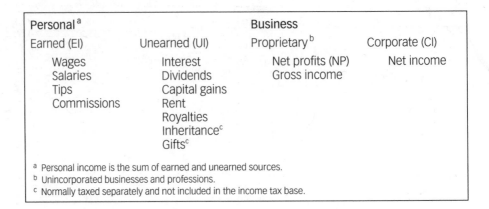

Personal[a]		Business	
Earned (EI)	Unearned (UI)	Proprietary[b]	Corporate (CI)
Wages	Interest	Net profits (NP)	Net income
Salaries	Dividends	Gross income	
Tips	Capital gains		
Commissions	Rent		
	Royalties		
	Inheritance[c]		
	Gifts[c]		

[a] Personal income is the sum of earned and unearned sources.
[b] Unincorporated businesses and professions.
[c] Normally taxed separately and not included in the income tax base.

States that authorized the income tax early on, most notably Pennsylvania, limited the local tax base to earned and **proprietary income** because of the relative ease of collecting the tax from employers. (All but two states require local administration of the income tax.) If the tax is based on gross income (no deductions or exemptions) and is withheld by the employer, wage earners usually do not file a tax return with the local government.

Although an income tax limited to earned income is less costly to collect and enforce, modern techniques of tax administration, especially the sharing of tax information between state and local revenue departments and the IRS, now make inclusion of unearned income in the local tax base administratively feasible. Consequently, states that have adopted the income tax more recently, most notably Maryland, define the tax base more broadly to include both earned and unearned income. Including unearned income makes the local levy more progressive. Since higher-income individuals receive a greater portion of their income from unearned sources, excluding this income makes the tax less fair by placing a greater portion of the tax burden on wage earners in the lower- and middle-income brackets.[2] A broad-based tax on both earned and unearned personal income distributes the tax burden more evenly across all income categories and is more equitable on the ability-to-pay basis. All versions of the income tax, other than payroll taxes, include the net profits of unincorporated businesses in their tax bases (see Figure 7–2).

Local income taxes differ from their state and federal counterparts in still another way: most are levied on gross income with no exemptions, deductions, or credits, which facilitates local collection and enforcement of the tax. Including adjustments to gross income increases the complexity and cost of administering the tax, especially if locally administered. On the other hand, itemized deductions for certain expenses and exemptions for dependents generally increase the tax's progressivity by reducing the tax burden on lower- and middle-income households. A number of local governments provide for these adjustments to gross income. Indiana and Maryland provide for optional local credits to tax liability that reduce liability for targeted purposes.

Piggybacking the local tax onto the state's income tax is a cost-effective approach to integrating such adjustments into the local tax. For example, Maryland counties' tax is collected along with the state liability by the state Department of Revenue. The local share is remitted to the taxpayer's county of residence. Figure 7–3 shows a portion of the Maryland tax return; line 9, local tax, is determined by multiplying state liability by the percentage applicable to the county in which the taxpayer resides. Maryland's approach reduces taxpayer compliance costs because only one

Figure 7–2
Income tax bases
used by local
governments.

Narrowest tax base ←				→ Broadest tax base
Earned only	Earned and proprietary	Personal and proprietary	Earned, proprietary and corporate	Personal proprietary, and corporate
Alabama	Ohio Pennsylvania	Indiana Maryland	Philadelphia Ohio	Michigan New York City

Getting to tax liability

Defining the income tax base involves more steps than is needed to define either the sales tax base or the property tax base. This is because of a number of adjustments designed to promote horizontal and vertical equity. The process involves the following steps:

Step 1: Define **gross income**. This involves listing all income subject to taxation. Here states can provide targeted relief, such as excluding from the tax base the interest income on bonds sold by local governments as well as by the state.

Step 2: Deduct **adjustments**. Adjustments are reductions in gross income designed to reduce or eliminate double taxation, such as with alimony payments, or the cost of earning income, such as job-related moving expenses.
Result: **Adjusted gross income (AGI)**. This is the beginning point for computing taxable income.

Step 3: Deduct **personal exemptions**. Some local and state governments, as well as the federal government, provide for a fixed dollar reduction in taxable income for each dependent in the household. These deductions promote horizontal and vertical equity.

Step 4: Deduct **standard (or itemized) deductions**. Usually individual income taxes provide for a standard deduction—a fixed dollar amount for each category of tax filers (single, married filing jointly, married filing separately). The standard deduction is designed to promote horizontal equity and reduce the need for retaining records on deductible expenses.

Alternatively, tax filers may itemize qualifying deductions, particularly if they have incurred deductible expenses that exceed the standard deduction. Depending on the marginal tax bracket of the taxpayer, the deductions represent significant reductions in tax liability. Most state revenue departments prepare analyses of the cost of these tax expenditures to state treasuries.
Result: **Taxable income**. This is the tax base to which the tax rate(s) is applied.

Step 5: Multiply the taxable income by the appropriate tax rate to determine tax liability. In states and the few local governments that use **graduated tax rate** structures, each bracket of income is subject to a separate tax rate, with higher brackets subject to progressively higher tax rates. In recent decades, states and especially local governments have gravitated toward flatter rate structures because progressive income tax rates may encourage higher-income households to migrate to lower-tax jurisdictions.

Step 6: Deduct **tax credits**. The final step is the application of any qualifying tax credits to tax liability. These dollar-for-dollar reductions in liability are particularly powerful tools for tax policy. A number of states offer **earned-income credits** to working families with moderate to low income. While most credits are capped at tax liability—that is, the credit cannot be greater than the tax liability—some states allow the earned-income credit to exceed liability, creating essentially a negative income tax by providing a cash subsidy to these families.

Figure 7–3   A portion of the Maryland tax return.

FORM
503
RESIDENT

MARYLAND TAX RETURN

2003
$

SOCIAL SECURITY #		SPOUSE'S SOCIAL SECURITY #
Your First Name	Initial	Last Name
Spouse's First Name	Initial	Last Name
PRESENT ADDRESS (No. and street)		
City or Town	State	Zip Code
Name of county and incorporated city, town or special taxing area in which you were a resident on the last day of the tax period (See Instructions)	Maryland county	City, town or taxing area

YOUR FILING STATUS—See Instruction 1 to determine if you are required to file.

1. ☐ Single (If you can be claimed on another person's tax return, use Filing Status 6.)
2. ☐ Married filing joint return or spouse had no income
▶ 3. ☐ Married filing separately   SPOUSE'S SOCIAL SECURITY NUMBER
4. ☐ Head of household
5. ☐ Qualifying widow(er) with dependent child
6. ☐ Dependent taxpayer (Enter 0 in Exemption Box (A)—See Instruction 7)

EXEMPTIONS—See Instruction 10

(A) Yourself ☐   Spouse ☐   Enter No. Checked (A) ___ × $2,400 $ _____
   Check here if you are   Spouse ☐
(B) ▶☐ ▶☐ ▶☐ ▶☐   Enter No. Checked (B) ___ × $1,000 $ _____
   65 or over Blind 65 or over Blind
(C) Dependent Children: Enter Total (C) ___ × $2,400 $ _____
   Name(s)   Social Security number(s)

(D) Other Dependents: Regular ☐ 65 or over ☐   Enter Total (D) ___ × $2,400 $ _____
   Name(s) and Relationship(s)   Social Security number(s)

(E) Enter Total Exemptions (Add A, B, C and D) ▶ (E) ___   Total Amount $ _____

Print your numbers like this - 0 1 2 3 4 5 6 7 8 9 - not like this Ø 4 7

Place your check or money order on top of your wage and tax statements and attach here with ONE staple.

	Dollars
1. Adjusted gross income from your federal return (See Instruction 11) ...... ▶	1
1a. How much of line 1 represents wages, salaries and/or tips? 1a	
2. Standard deduction (See Instruction 16) .... ▶	2
3. Net income (Subtract line 2 from line 1)	3
4. Exemption amount as computed above	4
5. Taxable net income (Subtract line 4 from line 3. GO TO TAX TABLE, page 18.)	5
6. Maryland tax (from Tax Table or Computation Worksheet)	6
7. Earned income credit ▶ 7a ____ Poverty level credit ▶ 7b ____ (See Instruction 18) Total	7
8. Maryland tax after credits (Subtract line 7 from line 6) If less than 0, enter 0.	8
9. Local tax (See Instruction 19 for tax rates and worksheet.) Multiply line 5 by your local tax rate .0 ____ or use the local tax worksheet	9
10. Local: Earned income credit ▶ 10a ____ Poverty level credit ▶ 10b ____ (See Instruction 19) Total	10
11. Local tax after credits (Subtract line 10 from line 9) If less than 0, enter 0.	11
12. Total Maryland and local tax (Add lines 8 and 11)	12
13. Contribution to Chesapeake Bay and Endangered Species Fund (See Instruction 20) .... ▶	13
14. Contribution to Fair Campaign Financing Fund (See Instruction 20) .... ▶	14
15. Total Maryland income tax, local income tax and contributions (Add lines 12, 13 and 14)	15
16. Total Maryland and local tax withheld (Enter total from and attach your W-2 and 1099 forms if MD tax is withheld) ▶	16
17. Refundable earned income credit (from worksheet in Instruction 21) .... ▶	17
18. Total payments and credit (Add lines 16 and 17)	18
19. Balance due (If line 15 is more than line 18, subtract line 18 from line 15) .... ▶	19
20. Overpayment (If line 15 is less than line 18, subtract line 15 from line 18) See line 23 . . .This is your REFUND ▶	20
21. Interest charges from Form 502UP ____ or for late filing ____ (See Instruction 22) Total ▶	21
22. TOTAL AMOUNT DUE (Add lines 19 and 21) .... IF $1 OR MORE, PAY IN FULL WITH THIS RETURN	22

For credit card payment check here ☐ and see Instruction 24. Direct debit is available only if you file electronically.

DIRECT DEPOSIT OF REFUND (See Instruction 22) Please be sure the account information is correct.
23. To choose the direct deposit option, complete the following information: 23a. Type of account: ▶ ☐ Checking   ☐ Savings
23b. Routing number ▶ _____   23c. Account number ▶ _____

Daytime telephone no.   Home telephone no.   CODE NUMBER   FOR OFFICE USE ONLY

Under penalties of perjury, I declare that I have examined this return, including accompanying schedules and statements and to the best of my knowledge and belief it is true, correct and complete. If prepared by a person other than taxpayer, the declaration is based on all information of which the preparer has any knowledge. Check here ☐ if you authorize your preparer to discuss this return with us.

Make checks payable to: COMPTROLLER OF MARYLAND. Write social security no. on check using blue or black ink. Mail to: Comptroller of Maryland, Revenue Administration Division, Annapolis, Maryland 21411-0001

Your signature   Date   Signature of preparer other than taxpayer   Preparer's SSN or PTIN
Spouse's signature   Date   Address and telephone number of preparer

03-50

Local Tax Rates

Your local income tax rate is relative to where you live and is collected by the Comptroller of Maryland as a convenience to Maryland's 23 counties and Baltimore City. Local officials set the rates and the revenue is returned to the local governments quarterly.

The local income tax is calculated as a percentage of taxable income, using line 31 on long Form 502 or line 9 on short Form 503. The local income tax rates range between 1.25% and 3.15% for tax year 2003.

2003 LOCAL TAX RATE CHART	
Subdivision	**Rate**
Allegany County	.0293
Anne Arundel County	.0256
Baltimore City	.0305
Baltimore County	.0283
Calvert County	.0260
Caroline County	.0263
Carroll County	.0285
Cecil County	.0280
Charles County	.0290
Dorchester County	.0262
Frederick County	.0296
Garrett County	.0265
Harford County	.0306
Howard County	.0245
Kent County	.0258
Montgomery County	.0295
Prince George's County	.0310
Queen Anne's County	.0285
St. Mary's County	.0310
Somerset County	.0315
Talbot County	.0179
Washington County	.0280
Wicomico County	.0310
Worcester County	.0125

tax return is filed. It also increases the equity of the local tax, because local adjustments to gross income are the same as the state's.

The special case of payroll taxes

Interest in payroll taxes has resurfaced as a result of Nevada's 2003 adoption of the tax, which is currently at 0.65 percent. Several local governments have levied such a tax for a number of years, but Nevada is the first state to do so. The most widespread use of the payroll tax is in Alabama, where twenty cities levy a municipal occupation tax ranging from 0.50 to 2.0 percent of an employer's payroll. Generally, liability for payroll taxes falls on the employer; however, Alabama cities require the employee to file a return in the event that the employer fails to do so.

Because they usually have no deductions or other adjustments, payroll taxes can be particularly onerous on smaller businesses that have narrow profit margins, operate in a highly competitive environment, and depend on highly skilled labor—for example, computer software developers. To accommodate such entrepreneurs, some local governments exempt a portion of the payroll from taxation. The 1 percent tax in Newark, New Jersey, begins after the first $2,500 of payroll costs per calendar quarter. San Francisco exempts from its 1.5 percent tax any employer who would not owe more than $2,500. Los Angeles applies a flat $33 for the first $4,000 of payroll and then $8.25 for each additional $1,000 of payroll. Chicago makes it even simpler: $4 per employee per month, regardless of salary. The tax applies only to businesses that employ fifty or more full-time workers, and employees must earn more than $900 in a quarter to be considered taxable.

While employers are generally liable for the payroll tax, the tax is likely to fall on employees in the form of lower wages, particularly in industries employing lower-skilled workers. However, this may not be true in businesses where the demand for workers is more competitive. In general, the tax does not rate well on horizontal or vertical equity, and it likely has a negative impact on economic growth in the long term, particularly in sectors that rely on highly skilled, higher-cost employees, such as those in engineering and technology development.

Local taxation of corporate income

Another issue concerns the treatment of corporate income. New York City, Philadelphia, and local governments in Kentucky, Michigan, Missouri, and Ohio levy a tax on corporate income. In these cases, the starting point for determining local tax liability is federal taxable income.[3] Usually the same tax rate is applied to corporate income as is used for wage and unincorporated business income. Unlike other Michigan cities, Detroit taxes corporations doing business within its limits at a rate of 1 percent compared with a rate of 2.5 percent on residents' income and 1.25 percent on commuters.

Two problems limit the potential for more widespread use of a corporate income tax at the local level. First, administration of the tax is complex because it is difficult to allocate net income of multijurisdictional corporations to the taxing jurisdiction. Second, the tax adversely affects economic development because it is perceived as creating an unfavorable business environment. Because the local tax can be applied only to that portion of a corporation's net income attributable to the taxing jurisdiction, piggybacking the local tax onto the corporation's state tax return is not feasible. Hence, the corporate portion of the tax must be administered locally. For corporations operating in more than one city or state or country, a formula must be developed for allocating the taxable income of corporations to each local jurisdiction in which they do business. The **three-factor formula,** used by some states, apportions net taxable income according to the portion of a firm's payroll, property, and sales occurring within the taxing jurisdiction.[4] However, some cities deviate from this formula or weigh the three factors differently, increasing the cost of compliance for corporations. For example, Dayton, Ohio, uses only total sales to allocate taxable income to the city, and Lexington and Louisville, Kentucky, use just sales and payroll.

Although the problems of administering a locally levied corporate income tax are significant, they are not insurmountable. The more serious limitation is the perceived effect of the tax on local economic development. As noted in Chapter 2, perceptions are more important than facts in forming taxpayer attitudes toward local government revenue policies. While a locally levied corporate income tax may lower the property tax burden on business, it is widely perceived by corporate executives as indicative of an unfavorable business climate. In a period of increasing interlocal competition for business investment, few local governments can afford to convey such an impression.

Summary

Corporate income should not be taxed at the local level because of administrative complexity and the potentially adverse effect of the tax on business location decisions. The Maryland local income tax, which is a surcharge on a taxpayer's state tax liability, is an excellent example of an equitable and effectively administered local personal income tax. The tax extends only to the income of individuals and unincorporated businesses and is remitted along with the taxpayer's state tax, which greatly simplifies compliance for taxpayers and enforcement for government.

Issues in the design of a local income tax

Many of the same issues that local governments encounter when considering the adoption of a general sales tax or an excise tax appear with respect to the income tax. These issues include the following questions:

- Does an income tax adversely affect the location decisions of households or businesses?
- Does it reduce the property tax burden or merely increase local government spending?
- Should commuters be taxed by their jurisdiction of residence or employment?
- How much discretion should local governments have in adopting and administering the tax?

Effects of an income tax on the local economy

The greatest source of controversy related to a proposed income tax concerns its potential effects on business and household location decisions. The common assumption is that the tax will drive businesses and families out of the jurisdiction. Because of the greater visibility of the income tax, fears of adverse economic effects will be especially strong, and a proposal to adopt the tax will likely evoke even greater opposition than either a general sales tax or an excise tax. Opposition will also develop because income is already taxed by forty-three states and the federal government.

The tax's effect on business investment has been the subject of some research. In their study of the effect of city taxes on property values, Katharine Bradbury and Helen Ladd found that increases in local income tax rates reduced property values—and thus property tax revenue—over the long term.[5] At least part of the decline in property values was caused by disinvestment by existing businesses and households and by a decline in new investment by nonresident firms. These authors concluded "that the net effect of shifting away from property taxes toward income taxes is to reduce the size of the property tax base."[6]

In a study of the wage tax levied by Philadelphia, Pennsylvania, John Gruenstein examined the tax's effect on job creation.[7] He found that employment declined by between 1 and 2.5 percent for every 10 percent increase in the income tax rate. It should be noted that Philadelphia's tax rate—4.4625 percent of gross earnings—is the highest of any local government in the United States, which may have made taxpayers more sensitive to changes in it. Also, because municipalities surrounding Philadelphia do not levy an income tax, the relative ease of tax avoidance may have affected Gruenstein's results.

In a far more recent study of four major U.S. cities, Andrew Haughwout and colleagues found that in the case of both New York City and Philadelphia, changes in income (New York) and wage (Philadelphia) tax rates adversely affect job creation.[8] Both cities rely heavily on income-based taxes, and both are surrounded by communities that do not levy the tax, creating border-city effects that give households and businesses powerful incentives to relocate to the suburban areas. According to the authors' analysis, between 1971 and 2001, New York City lost 331,000 jobs because of income tax increases, and Philadelphia lost 173,000 jobs because of increases in its wage tax rate.

These studies indicate that taxes do affect business investment and job creation. It is also reasonable to expect households and businesses to be more sensitive to rate changes in the local income tax than in the property tax. While the property tax is nearly universally levied and thus unavoidable, taxpayers can more easily avoid the income tax by locating in neighboring jurisdictions where it is not levied. Regional adoption of the tax plays a critical part in building taxpayer tolerance. As noted in Chapter 1, in sensitive policy areas such as the adoption of a local income tax, regional precedent in demonstrating a policy's viability is essential for its dissemination. In a report on taxpayers' attitudes toward local taxes, the Pennsylvania Economy League noted that "because of its established and widespread use in Pennsylvania, the local earned-income tax, despite its lack of progressivity, does not appear to engender notable taxpayer resistance."[9]

Effects of an income tax on local government budgets

Like other revenue diversification measures, adoption of a local income tax is often introduced as a way of reducing the property tax burden. This justification is most often made when income tax authority is extended to local governments other than central cities. For example, Indiana counties levying an income tax under the County Adjusted Gross Income Tax (CAGIT) statute were initially required to reduce their property tax levy by an amount equal to the revenue from the income tax. The statute was amended, permitting counties to use some of the income tax return to offset lost general revenue–sharing funds and even to increase spending. Subsequently counties were given separate authority to levy a tax for economic development. Currently eighty-eight of Indiana's ninety-two counties levy an income tax under one or more of these statutes.

It is somewhat curious, however, that local income taxes have gained a level of acceptably in some of the more politically conservative areas of the nation. Whether this is the result of historical events or underlying social mores is debatable. The fact that these taxes have become accepted sources of local revenue in this part of the nation and that they seem to work effectively at providing revenue diversity makes them worth further analysis, particularly regarding their effects on local spending levels.

Taxing commuters

For central cities with a declining property tax base, an income tax offers an appealing tool for reaching nonresidents who work in the city and benefit from its role as a regional center of economic activity. Several major cities that levy an income tax derive a considerable portion of their tax revenue from commuters. For example, Cincinnati, Ohio, estimates that it receives at least 40 percent of its income tax revenue from nonresidents, and Philadelphia estimates that about one-fourth of its wage tax revenue is paid by nonresidents.

The taxation of commuters is a source of considerable controversy, especially between central cities and surrounding suburban communities. State legislatures have resolved this issue in one of three ways (Figure 7–4). At one extreme are states giving the jurisdiction of employment first claim to the income of commuters. For example, the 1.25 percent tax on earned income levied in Wilmington, Delaware, applies to commuters as well as to residents of the city. Until 1983 Philadelphia applied the same rate of 4.3125 percent to the wages of both residents and commuters; the city now taxes commuters at a lower rate of 3.8801 percent. States that give the jurisdiction of employment first claim to commuters'

Figure 7–4
Strategies for taxing commuters.

Tax credited to jurisdiction of employment	Commuters taxed at a lower rate than residents	Tax credited to jurisdiction of residence
Kentucky	Michigan	Indiana[a]
Ohio	Philadelphia	Maryland
Kansas City, Missouri	Yonkers, New York	New York City
St. Louis, Missouri		Pennsylvania[a]
Wilmington, Delaware		

[a] Indiana counties and Pennsylvania municipalities, except Philadelphia, may tax commuters only if the jurisdiction of residence does not levy the tax.

incomes generally overcompensate central cities for their services to commuters and actually create an incentive for these governments to export a large portion of the local tax burden. Because they have no voting privileges in the jurisdiction of employment, commuters complain that such levies constitute "taxation without representation."

At the other extreme are states such as Maryland, which give full credit for tax liability to the jurisdiction of residency. While this policy undercompensates jurisdictions with respect to commuters, it simplifies administration of the tax, especially where the local levy is piggybacked onto the state's. As a compromise between these two extremes, a few states (and Philadelphia) permit commuters to be taxed at a lower rate than that levied on residents. For example, Michigan limits the local tax on commuters to one-half the rate on residents. A study by William Neenan concluded that, in the case of Detroit in the early 1970s, this rate provided fair compensation for the benefits commuters derived from the city of employment.[10]

A related issue concerns the coordination of tax rates when municipalities and counties tax the same income. Currently this is an issue only in Kentucky, where cities, counties, and school districts may levy the tax, and in Pennsylvania, where municipalities and school districts may levy an earned-income tax. In Kentucky the city tax is credited against the county tax, with the county retaining any revenue that exceeds the city's rate. In Pennsylvania, non-home-rule municipalities must split the 1 percent tax rate evenly with school districts. Home-rule municipalities in Pennsylvania have no limit on the tax rate they may impose on residents.

As is true of the sales tax, the most equitable approach involves a countywide levy, with municipalities receiving a pro rata share of the tax revenue. Only Indiana uses this approach, under the newer of its two statutes granting counties the income tax option. The County Option Income Tax (COIT) program, which has been adopted by twenty-seven Indiana counties, requires that revenue from the tax be apportioned among counties, cities, and towns according to each jurisdiction's share of the property tax levy, excluding that levied for school purposes. This solution reduces both interlocal competition for household and business investment and the incentive for municipalities to become tax havens.

The taxation of commuters poses a thorny policy problem for lawmakers. The most equitable solution appears to be that used by Michigan, which permits commuters to be taxed by the jurisdiction of employment but at one-half the rate imposed on residents. A related issue concerns the division of revenue when the same income is taxed by overlapping jurisdictions. The solution used by the COIT program in Indiana appears to be the most equitable.

Administering a local income tax

Of the six states in which municipalities or counties levy an income tax, only Indiana and Maryland collect the tax on behalf of their counties and New York State does so on behalf of New York City and Yonkers. States are reluctant to collect the tax because of the perceived unpopularity of the local levy and the impression that state taxes are higher than is really the case. Local administration of the tax appears to be deeply entrenched, especially among cities levying the tax. For this reason, most local levies are limited to earned income and the net profits of unincorporated businesses. As noted earlier in the chapter, including unearned income in the tax base increases the equity of the tax burden, but this income should be collected as part of the state tax return to make enforcement cost-effective.

State administration of the tax, such as in Maryland, offers other benefits:

• Taxpayer compliance costs are reduced significantly because only one tax return is completed.

• Collection costs are lowered through centralization in one office at the state level.

• A more uniform level of enforcement can be achieved statewide because the same audit standards are applied to all tax returns.

• One audit performed on a return satisfies the needs of both state and local government.

Maryland has successfully implemented state administration of the county income tax without any evidence that local autonomy has been jeopardized. Centralized administration may increase taxpayers' tolerance for the local tax by reducing the time and irritation spent in completing a separate return for local tax liability.

A related issue concerns whether adoption should be left optional for local governments. Only Maryland requires adoption of the tax, while giving counties and Baltimore discretion in the tax rates they levy. Required adoption reduces any non-neutral effects created by taxpayers searching for nontax areas in which to locate.

Although state administration of the tax provides significant administrative savings, it may create a political liability for the state if taxpayers do not differentiate between state and local liability. Ideally, adoption should be statewide or at least at the county level to discourage households or businesses from moving to avoid the local levy.

Summary and recommendations

The following recommendations are drawn from the discussion in the chapter:

Use of the local income tax remains confined largely to states east of the Mississippi River, especially in large central cities with declining property tax bases. One of the strengths of an income tax is its capacity to extend the tax reach of a city to commuters who work in the city but otherwise bear no burden for financing its services.

Because the revenue from the tax is income elastic, local governments become more dependent on the tax over time as it displaces revenue from the less elastic property tax. As a result, local governments expose their operating budgets to greater instability whenever the local economic cycle turns downward and the income tax base contracts. For this reason, local governments should derive no more than $1.50 in revenue from the income tax for every $1.00 in revenue from the more stable property tax.

Most local governments limit the tax to earned income and the net profits of unincorporated businesses. This facilitates local administration of the tax because it can be withheld by employers. A few states permit taxation of unearned income, and still fewer permit taxation of the net income of corporations. Including unearned income in the tax base increases the tax's equity by shifting the burden to higher-income households, but it is more difficult to administer locally. Corporate income should not be taxed at the local level because of administrative complexity and the potentially adverse effect of the tax on business investment decisions.

Studies indicate that increases in the income tax rate adversely affect property values by discouraging investment by households and businesses. Evidence also exists that an increase in the local income levy reduces the number of jobs in a city.

The most thorny issue policy makers must resolve is the treatment of commuters: Should they pay taxes to the jurisdiction of employment or residence or both? One equitable solution, used by Michigan, limits the city tax on commuters to one-half the rate levied on residents. Another approach, used by Indiana, requires counties to share the revenue from the income tax with cities and towns on the basis of each jurisdiction's share of the property tax levy, net of school taxes.

Another issue concerns the administration of the tax. The most cost-effective approach involves piggybacking the local levy onto the state income tax, thereby reducing taxpayer compliance costs with the filing of only one tax return to satisfy both state and local needs. This also reduces the cost of administering the tax because of the economies of scale from centralization, and it leads to more uniform enforcement of the local levy since the same audit standards are applied to all tax returns. Maryland is the only state that requires local adoption of the tax, which reduces the inefficiency created by taxpayers searching for nontax areas in which to locate and the wasted resources used in avoiding the tax.

1 Elizabeth Deran, *City Income Taxes* (Washington, D.C.: Tax Foundation, Inc., 1967), 7–8.

2 Internal Revenue Service, *Statistics of Income 1985: Individual Income Tax Returns* (Washington, D.C.: U.S. Government Printing Office, 1987), table 1.4.

3 Catharine Kweit and Marilyn Rubin, "Local Business Income Licenses and Taxes," in *Proceedings of the Seventy-Sixth Annual Conference of the National Tax Association–Tax Institute of America* (Seattle, Wash., 1983), 194.

4 Ibid., 196.

5 Katharine L. Bradbury and Helen F. Ladd, "City Taxes and Property Tax Bases," National Bureau of Economic Research (NBER) Working Paper 2197 (Cambridge, Mass.: NBER, March 1987), 29.

6 Ibid., 30.

7 John Gruenstein, "Jobs in the City: Can Philadelphia Afford to Raise Taxes?" *Business Review,* Federal Reserve Bank of Philadelphia (May/June 1980): 3–11.

8 Andrew F. Haughwout et al., "Local Revenue Hills: Evidence from Four U.S. Cities," NBER Working Paper 9686 (Cambridge, Mass.: NBER, May 2003). Available at www.nber.org/papers/w9686.

9 Pennsylvania Economy League, *Local Taxes in Pennsylvania* (Harrisburg: Pennsylvania Economy League, no date), 73.

10 William B. Neenan, *Political Economy of Urban Areas* (Chicago: Markham Publishing Co., 1972), 291–292.

Service charges and regulatory fees

Be not the first by which the new is tried, Nor the last to lay the old aside.

—Alexander Pope

Service charges and regulatory fees

While sales and excise taxes have become increasingly prominent in local government budgets, services charges and fees represent the largest source of local revenue. This shift to charges has occurred in part because of taxpayers' resistance to higher tax burdens, particularly to increased property taxes, and in part because of the decline in federal aid described in Chapter 1. Service charges and regulatory fees are ideally suited to the "finance-it-yourself" environment that currently pervades all levels of government.

As previously discussed in Chapter 2, goods and services produced by governments can be divided into three categories: public, private, and mixed. The particular category into which a good or service falls is determined by whether it can be sold in units (its divisibility) and whether its benefits accrue solely to the buyer (its excludability). Public goods and services, such as snow removal, cannot be sold in units and benefit all citizens. They are therefore financed from general tax revenues. At the other extreme are private goods and services, which include the myriad of consumer goods available in the competitive market. Unlike public goods, these goods are sold in discrete units for a price, and nonbuyers are effectively excluded from enjoying any of their benefits. Ownership is evidenced by a receipt or title.

While most private goods are produced by the private sector, government also provides a large number of private services, such as water, sewerage, and electric power. Unlike the private sector, however, government rarely sells its services in a competitive market. It often assumes production of these services because the opportunity for profit is insufficient to attract a private provider (as in the case of public transit) or because the large capital investment naturally limits provision to a monopolist (as in the case of water service). Unlike the private sector, government has the choice of financing these services through charges to users of the service or through general revenues.

Between public and private goods lie merit (or mixed) goods and services, which are private goods endowed with a public purpose.[1] For example, a municipal airport provides individual benefits that can be denied to those unwilling to pay for them, yet it also benefits the whole community by improving business opportunities and thereby helping to create jobs. A portion of the cost of merit goods should, therefore, be borne by all taxpayers, with the remaining private portion of benefits financed through service charges to users.

Service charges are only one type of levy that governments use to finance the cost of private benefits from government-produced services. Figure 8–1 shows the range of benefits-based levies that governments use. User charges, such as an admission fee for a swimming pool or ice hockey rink, and utility service charges are typically levied under a local government's proprietary powers. State statutes usually grant municipalities (and, to a lesser extent, counties) the discretion to operate business-like services and levy a reasonable charge on their beneficiaries.

State laws also grant local governments limited regulatory powers for preserving and promoting the health, safety, and welfare of the community by issuing **licenses**

Figure 8–1

Benefits-based levies commonly used by local governments.

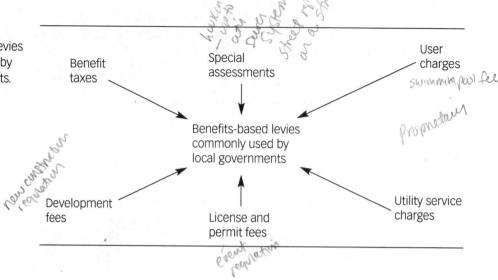

[handwritten annotations: "housing / use to on", "Development", "System", "street repairs on a street", "swimming pool fee", "Proprietary", "new construction regulation", "event regulation"]

and **permits.** A license authorizes an individual or business to engage in an on-going activity; for example, a bicycle license authorizes operation of a bicycle on local streets. By contrast, a permit authorizes a business or individual to undertake a particular task; for example, a parade permit authorizes individuals to use particular streets at a particular time for an organized parade. Within limits prescribed by law, governments charge a fee for a license or permit as compensation for the cost of regulating the activity. **Development fees,** such as impact and building inspection fees, compensate local governments for the cost of regulating new construction and for the impact of the construction on public services. Revenue from parking meters compensates government for the cost of regulating parking.

A few benefits-based levies derive their legal basis from the taxing powers of local governments. For example, in the case of a street improvement, a special assessment would recoup the value of private benefits accruing to property owners along the street. Revenue from the levy usually cannot exceed the increase in property value that results from the improvement. In some states, regulatory rather than taxing powers provide the legal basis for a special assessment, as in the case of a sidewalk installation.

In some cases, taxes with earmarked revenue are a type of benefits-based levy. A motor fuels tax earmarked for highway improvements constitutes a "charge" to vehicle operators that approximates their pro rata share of private benefits from using highways. Other benefits-based taxes were discussed in Chapter 6.

This chapter examines the first three types of benefits-based levies: user charges, utility service charges, and license and permit fees. The following chapter examines special assessments and impact fees on new development. For an increasing number of local governments, revenue from charges and fees now exceeds the total revenue from all taxes, including the property tax. Economically, charges and fees score high marks for both equity and efficiency. Politically, their luster is somewhat tarnished. They also pose policy issues that are quite different from those that local officials encounter with taxes. These issues include

• Obstacles to greater use of charges and fees

• Procedures for pricing services

• Determining the proportion of a service's cost to be recovered through charges to users

• Desirable provisions for a policy statement on service charges and fees.

[handwritten margin note: "Regulation vs taxing powers. ?"]

The following section reviews the role of service charges in local government, concluding with a discussion of the types of charges and fees commonly found in local government and the proportion of direct costs recovered from them. Subsequent sections consider policy and management issues associated with charges and fees.

The role of charges and fees in local government

The current "fend-for-yourself" fiscal era makes charges and fees attractive sources of revenue for financing services with private benefits. The accompanying sidebar summarizes some of their advantages. Undoubtedly, their greatest virtue is to reduce the wasteful use of some government-produced services, thereby reducing the pressure to expand public facilities to meet artificially inflated user demand and constraining the growth of the government budget. When a service is financed with tax revenue, users have no incentive to limit their use and therefore create an apparently greater demand, which governments feel obligated to meet. When the same service is *sold* to users, citizens will purchase only what they want, and consumption by those who use the service only because they think it is free will diminish. In the terms of economists, prices ration goods and services to those who value them the most, thereby maximizing economic efficiency.

As an illustration, consider the per capita water consumption in two hypothetical cities—Alpha and Delta. Alpha meters water use and charges users for the full cost of the quantity consumed, but Delta finances all water services through its property tax. Predictably, per capita water consumption in Delta greatly exceeds that in Alpha, because users who perceive the water as "free" have no incentive to control their level of use. The greater demand for water leads Delta to increase water production capacity well beyond that of Alpha.

Another effect of user charge financing is to constrain the growth of local government budgets by reducing demand for services. For example, a study of a large urban county conducted by the RAND Corporation indicated that charging a fee for the full cost of ambulance service would reduce emergency calls by one-third (as well as raising about $4 million annually).[2] Santa Ana, California, experienced a 40 percent reduction in false alarms after instituting a fee for such calls.[3]

Advantages of service charges and fees

Charges reduce wasteful consumption of some public services by heightening users' awareness of the cost of providing the service.

Because service charges are based on the quantity consumed by each user, they give local governments a clear indication of the level of service preferred by citizens, thereby reducing the tendency to expand government facilities to meet apparently increased demand.

Service charges are equitable: Those using the service pay in proportion to the benefits they receive from it. Those who don't use the service don't subsidize those who do.

Service charges improve local government productivity by increasing managers' awareness of the cost of services. Charges to users also slow the growth of local budgets by ensuring that decision making is based not on interdepartmental budgetary politics but on the relationship of service levels to demand.

Service charges provide a market-based alternative to regulating through rules and administrative orders. In other words, they can be used to influence private behavior toward socially desirable ends.

Economists are quick to note that prices reveal citizen preferences more accurately than the ballot box. Charging for government services provides a means of determining citizens' preferences by the amount of service they purchase. Voting provides only an indication of citizens' satisfaction with the overall package of government services and their cost.

Service charges also enjoy widespread acceptance by citizens. Public opinion surveys consistently show significant public support for increased use of service charges rather than increased taxes. As the following section shows, local governments have responded to citizens' preferences by increasing their use of charges.

Local government dependence on revenue from service charges

While local governments had begun to increase their dependence on service charges and fees prior to the ratification of Proposition 13 in 1978 and Proposition 2½ in 1980, the tax revolt accelerated this trend. A comparison of the role of user charges (service plus utility charges) versus property taxes in Tables 8–1 and 8–2 indicates how far this shift has gone. For municipalities, user charges represented 41.9 percent of general revenues in 2001, up from 40.8 percent a decade earlier; property taxes, on the other hand, decreased from 25.1 percent in 1991 to 22.8 percent in 2001. For counties, these shifts have been even more pronounced: user charges

Table 8–1
Municipal government dependence on user charges: Service and utility charges as a percentage of general revenues.

Revenue source	1991–92	1996–97	2001–02
Property taxes	25.1	22.7	22.8
All other taxes	22.3	23.9	24.2
Service charges	18.7	20.9	20.4
Utility charges	22.1	21.4	21.5
Other non taxes	11.9	11.1	11.1
	100.1	100.0	100.0
Total general revenue (in millions)[a]	$161,293	$202,674	$255,220

Source: U.S. Bureau of the Census, *Finances of Municipal and Township Governments,* 1997 Census of Governments 4, no. 4 (September 2000), table 1 (http://www.census.gov/prod/gc97/gc974-4.pdf); and U.S. Bureau of the Census, *Local Summary Tables by Type of Government: 2001-02,* table 2 (http://ftp2.census.gov/govs/estimate/02slsstab2a.xls).

Note: Percentages may not total 100% because of rounding.
[a] Total general revenue includes utility charges but excludes intergovernmental aid, liquor store income, and insurance trust revenue.

Table 8–2
County government dependence on user charges: Service and utility charges as a percentage of general revenues.

Revenue source	1991–92	1996–97	2001–02
Property taxes	43.5	38.6	38.4
All other taxes	15.0	17.0	17.1
Service charges	25.6	29.1	29.1
Utility charges	1.8	2.2	2.1
Other non taxes	14.1	13.1	13.2
	100.0	100.0	99.9
Total general revenue (in millions)[a]	$94,808	$122,161	$161,483

Source: U.S. Bureau of the Census, *Finances of County Governments,* 1997 Census of Governments 4, no. 3 (September 2000), table 1 (http://www.census.gov/prod/gc97/gc974-3.pdf); and U.S. Bureau of the Census, *Local Summary Tables by Type of Government: 2001–02,* table 2 (http://ftp2.census.gov/govs/estimate/02slsstab2a.xls).

Note: Percentages may not total 100% because of rounding.
[a] Total general revenue includes utility charges but excludes intergovernmental aid, liquor store income, and insurance trust revenue.

made up 31.2 percent of general revenues in 2001 compared to 27.4 percent a decade earlier, whereas property taxes dropped from 43.5 percent in 1991 to 38.4 percent in 2001.

Previous studies have found that smaller municipalities rely more heavily on service charges than larger cities, probably because the latter have more diversified revenue sources while the former have more limited tax bases. As is apparent from Tables 8–1 and 8–2, cities rely much more heavily on utility charges than counties do. For many cities, especially those with large amounts of tax-exempt state or federal property (such as university towns), utilities provide an important mechanism for subsidizing their general funds. Frequently, utility operations are required by local ordinance or charter to provide a return on investment to the city, as well as **franchise fees** comparable to what a private utility would incur for the exclusive privilege of providing utility services.

Table 8–3 illustrates quite vividly the different roles of user charges for county and municipal governments. In 2002, municipalities received $0.89 in revenue from charges for every $1.00 in taxes collected. Interestingly, this ratio did not change between 1982 and 2002, possibly indicating a moderation in the "fee fever." In municipalities, most revenue from charges comes from utility services, particularly water and electric power. Sewerage service also provides a significant amount of revenue, equal to about $0.15 for every $1.00 in taxes received.

Counties, on the other hand, derived only $.56 of every tax dollar from service charges in 2002, and much of that came from county-operated hospitals. This ratio reflects a significant increase since 1986, indicating the growing role of charges and fees in the revenue structures of county governments. Utility services provide only a small fraction of the revenue counties receive from all charges.

Table 8–3

Sources of service charge and utility revenue, 2002.

	Charges as a percentage of all tax revenues	
Type of charge	Municipalities	Counties
All charges	89.1	56.1
Current charges		
Airports	4.7	2.4
Highways	1.0	0.6
Hospitals	5.2	20.3
Housing and community development	1.3	0.2
Parking	1.0	0.1
Parks and recreation	2.8	1.1
Sea and port facilities	0.7	0.2
Sewerage	14.8	3.6
Solid waste	4.7	4.1
Other	7.2	19.7
Total	43.4	52.3
Utilities		
Electric	22.4	0.2
Gas	3.8	0.0
Public transit	2.3	0.4
Water	17.2	3.2
Total	45.7	3.8

Source: U.S. Bureau of the Census, *Local Summary Tables by Type of Government: 2001–02*, table 2 (http://ftp2.census.gov/govs/estimate/02slsstab2a.xls).

Cities in southern states depend most heavily on charges and fees, and New England states depend the least. Cities in California now derive about the same amount of revenue from service and utility charges as from taxes. Massachusetts cities and towns, however, derive about $.25 in charge revenue for every $1 in taxes, even though voters in both states ratified highly publicized tax limitation measures. This may suggest that while the tax limitation movement has encouraged greater use of service charges, regional precedent and local political attitudes play a much greater role in shaping the revenue structures of local governments.

Services financed by charges and fees

Local government policy makers are often astounded by the lengthy list of activities for which charges and fees are collected. The sidebar on page 163 lists some of the more common services for which local governments collect charges, and the sidebar on page 164 does the same for some of the more common regulated activities for which license and permit fees are assessed. For example, utility services, such as water and wastewater treatment, have long been financed by direct charges to users, including wholesale consumers such as governments. Some governments even generate a profit on these services, which is used to subsidize other tax-supported areas. The 1987 amendments to the federal Clean Water Act ushered in a new category of utility charges: stormwater drainage fees. To meet the federal mandate for water quality standards for runoff, many local governments, especially in flood-prone areas, adopted these fees, which are distinct from wastewater treatment fees. (Figure 8–2, on page 165, provides an example of a stormwater drainage fee used by the city of Denton, Texas.) Fees may be a flat rate per lot or, as in the case of Denton, scaled to lot size. Even more sophisticated fee structures consider the permeability of each surface area (lot or property boundary) and the expected amount of runoff it generates.

As resistance has grown to a greater dependence on taxes, local governments have looked to other services for which users can share in the cost. Tax-supported services funded through the general fund are not immune. Recreation and leisure, public works, police and public safety, planning, economic development, public health and sanitation, and public transit all have become candidates for at least partial cost recovery through user charges. In recent years, the search for chargeable activities has been enlarged to include advertising in public spaces, such as on government vehicles and buildings. Unlike utility services, for which revenue is accumulated in separate enterprise funds, revenue from these governmental services is typically comingled with tax revenue, which raises questions about the effectiveness of such charges at raising department managers' awareness of the cost of services.

While local governments generally have wider latitude in the rates they charge for services, state law and the courts have generally limited fees for licenses and permits to the cost of regulating the activity. Local governments have relied on their authority to promote the health, safety, and general well-being of their communities to license a wide range of private activities, including pet ownership, amusement and recreation, new construction, various professions and trades, food service, and land use. Seldom do the fees for these privileges cover the full cost of regulating the activity, and unless state or federal law stipulates otherwise, the revenues are almost always comingled with general taxes.

The tax limitation movement has pushed some local governments into imprudent ventures in their quest for non-tax revenue. As noted in Chapter 1 in the discussion of proprietary powers, local governments operate a host of "businesses," from radio stations to casinos, some of which have proven quite profitable. But other ventures have proven financially fatal. Gardena, California, a suburb of Los Angeles, entered the insurance liability business in the early 1990s as a way to

Services for which local governments commonly charge a fee

Recreation and leisure activities
Athletic fields (P)
Athletic leagues (F)*
Auditorium/civic center rental (F)
Boat harbors (F)
Concession rental (F)
Equipment rental (F)
Greens fees (F)
Law library (F)*
Parks (P)
Public library services (P)
Recreation center rental (F)
Recreation classes (F)*
Swimming pools (P)
Tennis courts (P)
Web-based data services (F)

Utility services
Connection (F)
Drainage (F)
Lateral permits (F)
Pro rata connection (F)
Retail wastewater service (F)
Retail water service (F)
Septic tank dumping (F)
Tap permits (F)
Temporary use of meter or hydrant (F)
Wholesale water and wastewater (F)

Public works
Abandoned-vehicle removal (F)
Barricades (F)
Curb and street cuts (F)
Maps (F)
Right-of-way access (F)
Weed cutting (P)

Police protection
Accident and offense reports (F)
DWI processing (F)
False alarm call (F)
Funeral escorts (F)
Other special-occasion escorts (F)
Police services at special events (F)
Serving warrants (F)
Vehicle impoundment (F)

Planning and economic development
Annexation (F)
Development guide or manual (F)
Fairgrounds rental (P)
Historic landmark designation (P)
Maps (F)
Plat processing (F)
Zoning variance (F)

Sanitation and animal control
Animal holding (F)
Animal impoundment (P)
Carcass retrieval (P)
Euthanasia (F)
Landfill (P)
Large-item solid-waste pickup (F)*
Litter abatement (P)
Rabies vaccination (P)
Solid-waste collection (F)
Street cleaning (P)

Health
Ambulance service (P)
Hospitals and nursing homes (F)*
Inoculations (P)
Mental health services (F)*

Transportation
Airport landing (F)
Bridge tolls (F)
Bus fares (P)
Hangar rentals (F)
Parking garages (F)*
Parking meters (F)*
Special-occasion bus rentals (P)

Miscellaneous
Advertising on public space (F)
Cemeteries (P)
Commodity sales (F)
Document search (F)
Election filing (F)
Farmers' market (P)
Meeting room rentals (F)
Photocopying records (F)
Public housing (P)
Vending machine space rental (F)
WiFi (wireless fidelity) service (F)

(F): Price should be set at full cost of providing the service.
(F)*: Full-cost pricing should be required only for certain classes of users; a partial subsidy should be provided for some users, such as the elderly, children, and nonprofit organizations.
(P): Fee for service should be set so as to recover only part of the cost of the service. A partial subsidy is justified for any one or all of the reasons discussed in the chapter.

control its liability insurance costs and provide a service to other cities facing the same constraints. Unfortunately, the city's company, Municipal Mutual, could not compete against the established insurance providers. By the end of 2004, the city was poised to file for bankruptcy, unable to repay the $30 million in debt it borrowed to fund the venture.

Activities commonly regulated by local governments

Animal regulation
Dog and cats (license)
Kennels (license)

Amusement and recreation
Bicycles (registration)
Billiard and pool halls (license)
Boats (license)
Camping (permit)
Carnivals and circuses (permit)
Coin-operated machines for entertainment (license)
Dance halls (license)
Fireworks (permit)
Fishing and hunting (license)
Massage parlors (permit)
Movie theaters (license)
Outdoor concerts (permit)
Parades (permit)

Building construction
Alarms (permit)
Billboards (permit)
Building (permit)
Building movers (license and permit)
Concrete contractors (license and permit)
Demolition (license and permit)
Driveway curb cutting (permit)
Electrical contractors (license and permit)
Elevator installation (permit)
Fence contractors (license and permit)
Grading (permit)
Heating contractors (license and permit)
Home repair (license)
Manufactured-housing installation (permit)
Plumbing contractors (license and permit)
Street excavating (permit)

Food service
Alcoholic beverage sales (license)
Food handlers (permit)
Restaurants (health permit)

Businesses and occupations
Bottled water (license)
Christmas tree sales (license)
Collection agency (license)
Distressed goods sales (license)
Dry-cleaning (license)
Electronic repair (license)
Flammable-liquid storage (permit)
Itinerant merchants (license)
Jewelry auction (permit)
Lawn sprinklers (license)
Motor vehicle repair (license)
Motor vehicle towing (license)
Parking lot (license)
Pawnbrokers (license)
Residential garage sales (permit)
Retail cigarette dealers (license)
Rug and carpet cleaners (license)
Sign permits (F)
Solid- and liquid-waste haulers (license)
Taxi and bus carriers (license)
Ticket brokers (license)
Tree service contractors (license)
Wood vendors (license)

Health care facilities and services
Ambulance drivers (license)
Hospital and convalescent home (license)
Private ambulance vehicles (permit)

Planning, zoning, and development
Barricades (permit)
Certificates of occupancy (fee)
Floodplain development (permit)
Plat approval (fee)
Waterway development (permit)
Zoning variance (fee)

Other
Charitable solicitation (permit)
Concealed weapons (permit)
Loudspeakers (permit)
Trash burning (permit)

Source: This is an updated version of an earlier list in Stanley E. Wilkes Jr., *A Guide to Revenue Administration for Small Cities* (Arlington: University of Texas at Arlington, Institute for Urban Studies, 1981).

Local governments often confront unrealistic expectations from citizens to reduce taxes while maintaining or even increasing services. In the case of revenue policy, governments are best served by incremental changes tested on a small scale before being expanded to the jurisdiction as a whole. There are no pots of gold awaiting discovery, and promises to the contrary are certain to lead to disaster.

Figure 8–2 Rate schedules for Denton, Texas, municipal utilities.

Consumer Information
Denton Municipal Utilities

ELECTRIC RATES

Residential

Facility Charge	$7.73/30 days (single phase)
	$15.45/30 days (three phase)
Energy Charge	
Winter (November-April)	4.34¢/KWH first 1,000 KWH
	3.94¢/KWH all additional KWH
Summer (May-October)	5.61¢/KWH first 3,000 KWH
	6.21¢/KWH all additional KWH
*Fuel Charge	3.80¢/KWH Energy Cost Adjustment

General Service Small

Facility Charge	$15.15/30 days (single phase)
	$20.20/30 days (three phase)
Demand Charge	$8.00/KW of demand/30 days

(Minimum demand is 70 percent of maximum monthly demand for May through October. First 20 KW not billed.)

Energy Charge – Customer with 20 KW or below:

First 2,500 KWH	6.75¢/KWH
All additional KWH	3.00¢/KWH

Energy Charge – Customer above 20 KW:

First 2,500 KWH	6.75¢/KWH
Next 3,500 KWH	
plus B2T KWH	3.00¢/KWH
All additional KWH	2.65¢/KWH
*Fuel Charge	3.80¢/KWH Energy Cost Adjustment

* The above fuel charge is effective as of 10-01-03. All fuel charges are subject to quarterly review and change. Call for current rate.

SOLID WASTE RATES

Residential Bagged Service

Bagged Service	$18.20/30 days - 2 collections per week
Recycling Charge	$2.07/30 days

Residential Containerized Service

Number of Containers	1	2
90-gallon container (nominal)	$15.00	$28.00/30 days
60-gallon container (nominal)	$13.00	$25.00/30 days
35-gallon container (nominal)	$12.00	N/A
Recycling Charge	$2.07/30 days	N/A

(Residential containerized service rates are based upon one collection per week.)

Commercial Front Load Service
Billing per 30 days

	Front Load
3 cubic yard container	$53.34
4 cubic yard container	$65.29
6 cubic yard container	$84.66
8 cubic yard container	$103.47

(All solid waste commercial rates based upon one service per week.)

Commercial Open Top (Roll-Off)

	Monthly Rental	Pickup (each)
20 cubic yard container	$81.70	$238.10
30 cubic yard container	$94.05	$291.85

WATER RATES

Residential

Facility Charge	
3/4" Meter	$9.55/30 days
1" Meter	$11.40/30 days
1 1/2" Meter	$16.25/30 days
2" Meter	$18.10/30 days

Volume Charge

Winter (Nov. - April)	Summer (May - Oct.)
$2.60/1,000 gallons	$2.60/1,000 gallons (up to 15,000 gals/30 days)
(all consumption)	$3.50/1,000 gallons (15,001 to 30,000 gals/30 days)
	$4.35/1,000 gallons (all over 30,000 gals/30 days)

Commercial/Industrial

Facility Charge	
3/4" Meter	$20.20/30 days
1" Meter	$22.20/30 days
1 1/2" Meter	$25.75/30 days ·
2" Meter	$31.65/30 days
Volume Charge	$2.87/1,000 gallons

WASTEWATER RATES
Residential

Facility Charge	$6.45/30 days
Volume Charge	$2.47/1,000 gals effluent

(Billing based on 98 percent of average monthly water billed from December through February.)

Commercial/Industrial

Facility Charge	$16.85/30 days
Volume Charge	$3.20/1,000 gals effluent

(Billing based on 80 percent of monthly water consumption.)

Equipment Services and Eating Establishments

Facility Charge	$16.85/30 days
Volume Charge	$4.42/1,000 gals effluent

(Billing based on 80 percent of monthly water consumption.)

DRAINAGE RATES

Residential

Square Feet in Block	Monthly Charge per 30 Days
0-600	$0.50
601-1000	$1.00
1001-2000	$3.35
2001-3000	$5.45
3001-4000	$7.60
4001-5000	$9.75
5001-6000	$12.00
6001+	$15.50

Non Residential

Square feet of impervious surface x $0.00186/30 days.

MISCELLANEOUS

A $10.00 late payment charge will be assessed on the fifth business day following the due date on any unpaid balance.

Interest of one percent per month will be added on all past due charges and account balances unpaid at the time of the current month's billing calculation.

More recently, local governments have introduced charges for the growing array of services spawned by new technology, such as access to online data and to wireless fidelity (WiFi), a city- or countywide broadband wireless network that provides high-speed Internet service to citizens at a fraction of the cost of other modes of service. As discussed briefly in Chapter 1, a number of U.S. cities are exploring the introduction of this service. Internationally, the technology has already gained acceptance. For example, residents of Taipei, Taiwan, now have access to the Internet through WiFi connectivity anywhere in the city. Not only does this technology make this service available at a low cost, but it also provides cities with a tool for attracting technology-dependent industries. Philadelphia is the largest and most recent U.S. city to enter this market. Unfortunately, self-serving interests in the private telecommunications industry, apparently anticipating the superior competitive performance of the public sector, have prevailed in at least thirteen states to pass legislation prohibiting local governments from providing telecommunication services to their citizens.

Fees for data services

With the convergence of digital data development through geographic information systems (GIS) and their accessibility through the Web, local governments have made such data available to citizens and business users, often for a fee. While local governments have generally charged fees for generating hard copies of maps and aerial photographs, more recently they have introduced fees for digital products such as online maps of political boundaries, plats, and centerlines for streets and alleys. For example, the city and county of Denver, Colorado, now charges a digital data fee for users of its online services. Fees are waived for contractors working on a contract with the city.

In the case of Denver, users must first complete and sign a GIS Data Request Form, which commits them to follow the city's GIS license agreement. The Web site provides instructions on (1) fee schedule and available products, (2) types of reference maps available, (3) the GIS ordinance and request form, (4) payment procedures, and (5) data delivery procedures. More information is available at www.denvergov.org under "Information Center: Online Services."

Fees for the use of public rights-of-way

Municipalities in most states have the authority to charge private utility companies for their use of public rights-of-way for service lines. Access to the right-of-way greatly reduces the utility's cost of doing business, and a usage or rental fee compensates the local government for granting that privilege. However, these rental fees (**right-of-way taxes,** or in some cases, gross receipts taxes as described in Chapter 6), especially for telecommunications providers, have come under increasing assault particularly with the advent of deregulation in the private utility world. The following recommendations clarify the role of charges for use of the public right-of-way.

Recommendation #1: If not already the case, state law should be modified to say that local governments are legally and economically justified in requiring compensation based on the fair market value of access to public rights-of-way. State law should make clear that if it does not charge for use, the city is acting irresponsibly as a trustee of the community's property.

Recommendation #2: Local governments should periodically reappraise the fair market value of the easements granted to telecommunications providers. This can be done by comparing what utilities must pay for access to rights-of-way in comparable markets and looking at the net income generated by the utility from serving an area. As competition in the telecommunications industry increases and as local exchange rates more closely reflect the true cost of service, the demand for access to public rights-of-way is bound to increase. Given the relatively fixed supply of public easement and the finite amount of space above and below ground level, the value of these easements will only increase in the next decade. Ideally, users of the right-of-way should be charged an annual fee based on the appraised value of the access. One advantage to such an approach is that it eliminates debate over what services to include or exclude from the base. An appraisal will at least provide a benchmark for the city and right-of-way users as to a reasonable rate, even if the local government continues to use a fixed percentage of gross receipts as a reasonable approximation.

With full deregulation of the telecommunications industry, cities should anticipate new entrants into the industry, many of whom may seek access to the public rights-of-way. These new entrants will be looking for opportunities to maximize income by serving low-cost/high-revenue customers, such as large institutions (universities, medical complexes, industrial parks) or concentrated population areas (apartment complexes, condominiums, central city business districts), with dedicated lines running along the public rights-of-way. In these cases, the economic value of the right-of-way may be justifiably higher than it is in the higher-cost/lower-revenue areas of the city or, especially, in unincorporated areas. An independent appraisal of the easement's fair market value will be particularly important in such cases in order to establish a "fair and reasonable" basis of compensation.

Cities may also want to test alternative pricing strategies, such as peak-period or block pricing for the use of streets. As a divisible and excludable good, use of rights-of-way should be viewed as any other private good and priced to reflect the variations in the marginal value it has to users in different parts of the city or even at different times of day. The technology may well emerge to allow more elaborate pricing structures.

Recommendation #3: Given the almost certain growth in demand for access to their rights-of-way, local governments may want to explore the feasibility of constructing and maintaining their own fiber-optic networks and then leasing capacity on those networks to private interests. The cities of Milpitas, California; Glasgow, Kentucky; and Gainesville, Florida, have all constructed fiber-optic networks that reduced their costs for telecommunications services significantly and increased their access to more services, including the Internet. However, not all efforts have been successful, a primary factor being the size of the potential end-user market. Local governments face the same economy-of-scale issues that private providers deal with daily.

Besides reducing the congestion that may develop if multiple providers build competing networks in the same area, a city-owned fiber-optic loop can be a tool for economic development. High-speed data communications and Internet access can attract industries that depend heavily on telecommunications, especially if the city can offer economies that are otherwise unavailable from the private sector. The network may also reduce municipal operating costs by making possible such services as automated meter reading, online reservation of city facilities, and online access to city services such as emergency medical services, continuing education, and recreation.

Source: These recommendations originally appeared in Robert L. Bland, "Franchise Fees and Telecommunications Services: Is a New Paradigm Needed?" *State Tax Notes* (February 10, 1997): 437–443. Copyright 1997 Tax Analysts. Reprinted with permission.

Issues in the adoption of service charges

When local governments review their services to determine which ones are candidates for charging fees, they must perform two tasks. In the first task, administrators must decide which services *can* be sold to users. This involves identifying activities that provide private benefits and whose benefits can be denied (with minimum expense) to those not paying for the service.

The second, more political, task involves deciding which services *should* be financed by service charges. In making this decision, managers must consider four issues.

First, is it more equitable to charge users for the service or to levy a tax? If beneficiaries from the service can be clearly identified and if nonpayers can be effectively excluded from enjoying at least some of the benefits of the service, then it is more equitable to charge users rather than taxpayers for the private benefits of the service.

Second, do surrounding cities, towns, or counties levy a charge for the service? Regional precedent makes it much easier politically for a local government to assess a fee for the same service.

Third, how do citizens feel about increases in local taxes? The more broad based the opposition to tax increases, the greater the pressure managers should place on supporters of new or expanded services to identify revenue sources for financing proposed services. Proponents of a new service should be routinely required to include the use of service charges in their proposals.

Finally, what effect will the charge have on the use of the service? Normally, charging a price for a service reduces demand. For some services that have widespread benefits to the community, however, such reductions are undesirable. For example, charging full cost for residential use of a landfill may increase illegal dumping along roadways and in vacant lots. When it comes to increasing prices, change in demand varies for different services (price elasticity of demand) depending on the availability of substitutes. For utility services, price elasticity is low; there are no substitutes short of reducing consumption, and going without the service is not an option in most cases. But for many other governmental services, consumer demand is more sensitive to price changes. The greater the price change, the greater the effect on service use. *For this reason, local governments should avoid large and irregular price increases.* Small, annual adjustments in prices have much less adverse effect on demand and on local government revenue yields.

Obstacles to the greater use of service charges

Although service charges are more likely than taxes to be accepted by citizens and although they provide an equitable and economically neutral revenue source, significant barriers exist to their expanded use by local governments. The accompanying sidebar summarizes some of those barriers.

Because of the political risks to public officials in altering established policies, regional precedent plays a key role in shaping local government revenue structures. Evidence of a policy's success in surrounding governments helps allay policy makers' fears for its success in their jurisdiction. Tradition also affects a local government's dependence on service charges. Introduction of new or increased service charges is much easier politically if a community has depended heavily on service charges in the past. If people "vote with their feet," as suggested in Chapter 1, these communities will attract other individuals with similar expectations for financing government services.

Users themselves also pose an obstacle to greater use of service charges. Because the benefit from a new service charge is spread among all residents through only a slight reduction in their effective tax burden, taxpayers have little incentive to mobilize in support of the fee. However, the cost of the new charge is highly visible to

Barriers to the increased use of service charges

The absence of a precedent among area local governments increases the political risk of being the first to charge for a particular service.

The benefits of charging for a service are widely dispersed among taxpayers through a slight (and most likely unnoticed) reduction in their effective tax burden. The charge is more apparent to users of the service who then have an incentive to lobby against it.

The piecemeal adoption of charges and fees in separate ordinances over time disperses them throughout the local code, which greatly complicates regular review and updating. Any change in the rates requires a separate amendment to each ordinance, and the staff time and effort

required for this task may not justify the small revenue increases that would result.

Antiquated state statutes that specify the maximum fees, especially for regulatory activities, unnecessarily complicate local governments' efforts to keep these levies current with the cost of the service.

Staff members may resist the imposition of new charges because they fear that the levy will reduce demand for the service and thereby jeopardize their position with the government.

Most service charges are regressive with respect to household income, prompting local governments to explore various ways of easing the impact of such charges on those least able to afford them.

users of the service, whose vocal opposition may make it more difficult for elected officials to support the fee. Only when all charges and fees are combined is their revenue significance apparent to taxpayers and policy makers. Yet service charges and regulatory fees are usually adopted not en masse but service by service, over time. Thus, one strategy for increasing their use may be to review rate adjustments en masse rather than piecemeal.

Another strategy for overcoming opposition is to levy a charge only for extra levels of a service.[4] For example, if weekly collection of residential refuse is financed from general revenues, a charge may be introduced for those wishing a second pickup during the week or for large-item pickup. Such a plan may help build public acceptance for service charges for refuse collection. Support can also be created through citizens' advisory groups and boards that review the merits of a charge or fee. In the case of an increase in an existing charge, adequate notification through radio and newspaper announcements must be given. Citizens resent being surprised by increases in rates for government services.

The piecemeal adoption of charges also poses a legal obstacle to rate adjustments. Because charges are usually adopted as part of an ordinance authorizing the service, adjusting charges requires amending a large number of ordinances, a task that demands considerable legal research on the part of government attorneys and monopolizes valuable agenda time for policy makers. For this reason, review of service charges and fees often occurs only during a financial crisis.

State statutes limiting charges and fees sometimes pose a barrier to increased use of service charges. State laws often limit license and permit fees, especially charges for court services. Unfortunately, state legislators generally review these rates only when state revenue is tight, which curbs local governments' ability to keep fees current with the cost of regulating the activity or providing the service.

Occasionally, local government staff may resist introduction of new charges, especially for services that have been financed from general revenues. Staff may express concern about a proposed charge's effects on demand. For example, charging for the use of tennis courts may reduce demand, depending on the availability of substitutes. An unspoken concern may be that a decline in use of a service will necessitate staff reductions. Departments have a vested interest in increasing demand for a service since their budget justification depends in part on usage. Some departments may view a shift to service charges as a threat to their budget base.

And there are other obstacles as well. Some charges, such as those related to building and new construction, have highly unstable yields, which complicates budget planning for local governments. Legal challenges also occasionally limit the use of charges and fees. For example, in response to Proposition 13, Inglewood, California, adopted a fire assessment fee based on the expected cost of fire protection for each property. The fee was dropped when its legality was challenged in a lawsuit.[5] Some observers have expressed concern about the fragmenting effect of service charges on the local budget process, especially when the revenue from charges is routinely earmarked and not subject to review along with other budget allocation decisions.[6] The fear is that this unbundling of the local budget may decrease community cohesiveness and damage support for activities not financed by earmarked revenues, especially services to lower-income groups.

Another concern is the adverse impact that service charges may have on low-income users, especially youth who rely on recreation programs. Local governments have experimented with several strategies for addressing this problem, including suspending the collection of charges during off-peak periods (e.g., offering a free day at the zoo or city pool), making vouchers available to qualifying low-income households (e.g., for public housing), and establishing differential pricing (e.g., a higher price for adults and a much lower price for children and youth). The electric utility department in Denton, Texas, gives rate payers an opportunity to add $1 to their monthly remittance, which a local human service agency administers as one-time assistance to qualifying users who are having difficulty paying their electric utility bills.

Increasing the role of service charges

Charges for utilities and other self-supporting services receive careful scrutiny by local government leaders because rates must be sufficient to recover all costs. Often an outside firm will undertake a rate study to ensure that the rate structure fairly distributes the cost of the service to users. Charges for tax-supported governmental services, however, rarely receive the same scrutiny, in part because they are not self-supporting and because charges supplement the tax-supported general fund. Because of the infrequent scrutiny these charges receive, rate adjustments—when they come—are substantial, often to compensate for a substantial revenue shortfall; this has the effect of depressing user demand for the service, at least in the short term.

A preferable approach is to *annually review* all government-type charges and fees and then adjust rates to reflect changes in the cost of service delivery. It is not necessary that a cost-of-services study (discussed later in this chapter) be performed annually. Once the benchmark cost of each service is determined through such a study, rates can be adjusted annually according to the consumer price index for the nearest metropolitan area. The accompanying sidebar summarizes the stages recommended for reviewing service charges.

List services   More systematic monitoring of charges for governmental types of services begins by asking each department to compile a list of services for which it currently levies a charge or fee. The budget office (or finance office if no separate budget office exists) should oversee this task. Departments should cite the legal basis for each charge along with information on the rate and amount of revenue it

---

Recommended stages in the review of charges on governmental types of services

1. Each department compiles a comprehensive list of all governmental (i.e., non-self-supporting) services for which it currently levies charges and fees.

2. The local government codifies these charges and fees by department or functional area for easy reference and amendment by ordinance.

3. As part of the preparation of the operating budget, each department estimates the revenue expected from each charge that it administers and the cost of providing each chargeable service.

4. As part of the detailed revenue analysis presented to local leaders, the budget or finance office compiles a list of all governmental types of services for which charges are levied and the percentage of each service recovered through the charge or fee. In consultation with each department, the budget office recommends adjustments in charges and fees where appropriate.

---

yielded during the previous fiscal year. (This task may already have been completed as part of the preparation of a revenue manual.)

Codify charges and fees by function Because legal authorization for charges is scattered throughout the local code, local governments should consider codifying charges and fees by category or function. One approach is to list all charges in one ordinance and all regulatory fees in another, making reference to the underlying ordinances authorizing their use.[7] An alternative is to group charges and fees by function and then adopt an ordinance setting the rates for each functional area.

Review charges and fees annually The third step involves each department reviewing the charges and fees it administers as part of the annual budget preparation process. Each department in Phoenix, Arizona, completes a "user fee analysis" form that identifies each service's total cost (direct and indirect), the expected revenues from the service at current rates, and the cost recovery ratio (revenues divided by cost).[8]

Recommend adjustments where appropriate As part of the detailed revenue analysis submitted to the city or county manager, the budget office includes a list of each governmental service for which a charge or fee is assessed and the proportion of cost recovered by the charge or fee. In consultation with each affected department, the budget office may include a recommendation for adjusting the charge or fee to better match the cost recovery target. For example, the Phoenix city council has established a minimum cost recovery ratio for each chargeable service. When the projected recovery ratio falls below that prescribed by the council, affected citizens groups and board and commission members consider a rate increase. Recommendations from departments for rate increases are then brought before the council for review and possible action.

While these four steps are necessary to improve the monitoring of charges and fees for governmental services, the following additional measures may be required to maximize the operational benefits of service charges.

Conduct cost-of-services study Periodically (although not annually), a **cost-of-services study** of governmental types of services should be undertaken to establish a baseline of the potential revenue available from users of each service. Such a study, typically undertaken by an outside consultant, also provides local government leaders with an objective reference point as to the proportion of costs that could be recovered through charges on users. Typically, a cost-of-services study identifies both **direct** and **indirect costs** for governmental services, which gives management a basis for better knowing the true cost of each service. More will be said on cost-of-services studies later in this chapter.

Introduce incentives   Managers may want to give department heads an incentive for pursuing the use of service charges by giving them greater discretion in the use of a portion of the charges they collect. The RAND Corporation has gone even further and suggested the creation of revenue centers within local government, also known as responsibility-centered management, which would strive for financial self-sufficiency and operate much like profit centers in a corporation.[9] Department heads should have some incentive for pursuing the use of service charges.

Summary

Administratively, the criteria for determining what services can be financed through charges are straightforward. If some or all of the benefits from the service accrue to identifiable individuals, and if those unwilling to pay for the service can be excluded from enjoying the benefits of the service, then the service can be priced. The more difficult political task involves identifying those services that *should* be sold. This involves examining the equity of a service charge, regional precedent, the citizens' tolerance of taxes as opposed to service charges, and the effect of a charge on demand.

This section has examined some of the legal and political barriers preventing local governments from making greater use of service charges and fees. The piece-meal adoption of a large number of charges and fees makes updating them legally complex and time-consuming. Political obstacles include the opposition of interest groups to a service charge, the indifference of taxpayers to the negligible benefits of a lower tax burden, and opposition from staff who fear that a service charge will adversely affect their budgets and staffing levels.

One approach to increasing the role of service charges and regulatory fees as a local revenue source is to design a strategy that integrates the review of all charges and fees into the budget preparation process. Another is to levy a charge only for extra levels of a service. Managers may also want to involve citizen groups and oversight boards in reviewing the rates for service charges and fees to monitor their impact on users and to alert local leaders to concerns that users may have with the administration of charges and fees.

Pricing public services

Once the decision to charge for a service has been made, discussion among public administrators and policy makers shifts to setting a fair price for the service. Most state laws and court decisions require that prices be reasonable and not arbitrary. In most states, local governments may earn a reasonable return on their investment (a profit), especially for enterprise services such as water, sewerage, and electric power.

Deciding on the right price for a service requires that public officials resolve the following issues:

- What proportion of the cost of a service should be recovered through service charges?

- How should the cost of a service be determined?
- How should rates be structured so as to reflect equitably the cost of serving different types of users?

Approaches to pricing services

A key policy issue that local governments must resolve is whether to price a service so that it recovers all or only a portion of the cost of the service. The common practice, especially for nonutility services, is to recover only part of the cost through service charges, with the remainder subsidized by general revenues. The sidebar on page 163 listing common services for which local governments commonly collect charges also identifies those services that should be priced at full (direct and indirect) cost, or at full cost for at least some users, and those for which partial cost recovery is justified.

The various pricing strategies available to local governments include **full-cost pricing, return-on-investment pricing, partial-cost pricing, competitive pricing,** and **marginal-cost pricing.**

Full-cost and return-on-investment pricing   Under most circumstances, enterprise services (e.g., utilities) should be priced at full cost, including both direct (production and distribution) and indirect costs associated with service provision. In some cases, a reasonable return on investment (i.e., a profit) is legally and administratively justified. Privately owned utilities earn a return on their investment, and it is reasonable for government-owned utilities to earn a comparable return. State and local laws vary in the amount of return authorized. For example, the Philadelphia Gas Commission permits an 8 percent return on investment for the city-owned natural gas distribution utility.[10] San Antonio, Texas, has authority to transfer to its general fund an amount equal to 14 percent of the gross receipts of the city-owned utilities, which the Texas Supreme Court ruled was reasonable.

Partial-cost pricing   For merit goods and services, a partial subsidy is usually warranted. This poses two issues that local governments must resolve when setting a price: (1) when should a subsidy be provided and (2) how much of a subsidy should be provided? For merit services, partial-cost pricing is justified when any of the following conditions exists:

- Some of the benefits from the service accrue to the whole community. For example, a rabies vaccination program reduces the risk of this disease for all pet owners, not just for those obtaining the inoculation. A portion of the program's costs should be funded from general revenues.

- The local government wants to stimulate demand for the service. For example, a county library provides long-term benefits to a community by enriching the community's quality of life. Policy makers can encourage library use by fully subsidizing its operations from general taxes or possibly by charging only a token fee for users.

- Enforcement of the charge at full cost would result in widespread evasion. For example, setting a fee for dog and cat tags at full cost may give pet owners an incentive to evade the purchase of these licenses. This situation then increases enforcement costs and creates an adversarial relationship between owners and the animal control unit. Partial-cost pricing may be justified under such circumstances.

- The service is used primarily by low-income households. For example, rental rates for public housing should be set below full cost, with the difference made up by subsidies from federal and state grants.

A checklist for estimating the private benefits of merit services

Question	Weight	Question	Weight
1. Does consumption of the service generate minimal spillover effects on other members of the community?	25	5. Would the imposition of beneficiary charges for the service lead to substantial revenues for the local government?	10
2. Is it possible to identify a specific beneficiary for this service?	20	6. Would benefit-based funding of this service result in enhanced efficiency?	10
3. Is the imposition of a beneficiary charge for this service statutorily and administratively feasible?	15	7. Would beneficiary charges for this service have negligible effects on the local government's competitive position?	5
4. Would the imposition of beneficiary charges for this service evoke negligible political opposition?	15		

When determining how much of the cost of a service should be recovered through charges to users, ask each of the foregoing questions of the service. Each "yes" answer is assigned the full weight from the right-hand column. Each "no" answer receives a value of zero. The total score suggests the percentage of the cost that should be recovered from service charges.

Source: Kevin Neels and Michael Caggiano, *The Entrepreneurial City: Innovations in Finance and Management for Saint Paul,* R-3123-SP/FF (Santa Monica, Calif.: RAND Corporation, October 1984), 13–14.

The second challenge for local governments is deciding how much of a subsidy is economically justified for services with spillover benefits to the community. In a study for St. Paul, Minnesota, Kevin Neels and Michael Caggiano proposed that each service be evaluated according to the seven questions listed in the accompanying sidebar. The sum of the points assigned to "yes" answers represents an estimate of the portion of full cost that should be recovered through charges. For example, using the suggested weights for these seven questions, a computer-based literature search by a public library should recover approximately 90 percent of its cost through user charges. The remaining 10 percent should be financed from general revenues.

Every local government should develop its own questions and weights on the basis of its values and preferences for using service charges. For example, Fort Worth, Texas, uses a similar approach but includes a question on the service's benefit to low-income users. The weight increases as the percentage of low-income beneficiaries declines.

Competitive pricing   A competitive pricing strategy considers the prices charged for comparable services by private or nonprofit providers or by surrounding local governments. For example, a village may set its admission price for a swimming pool to be competitive with the YMCA's charge. In the case of utility services, decision makers give particular consideration to the prices charged by surrounding jurisdictions and private suppliers. In the deregulated environment of today, especially for electric power and natural gas, public utilities must keep a close eye on the pricing practices of private providers who have an incentive to "cherry pick" (i.e., lure away the low-cost, high-revenue accounts).

Marginal-cost pricing   Another pricing strategy sets prices according to the marginal cost of producing the service: prices are set to reflect the cost of producing each additional unit of service. Economists support this approach because it leads to the most efficient allocation of resources in an economy. Since the price reflects the marginal cost, only consumers who value that additional unit will purchase it. However, this strategy poses significant administrative difficulties in determining the marginal cost of each service. It also leads to prices that do not always recover the full cost of producing a service. Some pricing structures may approximate marginal-cost pricing, such as peak-period and two-part tariff pricing, but pure marginal-cost pricing is rarely used in either the public or the private sectors.

Determining the cost of a service

Periodically, local governments should undertake a cost-of-services study to determine the full cost of providing chargeable services. For governmental services, usually a consolidated analysis for all services is undertaken at one time, with details on the cost (direct and indirect) of each service and the revenue potential from charges on users. For utility services, however, because of the complexity of their pricing structures and the amount of revenue generated, a separate rate analysis is prepared for each utility service by consulting firms that specialize in each type of utility. Knowing the full cost provides political, legal, and administrative benefits to local government managers and policy makers.

Rationale   Politically, a cost-of-services study or rate analysis provides a defensible basis for the price charged to users. In the case of merit goods and services, knowing the full cost also provides the manager with an indication of the value of the subsidy going to the service. Legally, cost analyses provide evidence of the reasonableness of a charge. They can buttress a government's contention that its prices were not arbitrarily set, particularly in cases where different rates are charged to different classes of users. For example, nonresidents may pay a higher water rate than residents because a rate analysis indicates that it is more costly to serve them. Finally, knowing the cost of providing services heightens administrators' awareness of the need to control costs. It aids managers in reviewing cost trends and their effect on budget allocations.

In-house or contract out?   A local government undertaking a cost-of-services study must decide whether to contract it out or use in-house personnel. Contracting out has several advantages, including giving citizens greater confidence in the objectivity of the cost estimates for each service, and does not divert valuable staff time from routine duties. However, if the local government has the necessary staff expertise, it may want to use in-house personnel because of their greater responsiveness to decision makers' information needs and the likelihood that the task will cost less to complete. Rate analyses are almost always contracted out because of the complexity of the task and of state and federal laws that affect the cost of providing services.

Costs to include   The objective of a cost-of-services study is to identify the cost of providing a service, but governments seldom maintain accounting information on the basis of costs (or expenses). Instead, budget information is maintained on the basis of expenditures (the value of goods and services purchased during the budget period), and these must be converted into costs (the value of the inputs used to produce the particular service during the budget period). The accompanying sidebar identifies the various types of costs that must be considered in a cost analysis.

Types of direct and indirect costs

Direct costs
Personnel: wages, benefits (vacation, insurance, sick leave, pension, employer's share of FICA taxes)

Other: equipment, supplies, contract services

Indirect costs
Administrative: general government (management, accounting, finance, purchasing, personnel, information technology, mail room), departmental administration (secretaries, department head), facilities

Other: operating (utilities), capital (space utilization)

Source: Adapted from Joseph T. Kelley, *Costing Government Services: A Guide for Decision Making* (Chicago: Government Finance Officers Association, 1984), 24.

Direct costs include those expenses that would be eliminated if the service were discontinued. Indirect costs result from the support (or staff) services provided by one department to other government departments, such as the cost of the city manager's office.

For utility services, local governments generally set rates so as to recover both direct and indirect costs. For services other than utilities, they almost never recover indirect costs, and recovery of full direct costs is even problematic because most of these services provide community-wide benefits. Park and recreation services, animal control, toll roads, public transit, and public health services all have community-wide as well as individual benefits.

One of the thorniest issues in cost analysis is the equitable allocation of indirect costs to each chargeable service. Support services, such as personnel or accounting, constitute indirect costs not only for line services but also for other support services. For example, the finance department provides accounting and payroll services to the water department and also to the personnel department, which is itself a support service for the water department. This complexity suggests the need for a series of simultaneous equations to determine the proper allocation ratio for the indirect costs of all government services.[11] Two less sophisticated procedures for allocating indirect costs—the consolidated allocation method and the step-down method—are usually used in cost studies.

The **consolidated allocation technique** involves summing the cost of all support services and then allocating these costs to each activity, including services sold for a price, using some allocation criterion such as each activity's share of the total budget or share of total salaries and fringe benefits. However, consolidated allocation completely ignores the interdependence of support services and thus allocates more support service costs to line activities (including chargeable services) than is justified.

The **step-down method** gives some consideration to the benefits that support services derive from each other. Support services are first ranked according to the amount of service each provides to all other support services. Line activities are not ranked. The benefits of each support service are then apportioned to all support services ranked below it. At least some compensation is thereby made for the benefits that support services derive from each other before indirect costs are allocated to line activities.[12] Properly allocating indirect costs will yield more accurate estimates of the true cost of providing services and provide a more accurate basis for pricing those services. However, the success of any allocation ratio ultimately depends on whether department heads are convinced that it is fair.

Structuring prices

Where the level of service consumption varies among users and where the cost of serving different user groups varies, charges should approximate the average cost of serving each group. Also, wherever possible, individual service use should be measured through metering or other means to ensure a more equitable allocation of the cost of providing a service. Metering is feasible for most utility services. In addition to the equity gains, metering ensures more efficient use of the service since the cost of wasteful consumption is borne by the user.

Local governments use one or a combination of several of the following pricing structures for their services: **flat-rate pricing, variable-rate pricing, block-rate pricing, peak-period pricing,** and **classification of users.**

Flat-rate pricing   In cases such as refuse collection for which measuring use is not feasible, a **flat fee** is usually assessed, based on the average cost of serving each class of user. Because flat fees provide no incentive to reduce wasteful consumption, they should be used only in cases where it is administratively infeasible to measure use. The monthly charge for residential bagged service for solid waste in Figure 8–2 is an example. Even the containerized service is a flat fee, although it increases as container capacity increases but at a declining rate because of the lower cost to collect each additional gallon (or cubic yard) of waste. The monthly residential drainage charge is also a flat fee, although it is scaled so that larger lots pay increasingly higher rates.

Sometimes, a flat fee is the most cost-effective way of allocating the cost among users. For example, the city of Austin considered charging each property owner for the cost of street cleaning on the basis of the number of linear feet of property fronting a street. The cost of collecting these data and justifying such an apportionment among property owners, without considering other factors such as street width and volume of traffic, made such a "metered" approach infeasible. The city instead resorted to a flat monthly fee of $2.60 for each residential property and $4.55 for each commercial parcel.[13] The anti-litter fee also pays for household hazardous-waste disposal.

Variable- and block-rate pricing   The variable rate, or **two-part tariff,** charges users a fixed rate (or facility charge) for the **fixed costs** of access to the service and a variable rate based on the volume of service used. Wastewater rates for the city of Denton, as shown in Figure 8–2 on page 165, use this pricing structure. A variation on the variable rate structure is a block rate structure, in which the volume rate changes for each block as consumption changes. A block rate structure reflects the fact that the per unit cost for overhead, capital, and operations changes as consumption changes. In some cases, as in the energy charge for wintertime use of electric power by residential consumers (see Figure 8–2), the block price declines as consumption increases. However, in the summer just the reverse occurs and higher levels of consumption move consumers into a higher-priced block. Such a pricing strategy approximates the marginal-cost pricing model.

Peak-period pricing   Peak period structures prices according to when a service is used. In cases where service cannot be stored, peak demand means that capacity must be built to satisfy peak usage. Charging the same rate for such service, regardless of time of use, means that off-peak-period users are subsidizing peak-period users. Public transit provides a good example. Fares should be higher during morning and evening rush hours to reflect the additional capacity in bus and rail service and the additional personnel required to meet demand during these periods. Similar capacity costs are incurred for water, sewer, electric power, and natural gas services. Both electric and water utilities for the city of Denton use peak-period pricing in combination with block pricing. Peak-period prices should vary according to the cycles in use of the service, such as by the hour, day, or season. For example, long-distance telephone rates reflect the daily and weekly cycles in telephone usage.

Pricing by classification of users   Classification of users may be according to type of user (elderly, children, handicapped), location of user (resident, non-resident), or location of service (transit zones). As shown in Figure 8–2, several utilities rely on separate price schedules for residential versus commercial/industrial users. Where costs vary by class of user, prices should be stratified so that low-cost users do not subsidize higher-cost users. Nonresidential rates are usually higher than residential rates because of the greater distance required to deliver services to nonresidents. However, the cost of serving different classes of users is not always the overriding consideration in classifying users; for example, adults generally pay a higher admission charge to recreation services than children do, but this does not reflect actual higher costs in serving adults.

Summary

This section has examined some of the issues encountered in pricing public services—for example, determining when a partial subsidy from general revenues is appropriate, deciding on the amount of a subsidy, and arriving at a reasonable rate of return for utility services. The discussion also addressed several important issues in costing services, including the sensitive issue of allocating the indirect costs of support services. Local governments use a number of pricing structures, including a flat fee, a variable rate structure, a block structure, peak-period pricing, and classification of users, as well as combinations of these approaches. The next section examines the administration of service charges and strategies for reducing collection costs.

Administering service charges and regulatory fees

Many of the issues associated with the collection and enforcement of service charges parallel those associated with the property tax, and most of the recommendations for improving the collection of current and delinquent property taxes apply to service charges as well, especially to those for utility services.

Collecting current charges and fees

Service charges are collected in one of two ways: at the point of sale (such as a rental charge for the use of recreation equipment or an admission charge to an ice skating rink) or on a periodic basis for the service used (such as a monthly statement for the quantity of water consumed). While the first approach eliminates the problem of delinquency, it is usually more costly to administer relative to the amount of revenue collected. Periodic billing of users yields the largest portion of revenue from service charges, especially for utility services. However, managing these accounts receivable creates many of the same problems a private firm encounters when it extends short-term credit to its customers.

One of the advantages of a billing system is that the cost of administering each account declines as the number of accounts increases. Local governments typically economize even further by piggybacking several utility and related service charges onto one billing system. For example, charges for water, sewer, solid-waste (refuse) collection, and electric power may be listed on one statement. While water usage is usually metered, sewerage charges are usually based on a proxy measure such as the average volume of water used during the winter months. Residential refuse col-

Strategies for improving collection of charges and fees

Current accounts

Design the utility statements to catch the attention of users and clearly communicate the amount of payment and the due date.

Keep account records current, especially mailing addresses; consider developing a consolidated database of utility and taxpayer accounts.

Provide for Web-based payment and automatic bank draft options now commonplace with many private firms. Allow payment by credit or debit card.

Adopt penalties and interest charges that make delinquency unrewarding.

Consider the cost-effectiveness of contracting out collection of current and delinquent accounts.

Delinquent accounts

Establish a legal basis and procedure for collecting delinquent accounts.
1. Establish liability for utility charges
2. Specify the steps for collecting delinquency charges and increase the intensity of each step in the process.
3. Use discretionary powers such as setoff provisions in contracts, attornment of rent, and liens on the property of delinquent customers.
4. Require a deposit.

Consider contracting out collection of delinquent payments to a private law firm.

Consider developing an amnesty program to reduce the backlog of delinquent accounts, especially for delinquent parking and traffic citations.

---

lection is usually a flat monthly fee, with higher fees for commercial and industrial customers.

Local governments should achieve at least a 95 percent collection rate on current accounts. That is, no more than 5 percent of the current charges for billed services should be delinquent. As with the property tax, achieving this collection rate depends on local economic conditions, including the unemployment level, and on the aggressiveness of the collection effort. The accompanying sidebar lists some strategies for improving collection of current and delinquent charges.

Improving the collection of current charges must begin with the design of the statement. Local governments tend to pack too much information onto the invoice, forcing customers to spend time trying to figure out how much they owe. Above all, invoices should make clear the amount currently owed, the basis for determining that amount (quantity used and rates), and the payment due date. If a discount is offered for early payment, this should also be indicated on the statement. However, evidence suggests that discounts do not significantly improve collection rates and that their costs do not justify their benefits to local governments.

One of the greatest challenges confronting those responsible for managing accounts receivable is keeping mailing addresses current. This same problem plagues property tax collections, and the solutions offered in Chapter 4 apply here as well. At a minimum, local governments should request notification of change of address from the postal service. In addition, the customer records for utility and property tax accounts should be consolidated into one database. This economizes on updating information (such as changes of address) and makes referencing payment histories much easier. Property owners who are delinquent in paying their property taxes are often delinquent on their utility payments as well.

More and more, governments are giving customers the option of using the Internet to pay recurring service charges as well as traffic or parking citations. As discussed in Chapter 4 with the property tax, citizens are growing increasingly comfortable with online shopping and payment options for their purchases. Extending this same option for government-provided services improves citizen satisfaction because of the convenience, enhances the image of local government as concerned about cost reduction, accelerates the collection of good funds through the payment of receivables with a credit or debit card or with a bank draft, and thereby reduces collection costs.

One of the most effective tools for controlling the turnover of accounts receivables is the imposition of penalties and interest for late payment. Both must be established in local or, less often, state law. A penalty is usually a flat charge that is applied once an account becomes delinquent. Interest is an additional variable charge that is applied each month (or day or week) that the account remains unpaid. In the case of utilities, local governments typically work out a payment plan with delinquent users that may involve charging only interest on the unpaid balance. During slow economic periods when unemployment rates increase, local governments typically see an uptick in the length of time their account receivables go unpaid. Prior to terminating service, utility providers typically notify the delinquent user by mail, followed by a phone call or personal visit if the account remains unpaid for more than a month. During extreme weather periods (the hottest part of the summer and coldest part of the winter), local utility providers must exercise extreme caution in order not to terminate service and thereby precipitate a tragedy.

In some cases, local governments may find it cost-effective to contract out collection to another local government or a private firm. This will more likely be true where the local government provides only one utility service and has few opportunities to piggyback a number of charges onto one statement. Penn Hills, Pennsylvania, contracts out the collection of current and delinquent sewerage charges to the same private firm that collects its earned income tax.

Collecting delinquent receivables

The sidebar on improving collections also includes suggestions for improving the collection of delinquent accounts. Considerable time and energy are spent by the finance office and the manager's staff in pursuing delinquent payments. An administratively sound program for collecting delinquent receivables must have a legal basis in local or state law as well as a policy statement specifying the procedures for collection.

Establish legal authority   The legal authority for pursuing delinquent accounts should ensure the following:

First, liability for utility charges must be established. This is particularly important for rental property, where customer turnover is higher and delinquent users are more difficult to track down.

Second, local law should clearly specify the steps for collecting delinquent charges. As a result of their proprietary powers, local governments usually have the authority to terminate service to delinquent users. However, customers are protected by the due process provisions of the Fourteenth Amendment and must be given adequate notice and an opportunity for an administrative hearing prior to termination of service. Local law should also specify when an account becomes delinquent—for example, three days following the payment due date.

Third, if state law permits the attachment of a lien on the property of delinquent customers, procedures for doing so should be specified in local law. Another approach used by some local governments is to include in all contracts a setoff provision whereby payment is withheld by the local government from contractors who are delinquent with their utility payment. An even more forceful measure, attornment of rent, is used in Ontario, Canada, for the collection of property taxes. Attornment, in effect, garnishees the rental payments owed to landlords who are delinquent with their utility payments.

Fourth, as protection against delinquencies, local governments require a deposit from customers and specify in law the amount of deposit and the conditions for waiving it. If the customer is a higher risk (or has a lower credit rating), a reasonable deposit would equal service charges for at least one month's service and perhaps more. Local governments should provide a reasonable rate of interest for the time they hold the deposit. It is common practice for local governments to return a deposit after the customer has demonstrated a pattern of prompt payments.

Contracting out collection Local governments should consider the cost-effectiveness of contracting out collection of delinquent utility payments to a private law firm specializing in this service. Contracting out often lowers the cost of collecting these accounts and avoids diverting staff expertise from routine tasks. Most important, it reduces the adversarial role of government with delinquent customers.

Amnesty programs One approach to reducing the backlog of delinquent receivables—both for services and for regulatory activities such as traffic and parking citations—has gained popularity with local managers in recent years: an amnesty program for delinquent accounts. The city of Chicago conducted a successful amnesty program for delinquent parking citations that reduced the number of outstanding citations by 250,000 and netted the city $9 million in revenue.[14] Unfortunately, amnesty programs are most attractive when local (and state) governments are facing severe revenue shortfalls. As a result, such programs tend to be poorly planned, communicated, and administered. Chicago's experience provides evidence, however, that with careful planning, aggressive enforcement *prior* to the amnesty period, and ramping up customer service capacity prior to the program's implementation, an amnesty program can significantly reduce delinquent receivables.

Designing a policy for service charges and fees

Chapter 2 described some of the benefits of adopting a revenue policy statement, including the opportunity to make explicit the assumptions underlying the financing of government operations. This section offers specific suggestions about the design of a policy statement on service charges and fees. Managers may want to propose a broad policy covering all types of charges and fees, with separate sections devoted to particular service areas, such as utility services, recreation and parks, sanitation, and health. The alternative is to adopt separate policy statements for each major service area.

A policy statement should address the following issues.

Integration with budget process First, as discussed earlier in the chapter, review of all charges and fees should be integrated into the budget preparation process. A policy statement should assign responsibility for overseeing implementation and review of this task. In Phoenix, Arizona, the manager, budget office, and internal auditor review department estimates of costs for chargeable services.[15] (The auditor also reviews service fees as requested by departments and the manager throughout the year.) The finance department then prepares a consolidated report on proposed fee adjustments approved by the manager for presentation to the city council.

Schedule for cost-of-services studies Second, a policy statement on charges and fees should specify the frequency with which a cost-of-services study will be undertaken and the cost-of-living index to be used in the intervening years to adjust rates.

Levels of subsidy   Third, a policy statement on charges and fees should provide guidelines on the types of services that will be priced at less than full cost and the level of subsidy provided. As noted earlier in the chapter, the city council of Phoenix, Arizona, has established a cost recovery ratio for every service for which a charge is levied. Services with projected recovery ratios below the prescribed levels are brought before council during budget review for a possible rate increase. Thornton, Colorado, classifies its park and recreation services into one of three categories: self-sustaining activities, partially sustaining activities, and services for which a token fee is charged.

Collection

Finally, a policy statement should provide guidelines on the collection of charges and fees. Guidelines are particularly important for utility services where delinquency is a problem. At a minimum, the policy should specify the amount of deposit required from new customers, the procedures for collecting delinquent charges, and the sanctions to be used against delinquent customers.

Summary and recommendations

On the basis of the discussion in this chapter, the following recommendations are made to assist local public officials in the use of service charges.

Local governments should make greater use of service charges because such charges provide an equitable source of revenue (those using the service pay in proportion to the benefits they receive) and promote efficiency by discouraging wasteful use of government services.

Service charges improve local government productivity by increasing managers' awareness of the cost of services. Charges to users also slow the growth of local budgets by ensuring that decisions are based not on interdepartmental budgetary politics but on the relationship of service level to demand.

An obstacle to increased use of service charges is their piecemeal adoption in separate ordinances, which means that they are dispersed throughout the code of local laws. Local governments should consolidate charges and fees in their code of ordinances. Another barrier to increased use of service charges is the political imbalance between the negligible benefits to taxpayers from a new charge and the noticeable cost to users of the service. This makes it politically difficult for elected lawmakers to support such proposals, especially if there are no significant benefits from a reduction in taxes. One strategy for increasing the use of service charges is to review adjustments in rates en masse rather than piecemeal. Support can also be created through citizens' advisory groups and boards that review the merits of an adjustment in charges.

As part of the budget preparation process, department heads should review all charges and fees annually and recommend rate adjustments as needed. These recommendations should then be presented to council as part of the annual budget review. Normally, charging a price for a service reduces the demand for it. The greater the price change, the greater the effect on service use. For this reason, local governments should make small, annual adjustments and avoid large, irregular adjustments in rates.

Deciding on a fair price for a service requires that managers know its cost and the subsidy, if any, that it receives. For services providing only private benefits, such as utility services, full-cost pricing (with possibly a return on investment) is appropriate. Partial-cost pricing is appropriate for services with some spillover benefits to the community or services for which local governments want to encourage demand.

A periodic cost-of-services study should be undertaken to establish a benchmark for the direct and indirect costs of each service. A sensitive issue in the costing of services is the allocation of the indirect costs of support services, such as those associated with the manager's office or accounting. An equitable basis should be found for allocating these costs to all activities, including those for which charges are not collected.

When the cost of serving different groups of users varies, charges should be stratified to approximate the average cost of serving each group. A flat-rate pricing structure is the simplest to design, but it is the least economically efficient because users have no incentive to ration their use of the service. Moreover, it is less equitable because those using less of the service subsidize those using more. Alternative pricing structures that more efficiently and equitably allocate costs include a variable rate (or two-part tariff) structure, peak-period pricing, and classification of users.

Managing the accounts receivable for service charges creates opportunities and problems similar to those encountered by private firms that extend short-term credit to their customers. Local governments should achieve at least a 95 percent collection rate on current accounts; no more than 5 percent of the current charges for billed services should be delinquent.

One advantage of a billing system is that a number of charges can be piggybacked onto one statement. Statements should communicate clearly to customers the amount owed, the date payment is due, and any discounts for early payment.

Local governments should adopt a policy statement on service charges and fees that assigns responsibility for annually reviewing rates as part of the budget process; specifies the frequency with which a cost-of-services study will be undertaken; and provides guidelines on the types of services that will be priced at less than full cost, the level of subsidy provided, and the collection of current and delinquent charges, including the amount of deposit required from new customers.

1 William G. Colman, *A Quiet Revolution in Local Government Finance: Policy and Administrative Challenges in Expanding the Role of User Charges in Financing State and Local Government* (Washington, D.C.: National Academy of Public Administration, November 1983), 9.

2 Anthony Pascal, *EBBF: A Guide to Installing Equitable Beneficiary-Based Finance in Local Government,* R-3124-HHS/SP/FF (Santa Monica: RAND Corporation, June 1984), 16.

3 Thomas L. McClimon and Yolanda Y. Rious, *User Fees: Towards Better Usage* (Washington, D.C.: U.S. Conference of Mayors and Arthur Young & Co., April 1987), 6.

4 Harvey E. Brazer, "User Charges in an Environment of Fiscal Limitation," in *Proceedings of the Seventy-Sixth Annual Conference of the National Tax Association–Tax Institute of America* (Seattle, Wash., 1983), 204.

5 Robert Cline, *Local Revenue Diversification, User Charges,* SR-6 (Washington, D.C.: U.S. Advisory Commission on Intergovernmental Relations, October 1987), 47.

6 Colman, A *Quiet Revolution,* 12.

7 Stanley E. Wilkes Jr., *A Guide to Revenue Administration for Small Cities* (Arlington: University of Texas at Arlington, Institute for Urban Studies, September 1981), 24–25.

8 "User Fee Annual Review Program" (Phoenix, Ariz.: City Auditor Department, December 2004). Available at http://phoenix.gov/auditor.

9 Kevin Neels and Michael Caggiano, *The Entrepreneurial City: Innovations in Finance and Management for Saint Paul,* R-3123-SP/FF (Santa Monica, Calif.: RAND Corporation, October 1984), 27–62.

10 Andre C. Dasent and George J. Whelan, "Government-Owned Utilities: A Rationale for Payments Made to Government Owners," *Government Finance Review* 4 (February 1988): 20.

11 Kyland Howard, "Determining Appropriate User Fees," *MIS Report* 19, no. 9 (Washington, D.C.: International City Management Association, September 1987), 9.

12 A case study of how to allocate indirect costs using the city of Amherst, Massachusetts, is provided in *Using User Fees: A Guide for Massachusetts Cities and Towns,* SP–129 (Amherst: University of Massachusetts, Cooperative Extension Service), 13–21.

13 City of Austin, Texas, *Solid Waste Services, 2004.* Available at www.ci.austin.tx.us/sws/rates.htm.

14 Matt Darst, "That's the Ticket: Lessons Learned from Chicago's Parking Ticket Amnesty Program," *Government Finance Review* 20 (August 2004): 46–50.

15 "User Fee Annual Review Program."

9 Impact fees and special assessments

Don't tax me, and don't tax thee; tax that man behind the tree.

—Senator Russell Long

Impact fees and special assessments

M ore and more, local governments that are experiencing rapid increases in population are relying on development fees to finance the capital cost of additional public facilities. Historically, developers have been required to dedicate on-site facilities as a condition of approval for their development. More recently, however, local governments have extended that responsibility to include off-site improvements needed to serve the new development. For example, developers may be required to finance arterial roads or an expansion of sewer treatment and water facilities needed to provide services to new residents.

Impact fees are charges to developers for off-site improvements that the local government must provide to serve the new development. **Connection charges** are another type of levy used to recover the cost of off-site improvements. While impact fees provide up-front financing for the expansion of public facilities, connection charges allow the developer to buy into the existing capacity of public facilities. A third approach is to require developers to **dedicate improvements**—such as new streets, lighting, and drainage—as a condition for local government approval of the new subdivision.

Impact fees and similar levies for off-site improvements have become popular with local governments whose populations are growing rapidly and whose public facilities are at capacity. Traditionally, the cost of adding facilities has been borne by all users through increased charges and taxes. However, the advent of the tax limitation movement and the retrenchment in federal aid have made it increasingly difficult for local governments to sustain this method of financing additional public facilities. Local governments in Arizona, California, Colorado, Florida, Texas, and Washington, in particular, use impact fees extensively to partially shift the burden of new growth to new residents.

Special assessments, another form of benefits-based financing of public facilities, capture the increase in property values that results from public improvements. By shifting part of the cost of public improvements to property owners who benefit from increased property values, special assessments promote equity. For example, widening a street through a commercial area of town increases the volume of traffic through the area and property values for owners of businesses adjacent to the project. An assessment equal to the increase in each property's value eliminates any windfalls these property owners would otherwise have received at other taxpayers' expense.

Prior to the Depression, local governments used special assessments extensively to finance street improvements and the installation of water and sewer lines. During the Depression, widespread default on debt backed by special assessments resulted in the virtual abandonment of this method of financing public improvements. However, special assessments have made a comeback in recent years. At a developer's request, the local government creates a special assessment district to obtain tax-exempt financing for public improvements in the district.[1] The narrower definition of public-purpose debt in the Tax Reform Act of 1986 limits this use of special assessment financing to public improvements such as streets and utility systems.

This chapter treats some of the management and policy issues that local governments encounter in the adoption and administration of impact fees and special assessments, including

- What are the steps involved in adopting an impact fee?
- What effect do impact fees have on the cost of new housing?
- What are the legal obstacles to impact fees?
- What procedures do state laws usually require for the adoption of special assessments?
- What legal and administrative issues do local governments encounter when using special assessments?

Impact fees

Impact fees are most widely used by governments in the Sun Belt states, where heavy population migration has strained existing public facilities. Advocates claim that impact fees reduce the financial burden on current residents, who would otherwise share the cost of new facilities through higher taxes and service charges. Understandably, impact fees on new development are popular with current residents and unpopular with developers.

Cities in Colorado have the longest experience with impact fees, although the fees are most widely used by cities and counties in California.[2] Florida, where use of these levies is growing, holds the distinction of having the most well-developed case law on the use of impact fees. Another trend has been for states to grant explicit authority for the fees in statutes rather than relying on local governments' regulatory powers. At least twenty states have adopted enabling legislation since 1987 when Texas was the first to do so.[3]

Impact fees were initially used to finance off-site expansion of water and sewer treatment facilities. During the 1970s, their use was extended to cover the cost of expanding arterial roads serving a new development; solid-waste disposal capacity; storm drainage; beach and park acquisition; and police, fire, school, and public transit facilities. Although state courts have generally upheld these extensions as long as evidence indicates that the new development has created the need for additional facilities, impact fees continue to pose difficult political and legal questions for local government managers and policy makers.

Adopting and administering impact fees

Figure 9–1 identifies the steps that local governments generally take to adopt an impact fee ordinance. States statutes and court rulings now generally require that the revenue from the fee not exceed the cost of constructing the facilities needed to serve a new development. The critical stage in fee adoption is the process of documenting the cost of capital improvements needed to serve new residents; costs, in turn, depend on reasonable assumptions about land use and projections of needed capital improvements. Once these costs are determined, policy makers must decide what portion will be covered through an impact fee and what portion should be paid from other revenues.

Figure 9–1
Stages in the adoption of an impact fee.

| Prepare land use plan | → | Define service areas and determine capital needs in each | → | Develop capital improvements plan and prepare budget | → | Determine capital improvements needed to serve new residents | → | Adopt impact fee by ordinance or order | → | Establish accounting guidelines for recording use of revenue from fee |

Designing an impact fee   The first issue to resolve in the design of an impact fee is the type of improvements to be financed. Although an increasing variety of improvements are financed by impact fees, water and sewer facilities are the most common. Compared with local governments in other states, those in California and Colorado use impact fees for a wider variety of purposes, including school buildings, storm drainage, and arterial road improvements.

The second issue is the basis for liability. While state law, such as Texas's, may specify the procedures and formulae for calculating fees, more than likely the statute has left such administrative details to specification in local ordinance. The first step is to determine the service area to which the fee will be applied; for some improvements such as parks, this may be city- or countywide; for others, such as for storm drainage, the calculations will be for a particular region or sector of the jurisdiction. The next step is to develop a decision matrix to allocate the costs for off-site improvements needed by the new development to that geographic area. For water and wastewater improvements, fees are often assessed on a per housing unit basis. For commercial and industrial development, an even more sophisticated formula may be necessary that takes into consideration the effluent created by the development and the cost of treating it.

The third issue in designing an impact fee is whether the fee should be stratified by type of property (residential, commercial, or industrial) or by the location of the property (inside or outside corporate limits, or by zones). Impact fees for roads, fire protection, and park improvements are often based on zones, with higher fees charged in zones requiring more improvements. Fees may also vary according to whether the development is inside or outside the corporate limits of the local government but within its planning jurisdiction.

Once the fee's scope and structure have been determined, a fair rate must be set in the ordinance, based on the cost of constructing the public facilities needed to serve the development. State courts have become more insistent that local government accounting procedures provide assurance that the funds will be used to construct facilities that benefit new residents. The ordinance should specify the design of the fee, including the types of improvements it will finance (the fee's scope), the basis for determining each property's liability (the fee's structure), and whether different rates will be charged to different classes of property according to the cost of serving each type (fee stratification). The ordinance should then specify the collection procedures, including when the fee is collected, how the fee will be phased in initially, and the procedures for accounting for receipts and disbursements.

Collecting impact fees   The preference among local governments is to collect impact fees along with other fees when a building permit is issued. In a nationwide study of municipalities charging sewer impact fees, more than 70 percent collected the fee when a building permit was issued, and about 15 percent collected the fee at the plat approval stage.[4] Although collection at the building permit stage is more administratively convenient, collection at the plat approval stage gives the local government control over the funds much earlier. Sometimes local governments allow split payment of the fee, with half due at plat approval and the balance due when a building permit is issued. If a formula is used to determine fee liability, collection at the building permit stage is more appropriate since more information is available to compute liability.

Impact fees should be phased in over at least a two-year period to give developers an opportunity to shift the fee backward to landowners through capitalization and to reduce the likelihood that the cost of the fee will be borne by builders' existing inventory of residential or commercial development.

The final issue in fee collection is ensuring that receipts and disbursements are carefully accounted for. Whether the fee is based on the regulatory powers of local government or on specific statutory authority, revenues cannot exceed the cost of providing the needed facilities. Usually, governments adopting an impact fee establish a separate fund in which to record receipts and disbursements. Some establish a restricted set of accounts within existing capital improvements funds. State courts have generally looked much more favorably on fees that have been segregated either through a separate fund or in restricted accounts of an existing fund.

Objections to impact fees

Local governments considering an impact fee will encounter at least three objections to its adoption. First, opponents will contend that the fees increase housing costs, especially for low- and moderate-income families, thereby stifling economic growth in the community. Second, some may argue that impact fees are unfair because they require new residents to pay twice for public facilities—once through these fees and again through taxes and utility service charges used to retire the debt on existing facilities. Third, opponents believe that impact fees unfairly benefit current residents by giving them access to expanded public facilities (such as wider roads and larger water treatment capacity) without requiring them to bear the cost of that expansion.

Impact fees and housing prices   Developers and builders often oppose impact fees because of their potential inflationary effect on housing prices. An impact fee of $3,000 per house is assumed to increase housing prices by at least $3,000, and probably more after the builder includes financing costs associated with the fee. Intuitively, it appears that the final buyer of a home would bear the cost of the impact fee. Certainly, developers and builders will not bear the cost if they can pass it on to the buyer. However, economic theory and market analysis indicate that this is rarely the case. Because the housing market is competitive and many comparable substitutes exist (in both new and used housing), new housing prices are determined by relative supply and demand, not by the cost of production. If in the short term the demand for housing exceeds available supply, then prices will rise. Conversely, prices will fall whenever supply exceeds demand.

With few exceptions home buyers are extremely sensitive to prices because of the large investment and risks involved. In most markets, substitutes are readily available. Rarely do all local governments in a region levy an impact fee, and when they do, the fees are seldom set at the same rate. Where comparable housing is available in communities with a lower impact fee or no fee at all, builders will be unable to shift the impact fee's cost forward. If a house sells for $100,000 in a community without an impact fee, then comparable housing in surrounding communities with an impact fee cannot sell for more than $100,000—regardless of the cost to the builder.

If competitive market forces prevent the impact fee from being shifted forward, who bears the cost? In the short term (one to three years) after adoption of a fee, builders will likely bear most of the cost on their existing inventory of housing—either accepting lower profits or cutting their costs by downsizing lots or structures or by using lower-quality materials. However, if the fee is phased in by the local government over two or three years, much of its short-term adverse effects on builders and developers can be avoided, possibly reducing some of their opposition to the fee.

In the long term, the cost of impact fees is shifted *backward* to landowners in the form of lower prices for undeveloped land. That is, fees are capitalized into land values. Why? The following scenario, cited by Thomas Snyder and Michael Stegman, illustrates the usual procedures developers follow in determining their bid price for raw land:

Officials from two large development companies in Orange County, California, described how they decided on the price they would pay for raw land. Their land pricing began with as good an estimate as possible of the likely sales price of the finished house. . . . From the market-determined sales price the developers subtracted all hard and soft costs of production, including the asking price of the land. The amount left over equaled the residual profit to the developer. If that amount was below the company's targeted profit per housing unit . . . [the company] would lower its bid price for the land until its targeted rate of return could be achieved.[5]

In other words, as building costs increase, including an impact fee, the price that developers are willing to bid for the land declines. The following conditions are necessary for the backward shifting (capitalization) of impact fees:

• Home buyers are price sensitive; that is, they comparison shop for housing, seeking the lowest-priced home with the desired structural and neighborhood amenities.

• Substitute housing is readily available in nearby communities offering comparable public services, particularly public schools.

• Not all governments in the region levy an impact fee, and the rates among those with a fee vary.

Except in those rare cases when buyers are insensitive to price (i.e., they will pay whatever it costs to buy a house in the desired community, especially for high-priced, custom-designed homes) or comparable housing is not available in adjoining communities, the cost of impact fees will ultimately be borne by landowners, regardless of who writes the check for the fee. However, if impact fees are levied at a uniform rate by all communities in the region, their cost will be shifted forward to the final buyer as a higher price for housing.

Several formal studies have validated the backward shifting of the fee onto property values.[6] In one particular analysis using property values from Dade County, Florida, the researchers found that not only do land values decline by an amount equal to the capitalized value of the impact fee, but housing prices increase about half again the cost of the fee. Arthur Nelson and Mitch Moody posited that the increase in housing values may result from the leveraging effect of impact fees (such as being used to provide matching funds for federal or state grants) or that because of the fee, home owners are assured of a certain level of service regardless of the impact of growth.[7]

A related question concerns the impact of these fees on the local economy. Some have argued that impact fees slow local development through increased housing (and commercial/industrial) costs and thus lower local employment levels. If this is the case, communities with impact fees should have lower rates of growth in employment, other things being equal. Nelson and Moody tested this question using data from Florida's sixty-seven counties, half of which have adopted impact fees.[8] They concluded that, rather than slowing growth, impact fees actually aid growth. They conjectured that impact fees assure new arrivals that services will be available to meet their needs regardless of the rate of growth, and they assure developers that services will be available in the areas from which the fees are collected. The irony may well be that impact fees have become a developer's ally rather than albatross.

Unfairness to new residents Another objection to impact fees is that they subject buyers of new homes or commercial space to a double payment for public improvements—once through the impact fee for new facilities and again through taxes and service charges used to retire the debt that financed existing facilities. If fees are borne by the landowners rather than by the final buyer, the double payment problem does not exist. However, most new arrivals to a community believe that they, not the landowners, bear the cost of the impact fee. Local governments typically deal with this perception by lowering impact fees by an amount equal to the portion of taxes and service charges used to service the debt on existing facilities. In fact, local governments usually set fees well below the full cost of constructing additional facilities, partly to correct for double payment, but mostly to decrease the visibility of fees and thus defuse political opposition.

Windfall to current residents   Current residents benefit in two possible ways from the adoption of an impact fee. First, existing facilities were financed in part by previous generations of residents who recognized the need to provide adequate capacity for their own use as well as for that of later generations. Impact fees alter this pattern by shifting the cost of expansion to new residents. Current residents reap a windfall because they benefit from the investment of previous users without bearing the cost of providing facilities for successive generations.

What of the second benefit to current residents, who are assured of an adequate capacity in public facilities without having to pay for it? If the indirect benefits to current residents are considered significant, then impact fees should be lowered to shift a greater share of the cost of new improvements to current residents.

These three objections to impact fees—their effect on housing prices, the double payment problem, and the windfall to current residents—do not nullify their equity or efficiency. Impact fees often provide a politically acceptable means of financing needed expansion in public facilities without unfairly burdening current residents. Once a local government decides to adopt an impact fee, determining the legal basis for the levy then becomes the critical issue.

Impact fees and the law

Local government managers and policy makers must give careful attention to the design of a legally defensible impact fee. Legal challenges to impact fees typically focus on two issues. First, what is the basis in state statutes for the fee? Second, do impact fees violate the constitutionally guaranteed protections of due process and equal protection or represent an unconstitutional taking of private property?

Statutory tests of validity   Local governments rely either on specific authority in state statutes or on their regulatory powers—their power to promote the community's health, safety, and general welfare—to levy an impact fee. Virtually all local governments have established the authority to regulate land use. Planning, zoning, and subdivision control statutes often refer to these regulatory powers. Such powers are inherently broad, and state courts have recognized that it is impossible for legislatures to enumerate all the duties that qualify as promoting health, safety, and general welfare. Because they are designed to ensure an adequate supply of public facilities, impact fees represent a logical extension of a local government's responsibility to regulate land use in the public interest. As a regulatory measure, however, an impact fee cannot exceed the cost of providing additional capacity; if it did, the fee would constitute a tax, and the courts would look to state statutes for specific enabling legislation.

Relying solely on regulatory powers has resulted in too much ambiguity for developers and local planning and engineering staff, precipitating costly litigation. In response, at least twenty states have adopted legislation specifying (1) the type of public improvements that can be funded by impact fees, (2) that an analysis of the costs imposed by new development and the service area be undertaken, (3) at what point in the development process fees may be collected, (4) the accounting procedures for impact fee revenues, and (5) the length of time the revenue may be held by the local government before it must be used.[9]

Constitutional tests of validity   Litigation involving impact fees routinely challenges their constitutionality on two grounds: first, they are held to violate due process and equal protection; second, they are held to constitute a taking of private property without just compensation. The state courts' task is to determine when local government regulatory powers violate constitutional guarantees.

When impact fees are challenged as a violation of due process, they are held to be arbitrary and unreasonable, thereby denying property owners equal protection under the law. State courts have developed three tests to determine whether an impact fee does in fact violate due process and equal protection. The earliest and most restrictive test was promulgated in 1961 by the Illinois Supreme Court, which stated that impact fees are reasonable and not arbitrary only if they are "specifically and uniquely attributable" to the new development.[10] That is, new development has to be the sole beneficiary of improvements financed with an impact fee. Since most off-site improvements involve the expansion of facilities used by the entire community, few improvements satisfy this test.

The second and most permissive test was promulgated a decade later by the California Supreme Court, which held that only a "reasonable relationship" had to exist between the development where the fee is assessed and the beneficiaries of the service. The need for expanding service capacity does not have to originate with the development, although the development must benefit from those facilities to some extent.[11]

A third test, which is emerging as the preferred standard among state courts, requires that a "rational nexus" exist between the new development and the facilities financed with an impact fee.[12] According to this test, first adopted by the Wisconsin Supreme Court in 1966, a rational nexus exists if the local government can demonstrate that the population growth from new development has created the need to expand existing facilities (the "needs test") and that home owners paying the fee are also the ones benefiting from the expanded facilities (the "benefits test"). In *Nolan v. California Coastal Commission* (1987), the U.S. Supreme Court added its support to the **rational nexus test** by ruling that there must be a rational nexus between a regulatory measure (such as an impact fee) and the benefits from the measure.

With respect to the second constitutional challenge, impact fees may constitute a taking of private property without fair compensation if they are not proportional to the cost of adding public facilities to serve the new development. Fees in excess of such costs may be considered confiscatory and thus an unconstitutional taking of property.[13] Along these lines, state courts have also ruled that impact fees cannot be used to modernize or otherwise upgrade existing facilities at the expense of newcomers.[14]

Developing a legally acceptable fee ordinance   The following guidelines, which are based on the foregoing discussion, will help local governments prepare an ordinance or order levying an impact fee:

- A local government contemplating the adoption of an impact fee would be wise to secure competent legal expertise early in the process to ensure that the ordinance meets legal standards and to better prepare the government for possible litigation.

- Prior to adopting an impact fee, the local government must document the improvements needed to serve new growth and the cost of those improvements.

- The impact fee should not provide more revenue than the cost of the needed improvements. In fact, the fee should be lower than the cost of the improvements, with the difference being made up by current residents based on their assurance of adequate capacity in public facilities.

- The ordinance or order adopting an impact fee should refer to the state statute that authorizes the levy as an exercise either of the local government's regulatory powers or of its taxing powers.

- The local government should be able to document that the fee was not used to renovate existing facilities that have deteriorated as a result of neglect or use.

- The ordinance should make clear the types of development subject to the fee, whether redevelopment is subject to the fee, and whether tax-exempt property (including that of other governments) is subject to the fee.

Summary

Impact fees provide local governments with a means of shifting the cost of additional public facilities to those who benefit from them. The ordinance that levies the fee should specify the types of improvements financed by the fee, the basis for determining liability, and whether rates should be stratified by the type or the location of property. The fee ordinance should also specify when in the development process the fee will be collected. Most governments collect it at the building permit stage along with other development-related fees. Local governments should develop accounting procedures capable of documenting that fees were used to finance projects directly benefiting those paying the fee.

Impact fees remain popular with current residents in rapidly growing parts of the country, who see them as a more equitable way of providing additional service capacity than relying on taxes and service charges on all residents. However, opponents contend that impact fees increase the cost of housing, are potentially unfair to new residents, and provide a windfall in benefits to current residents. In fact, except under unusual market conditions, impact fees are capitalized into lower land values rather than being shifted forward to buyers (or renters) as higher prices for housing or commercial space.

Legally, impact fees have been challenged on both statutory and constitutional grounds. In order to reduce the ambiguity and ensuing litigation when local governments rely on their regulatory powers to levy impact fees, most states have resorted to specific enabling legislation that defines the procedures and types of improvements for which impact fees can be collected. State courts have generally held that impact fees do not deny due process or equal protection as long as a rational nexus exists between the need for additional capacity in public facilities and the growth from new development.

Special assessments

Special assessments are levies on property owners for the increased property values created by a public improvement. The amount of a property's assessment is computed as a pro rata share of the costs of the project not to exceed the increase in the property's value attributable to the project. Rarely do special assessments recover the full cost of a project. Essentially, special assessments capture the private benefits from an improvement financed in part by general revenues. They differ from other benefits-based levies, including impact fees, in that the maximum assessment is the increase in property value created by the improvement, regardless of the extent to which beneficiaries use the facility. Traditionally, special assessments have been used for street improvements, including curbs, gutters, sidewalks, storm drainage, and street lighting. Some local governments use assessments to partially finance the installation of water and sewer lines. More recent uses include financing the construction of recreational facilities and off-street parking.

Unlike impact fees, special assessments are levied under the taxing powers granted to local governments in state law. Municipalities in all states have authority to levy assessments, and counties and special districts also frequently have statutory authority to adopt special assessments.[15] Heaviest use of these levies is made by local governments west of the Mississippi River, especially those in Pacific Coast states.

While impact fees are generally collected prior to the construction of the facility, state laws usually prohibit collection of special assessments until the project is completed, at which point property owners have the option of paying their assessments in installments over a number of years, usually at very favorable interest rates. When financing a project with assessments, a local government must finance the construction phase with general revenues and then reimburse itself as special assessments are collected. When impact fees are used, beneficiary financing is up front, which places less of a drain on the local government's general revenues.

The remaining sections of this chapter examine the adoption of special assessments, their legal basis, and issues in their administration.

The special assessment process

Politically, special assessments offer governments several advantages for financing capital improvements. First, they promote intrajurisdictional equity because all taxpayers need not bear the full cost of an improvement that increases the property values of a few property owners. Second, a local government may establish a special district that is coterminous with a new development and authorize a special assessment on property owners in the district to finance part of the cost of public improvements. The local government then issues tax-exempt debt (sometimes called special assessment bonds), which is repaid from the assessments and which enables developers to lower their financing costs. Occasionally, politically independent special districts, such as municipal utility districts in Texas, use special assessments for development-related improvements, such as water and sewer lines.

Figure 9–2 summarizes the stages that local governments levying a special assessment generally go through. First, projects may be initiated as a result of either citizen initiative (voluntary assessment) or government initiative (compulsory assessment). If the project is citizen initiated, usually a majority of the affected property owners (or owners of a majority of the affected properties) must sign the petition requesting the project. A local government's special assessment policy should specify the procedures for circulating a petition, the qualifications for signing the petition, and the types of projects that will be financed with an assessment.

If the special assessment is initiated by the local government, state statutes usually specify the procedures for proceeding with the project. In these cases, successful use of special assessments requires that affected property owners be involved early in the process. For example, once a project has been proposed for special assessment financing in Fort Worth, Texas, a personal letter is sent to each property owner describing the proposed project, its total cost, the estimated assessment on the property, and the construction schedule.

The second stage in the process is the completion of a feasibility study, which should determine the need for the project and its estimated cost, including the indi-

Figure 9–2
Stages in the adoption of special assessments.

Initiate project ➤ Complete a feasibility study ➤ Hold public hearing on project's feasibility ➤ Authorize project ➤ Prepare and mail assessments ➤ Hold public hearing on assessment roll ➤ Issue assessment certificates

rect costs to the local government for project administration. During this phase, local government policy makers should establish by ordinance the project's boundaries (or create an assessment district), identify the properties affected by the project, and authorize an appraisal study to determine the project's effect on the value of each property. At this point, policy makers may authorize preparation of a preliminary assessment roll that identifies each property's legal boundaries and the name of the property owner.

Once the project's feasibility has been demonstrated, state laws typically require that city council or county commissioners conduct a public hearing giving affected property owners the opportunity to voice their opinion of the proposed project. In some states, the law requires an extraordinary majority (e.g., two-thirds) of affected property owners to approve creation of the special assessment district. During this stage, owners may also be notified (on the basis of the appraisal study) of the estimated increase in their property's value that will result from the improvement. On completion of the public hearing, policy makers adopt an ordinance authorizing the project's construction and then proceed with the awarding of contracts.

Following project authorization and on completion of the appraisal study that was conducted during the second stage, each property's assessment is determined, the assessment roll is updated to include this information, and property owners are notified of their assessment for the project's cost. Property owners may appeal their assessment (a pro rata share of the project's costs not to exceed the estimated increase in their property's value attributable to the project) at the public hearing on the assessment roll, which may be combined with the public hearing on the project's feasibility or held separately. After hearing the evidence, lawmakers may adjust assessments downward.

The aspect of special assessments that is legally contested most often is the allocation of construction costs to affected property owners. State law usually specifies the basis for allocating a project's cost among property owners, which is almost always according to the number of feet fronting the improvement (i.e., a front-foot basis). Although by law the maximum assessment equals the increase in value attributable to a public improvement, local governments rarely levy assessments at this level. For example, as a matter of policy a local government may decide to assess property owners only one-third of the cost of a project (which may be lower than the resulting increase in property value) in residential areas but two-thirds of the cost for improvements in commercial areas—with the balance in both cases paid from general revenues.

Although costs are usually allocated among property owners on a front-foot basis, an appraisal study may reveal that the project's benefits are not uniformly distributed. In this case, the assessment of each property must be adjusted to reflect any differences. State courts have become more insistent that assessments be linked to a property's enhanced value and not based simply on a rigid application of the front-foot rule. Costs may also be allocated on a per acre or per lot basis, especially for water and sewer installations. In some cases, a zone method may be used whereby properties closest to the improvement bear a greater portion of the cost.

Even though the assessment roll is normally prepared much earlier, state law usually requires that the project be completed and accepted by the city or county before assessments can be collected. On acceptance of the completed project, the local government issues assessment certificates to property owners. Each certificate includes the amount of the assessment, a legal description of the property, and the terms of payment—including the number and frequency of installments and the rate of interest if the fee is paid in installments. Issuance of the certificates, which is by ordinance, also fixes a lien against the property, which remains in force until the assessment is paid in full.

The legal basis for special assessments

Unlike impact fees, which depend on implied local powers to regulate land use, special assessments are explicitly authorized in state law under the taxing powers granted to local governments. Yet assessments are not taxes per se, since they are not levied at a uniform rate on all property in the jurisdiction; they apply only to those properties benefiting from a public improvement. The maximum assessment is the increase in property value attributable to the improvement. Any levy exceeding this constitutes a taking of private property without just compensation and thus violates the eminent domain provisions of state and federal constitutions.

Enabling legislation usually specifies which levels of local government may levy assessments, the general procedures for adopting an assessment, the types of improvements that can be financed with a special assessment, the basis for allocating costs (front-foot, per lot, zone), whether payments can be made in installments, and the maximum interest rate on installment payments. State laws usually leave less clear whether assessments extend to tax-exempt property. For example, in Missouri, tax-exempt property is subject to special assessments, but in Texas it is excluded because assessments are viewed by the courts as a form of taxation.[16] Enabling legislation may also specify the maximum portion of a project's cost that can be collected from assessments. For example, Texas law limits street assessments to 90 percent of the project's cost or of the increase in property value that results from the project, whichever is less.[17]

As noted earlier, the most litigated aspect of special assessments is the allocation of design and construction costs to individual properties. Street improvements in residential areas pose the greatest problem, since they do not necessarily increase property values. The Texas Supreme Court held in 1983 that property values may actually decline as a result of additional traffic, noise, and pollution: "There is no presumption of special benefits which arises simply by virtue of the improvement of a city street. Improvement of a street may cause a decline in the value of residential property."[18]

Because of the difficulty of demonstrating increases in property value for residential areas, some local governments restrict special assessments to commercial strips, where increases in property value are greater. Generally, special assessments can be used to recover a greater share of the cost of an improvement in a commercial strip than in a residential area. Furthermore, the cost of administering assessments declines for commercial areas because the increased property values are easy to document.

Administering special assessments

In most states, special assessments become a lien on the property once the final appraisal roll is certified. If a "due on sale" or "due on platting" clause is included in the assessment certificate, the outstanding balance of the assessment becomes payable at the time of sale or platting.[19] Such a provision protects governments from having to collect assessments after a property has been sold, especially in cases where ownership is turned over quickly. In some states, the special assessment lien is subordinate (takes a lower priority in the event of foreclosure) to the lien for property taxes; in other states (such as Texas), constitutions prohibit governments from foreclosing on special assessment liens against homesteads.

Special assessments are costly to administer. Legal advisers and fee appraisers can be expensive, especially for more complex projects or projects that involve a large number of property owners. In addition, the in-kind cost of assessments can be considerable because of the time spent by policy makers in conducting hearings and by managers in negotiating agreements. Local governments should not adopt special assessments unless they have a sufficient volume of projects to benefit from the administrative economies of scale.

State laws usually specify the frequency of installment payments and the number of years an owner's debt may be carried. Oregon authorizes semi-annual payments over a ten-year period and permits deferred assessments on the homesteads of senior citizens until the property is sold or the owner dies.[20] Assessment certificates should also specify the rate of interest on the outstanding balance of an assessment, which is often pegged to the interest rate the local government incurs on its debt. Finally, local governments may want to establish a revolving fund to reduce the amount of up-front funding they must provide from other sources for projects financed by assessments. For example, Missouri cities may issue debt to provide the capital for such a fund and then repay the debt with revenue from special assessments.[21] This procedure provides up-front financing for project construction in a way that avoids draining a city's general revenues.

Summary

Special assessments provide local governments with a means of capturing the increased value that accrues to property owners from the installation of a public improvement. Not only do special assessments promote intrajurisdictional equity by capturing these private benefits, but they also lower developers' financing costs by giving them access to tax-exempt debt backed by the assessments.

Projects financed by special assessments may be initiated by property owners (including developers) or by the local government. Once a feasibility study has been completed for the proposed project, a public hearing is conducted to determine property owners' level of support for it. During this period, an assessment roll is prepared identifying the affected properties and their owners and estimating each property's assessment. Property owners are notified of their assessment for the project's cost and are then given an opportunity to contest the assessment at a public hearing. The final step is certification of the assessment roll by local government policy makers and the issuance of assessment certificates to property owners.

Because special assessments are levied under the taxing powers of local government, specific authority must be granted in state law for these levies. Every state grants municipalities the authority to levy assessments, and most extend the same authority to counties and less frequently to independent special districts, such as utility districts. Enabling legislation specifies the general procedures that local governments must follow to levy an assessment, the method for allocating the costs of the project, and the terms of payment for property owners affected by the project.

Administratively, assessments are costly, particularly for improvements in residential areas, where the increases in property value are less apparent, or for projects that involve a large number of property owners. Local governments are advised to use special assessments only when they can gain some economies of scale by spreading administrative costs among several projects.

Summary and recommendations

The following recommendations for the use of impact fees and special assessments are based on the discussion in this chapter:

The critical stage in the process of adopting an impact fee is documenting the cost of capital improvements needed to serve new residents. Costs depend on reasonable land use assumptions and projections of needed capital improvements.

The ordinance levying the fee should specify the types of improvements financed by the fee, the basis for computing each property's liability, and whether the fee will be collected at the point of platting or when a building permit is issued.

The principal objection to impact fees is that they will increase the cost of housing in the community. In fact, in the long term, fees are capitalized into lower prices for undeveloped land. However, in the short term after adoption of the fee, builders will likely bear the fee's cost on their existing inventory of property. In order to reduce this burden, it is recommended that local governments phase in the fee over a two- or three-year period, giving developers and builders an opportunity to adjust their bid prices for raw land to compensate for the fee.

Evidence from formal research has found that impact fees result in lower land values, as expected from theory. But they also benefit developers and their customers by assuring them of adequate capacity in the public services financed by the fees. Such assurance appears to increase property values much like higher-quality schools result in increased property values.

Careful attention must be given to designing a legally defensible fee. This involves securing competent legal expertise early in the process to ensure that the ordinance meets legal standards, adequately documenting the improvements needed to serve new growth and the cost of those improvements, and setting a fee rate that fairly compensates the local government for the cost of those facilities.

Successful use of special assessments requires that affected property owners be involved early in the process. The local government may want to survey owners about their attitude toward a proposed project and their willingness to pay an assessment for part of the cost of the project.

The most legally contested aspect of special assessments is the allocation of construction costs to affected property owners. Local governments should authorize an appraisal study to document the increased property values from the project.

Assessment certificates should include a "due on sale" or "due on platting" clause to reduce the risk of having to collect the assessment after the property has been sold or developed.

The most litigated aspect of special assessments is the basis used to allocate project costs to individual properties, especially for projects in residential areas. Local governments may want to restrict assessments to commercial strips where increases in property value are greater and easier to document.

Because special assessments are costly to administer, there should be a sufficient volume of projects capable of being financed in part by assessments to provide some economies of scale in their administration.

1 Thomas P. Snyder and Michael A. Stegman, *Paying for Growth: Using Development Fees to Finance Infrastructure* (Washington, D.C.: The Urban Land Institute, 1987), 66.

2 Ibid., 74.

3 Lawrence W. Libby and Carmen Carrion, "Development Impact Fees," CDFS-1558-04 (Columbus: Ohio State University Extension Service, 2004). Available at www.ohioline.osu.edu/cd-fact/1558.

4 James E. Frank, Elizabeth R. Lines, and Paul B. Downing, "Community Experience with Fire Impact Fees: A National Study" (Tallahassee: Florida State University, Policy Studies Program, 1985), 17.

5 Snyder and Stegman, *Paying for Growth,* 98.

6 Keith R. Ihlanfeldt and Timothy M. Shaughnessy, "An Empirical Investigation of the Effects of Impact Fees on Housing and Land Markets" (Cambridge, Mass.: Lincoln Institute of Land Policy, 2002); John Yinger, "The Incidence of Impact Fees and Special Assessments," *National Tax Journal* 51 (March 1998): 23–41.

7 Arthur C. Nelson and Mitch Moody, "Paying for Prosperity: Impact Fees and Job Growth"

(Washington, D.C.: The Brookings Institution, Center on Urban and Metropolitan Policy, June 2003). Available at www.brookings.edu/es/urban/publications/nelsonimpactfees.

8 Ibid., 9–16.

9 Martin L. Leitner and Susan P. Schoettle, "A Survey of State Impact Fee Enabling Legislation," in *Exactions, Impact Fees, and Dedications,* ed. Robert H. Freilich and David W. Bushek (Chicago, Ill.: American Bar Association, State and Local Government Law Section, 1995), 60–86.

10 *Pioneer Trust and Savings Bank v. Village of Mount Prospect,* 176 N.E.2d 799, 804 (Ill. Sup. Ct. 1961).

11 *Associated Home Builders v. City of Walnut Creek,* 4 Cal.3d 633, 94 Cal. Rptr. 630,484 P.2d 606 (1971), *app. dism'd* 404 U.S. 878 (1972).

12 *Jordan v. Village of Menomonee Falls,* 137 NW.2d 442 (Wisc. Sup. Ct. 1966).

13 Terry D. Morgan, James B. Duncan, and Bruce W. McClendon, "Drafting Impact Fee Ordinances: Legal Foundation for Exactions," *Zoning and Planning Law Report* (July–August 1986): 53.

14 James B. Duncan, Norman R. Standerfer, and Bruce W. McClendon, "Drafting Impact Fee Ordinances: Implementation and Administration," *Zoning and Planning Law Report* (September 1986): 58.

15 Snyder and Stegman, *Paying for Growth,* 35.

16 *Special Assessment Procedures for Missouri Municipalities* (Jefferson City: Missouri Municipal League, September 1986), 3; and Robert L. Bland, *Financing City Government in Texas: A Revenue Manual for City Officials* (Austin: Texas Municipal League, 1986), 143.

17 Bland, *Financing City Government in Texas,* 142.

18 *Haynes v. City of Abilene,* 659 SW.2d 638 (Tex. 1983).

19 Bland, *Financing City Government in Texas,* 148.

20 *Financing Local Improvements by Special Assessment* (Eugene: University of Oregon, Bureau of Governmental Research and Service, January 1982), 19.

21 *Special Assessment Procedures,* 7c.

Glossary

Ability-to-pay principle   A basis for distributing the tax burden. According to this principle, on which the progressive rate structure used by the federal and many state personal income taxes is based, those with a greater capacity, as measured by annual household income or wealth, should bear a greater relative share of the burden. As household income increases, a higher rate of taxation applies for each additional dollar of income.

Accounts (or taxes) receivable   An accounting term that refers to a type of asset created when a utility service is provided or a tax is levied. Accounts receivable represent the outstanding amount of money owed for the service or tax liability. They are recognized as assets and are considered revenue whenever they have been earned (i.e., when utility service has been provided) or when they are available (tax receipts are expected to be available for current-year operations). Once the utility user or tax-payer pays the liability, the receivable is reduced and cash is increased.

Acquisition-based appraisal   A standard for valuing real property that uses the property's most recent selling price. Whenever ownership changes, the selling price becomes the property's new appraised value. Annual increases in assessed (taxable) value, which are usually capped in state law, are then bench-marked to the appraised value. Proposition 13 introduced the use of this new standard for valuing property.

Acquisition value   First introduced by Proposition 13, this valuation standard adjusts appraised and assessed values only when a real estate sells. The property's appraised value is set at the selling price, and that value becomes the new base for any annual adjustments in assessed value. Some states limit this valuation standard to single-family residences only, while others, such as California, extend it to all types of real property.

Adjusted gross income   The sum of all taxable income, excluding income excluded from the tax base, less adjustments for income already taxed or for the cost incurred in earning that income (e.g., the cost of an employer-mandated relocation) or certain other adjustments (e.g., for individual retirement accounts).

Adjustments   Reductions in gross income designed to reduce or eliminate double taxation, such as with alimony payments, the cost of earning income, or job-related moving expenses. Adjustments are also made for standard and itemized deductions and personal exemptions, which reduce taxable income, and for credits, which reduce tax liability.

Agglomeration economies   Reductions in operating costs that result when firms in the same industry locate in a common geographic area in order to benefit from the savings that come from sharing the costs of specialized services or accessing a specialized pool of labor. Such concentrations of industries may be driven by natural forces or fortuitous historical events.

Amnesty   A controversial revenue enforcement measure used to collect delinquent taxes, fines, and charges. As a one-time incentive, the penalty is reduced or eliminated in reward for payment during the amnesty period. Amnesty programs provide a one-time infusion of revenue for local governments and are always accompanied by a promise from the local government to elevate enforcement efforts following the amnesty period.

Announcement effect   Taxpayers' anxiety resulting from a high nominal (or statutory) tax rate. A high nominal tax rate does not necessarily imply a high tax burden, which the local government can lower by awarding partial exemptions or exclusions.

Apportionment   The allocation of a tax base or of tax revenue when claimed by more than one taxing jurisdiction. In the case of local governments, apportionment is an issue for allocating the taxable income of commuters and of corporations with operations in multiple jurisdictions or countries. In the case of the sales tax, apportionment is an issue when consumers live in one jurisdiction but make their taxable purchases in another.

Appraisal roll   The end product of the appraisal phase that lists the name and address of each property's owner, the certified appraised value of the taxable portion of the property, and a legal description of the property.

Appraised value   An estimate of a property's market value for tax purposes using legally specified standards of valuation. The appraisal process begins with the discovery of property, identification of owners, valuation, notification of owners of their property's estimated market value, a hearing and appeals process, adjustments to the estimated value based on evidence provided in the hearing, and a final certification of value.

Arbiter community   A community characterized by a high per capita revenue effort but a low capacity to provide necessary revenues. Arbiter communities typically have relatively high expectations for public services but limited

revenue capacity to meet those needs, requiring the manager to arbitrate among the factions competing for the already stretched local budget. Older central cities and counties dominated by manufacturing fall into this category.

Assessed value   The basis for levying the property tax, representing the taxable value of a property, net of deductions and other adjustments. A property's *appraised* value is adjusted downward by means of partial exemptions (such as a homestead exemption) or fractional assessment to determine its *assessed* value. This value provides the basis on which the tax burden is distributed to property owners.

Assessment cap   A statutory provision, usually statewide, that limits annual increases in property assessments to the cost of living or a specified percentage, whichever is less. Assessment caps are intended to limit extraordinary increases in taxable values and the revenue windfalls to local governments that such increases produce. Unfortunately, these caps introduce significant horizontal inequities into the distribution of the property tax burden since lower-valued properties tend to increase in value at a lower rate than higher-valued properties.

Benefits-based tax   A type of tax that allows a local government to recover at least part of the cost of a public service from those who benefit from that service. Examples include room taxes on hotel and motel occupancy, levies on gasoline and other motor fuels, and franchise taxes on utilities for the use of public rights-of-way.

Benefits-received principle   A defensible basis for tax equity that states that those who benefit from a public service should bear a proportional cost of the service. The more private the benefits from the service, the greater the proportion of its cost that should be recovered from beneficiaries through either direct charges or taxes. The most widespread application of this principle is in the use of charges for public services, such as toll roads and utility services. Benefits-based taxes are also an example of the application of this principle of equity.

Block-rate pricing   A variation of the variable-rate pricing structure in which the rate changes across levels of consumption. This pricing strategy divides consumption into blocks and then prices each block separately according to the per unit variable costs for providing service for each level of consumption. Such a pricing strategy approximates the marginal-cost pricing model.

Border-city/county effects   The negative economic consequences when tax rates or service charges differ substantially among local governments within a region, thereby violating the principle of tax neutrality. Households and businesses make economic decisions on the basis of tax (or service charge) considerations. Such behavior creates a net drain on the productive output of the local economy. States have a responsibility to promote neutrality through policies that encourage broader-based, flatter-rate taxes, especially at the local level of government.

Capitalization of taxes and fees   The backward shifting of changes in property taxes and impact fees to landowners in the form of lower prices for their land. A tax increase reduces the value of the land; that is, the tax burden has been capitalized into land values, and the cost of the tax increase is borne by the landowner. The reverse occurs for tax (or fee) decreases.

Caretaker community   A smaller, more rural community that has a low revenue capacity and low revenue effort. Caretaker communities generally obtain their revenues from a modest property tax, a limited number of license and permit fees, and some service charges.

Circuitbreaker program   A state-funded property tax relief program, usually to low-income home owners or renters or both, through a tax credit or rebate on the state personal income tax. Such programs have the advantage of targeting tax relief to the most needy

property owners; however, they are more administratively costly than across-the-board exemptions and can adversely affect state budgets during economic downturns.

Classification of property   A tax relief measure whereby states classify property by use, applying a different tax rate or level of assessment to each class. Property classification schemes generally favor residential over income-producing property and introduce horizontal inequities into the property tax.

Classification of users   A pricing strategy that classifies users by type or location of the user or by location of the service. Prices are then stratified by categories so that low-cost users do not subsidize higher-cost users.

Coefficient of dispersion   A statistical measure of appraisal performance that measures the average deviation in the level of appraisals (appraised value divided by sales prices) from the median level of appraisal. Coefficients range from +1.00 to –1.00, with zero as perfect appraisal uniformity. That is, all properties within each appraisal class, if applicable, in a jurisdiction are appraised at the same percentage of market value in that class.

Collection rate   The proportion of currently due tax or utility payments collected prior to the date due. A desired collection rate is usually not less than 95 percent of all the current liability for each revenue source. Collection rates are affected by local and national economic conditions, particularly unemployment and bankruptcy rates. The higher the collection rate, the lower the delinquency rate.

Competitive pricing   A pricing strategy that considers the prices charged for comparable services by private or non-profit providers or by surrounding local governments.

Connection charge   A type of levy used by governments to recover the cost of off-site improvements by requiring a developer to buy into the existing capacity of public facilities, which effectively shifts to new development some of the cost of building these facilities.

Consideration *See* Sales price.

Consolidated allocation technique A method for allocating indirect costs that involves summing the cost of all support services (purchasing, personnel, central administration, budget, etc.) and then apportioning those costs to direct services for which a fee is collected. Indirect costs are then allocated on the basis of each chargeable activity's share of the total budget, or share of total salaries and fringe benefits, or a similar measure of relative size. This method ignores the interdependence among support services and thus allocates more of the cost of these support services to chargeable services than is justified.

Constant yield rate A hypothetical tax rate that will yield the same amount of property tax revenue produced in the preceding year using the current year's tax base. This rate, computed as the first step in the truth-in-taxation process, is the benchmark used by taxpayers to compare with the actual rate adopted by the governing board.

Consumption community Typically an upper-middle-income area whose residents value locally produced public services and are willing (effort) and able (capacity) to pay for good services. Consumption communities rely primarily on the property tax and possibly the sales tax but also make extensive use of service charges and regulatory fees.

Cost method A method for valuing property, especially for unique properties or intermediary facilities like warehouses, that uses the cost of materials and labor, less depreciation, for replicating the structure plus the value of the land on which the structure stands.

Cost-of-services study An analysis, usually undertaken by a consulting firm, that determines the full cost of providing services, especially those in the general fund for which fees may be charged. The

study usually identifies both the direct and indirect costs of providing a service, thereby providing a basis for pricing the service that is defensible to users.

Cyclical change Shifts in the business cycle, economic upswings and downturns, both national and regional, that affect the overall economic stability of that region.

Dedicate improvements A common requirement in land use controls that developers install at their own expense certain public improvements, such as streets, sidewalks, lights, and storm drainage, that are needed to serve a new development.

Development fees Charges by local governments to compensate for regulating new construction and for the impact of that construction on public services. Impact fees for off-site improvements and building inspection fees are examples.

Direct costs Expenses that are attributable to the production of a particular service (such as wages, benefits, and FICA contributions) and other production costs (such as equipment, supplies, and contract services) that would be eliminated if the service were discontinued.

Earned income Earnings from wages, salaries, tips, and net profits of unincorporated businesses.

Earned-income credit An adjustment to tax liability available to low- and moderate-income workers that allows taxpayers to reduce their income tax liability. The credit is usually given on a sliding scale that takes into consideration household income and the number of dependents. Some states allow the earned-income credit to exceed liability, creating a negative income tax by providing a cash subsidy to qualifying households.

Effective property tax burden A measure of the relative impact of the property tax. It is the ratio of property tax liability to the market value of a property or, in the aggregate, the ratio of total property tax revenue to the sum of the market values of all taxable property in a taxing jurisdiction.

Effective yield rate *See* Constant yield rate.

Enterprise funds A group of funds used to account for operations that are financed and operated like private business enterprises and for which the cost of providing the service is primarily through user charges. Activities accounted for through enterprise funds are usually expected to be financially self-supporting or nearly so.

Equalized value An adjustment to assessed value made by a state agency in order to bring assessments into closer conformance with a common statewide assessment ratio. Equalized values ensure equity in the allocation of state aid, especially for public education.

Equity The approach to establishing a revenue structure that promotes fairness to all sectors and citizens in the community. Fairness is established by imposing benefits-based levies, minimizing tax favors, balancing the burden on the poor and the wealthy, and recognizing that the perception of fairness varies by community and through time. Equity is evaluated horizontally (across taxpayers in comparable economic status) and vertically (the extent to which taxpayers in different economic situations are treated differently by the tax code).

Estate tax A wealth-based tax that is imposed on a deceased individual's property prior to that property being distributed to heirs according to the terms of the decedent's will.

Excise (or selective sales) tax A levy on a specific type of transaction at a rate specific to each type. Excise taxes, also known as selective sales taxes, are levied separately from a general sales tax and are usually based on separate statutory authority.

Fees-for-service A generic term that refers to the wide range of levies imposed by governments on a *quid pro*

quo basis. Fees levied under a government's proprietary powers include services charges or utility charges, whereas fees levied under a government's regulatory powers include license and permit fees or, in some cases, even impact fees on developers.

Fixed costs Costs that do not vary with the level of service production, such as debt service, rental payments, and insurance contributions.

Flat-rate pricing A pricing strategy that charges users a uniform fee based on the average cost of serving all users. While it is simple to administer, a flat fee requires that users whose costs are below average must subsidize those whose costs are above average. In addition, this pricing strategy creates no incentive to reduce wasteful consumption and should be used only when it is administratively infeasible to measure consumption.

Fractional assessment The assessment of taxable property at less than full market value. This adjustment to taxable values may be set intentionally at less than 100 percent or may, de facto, be at a fraction of full value.

Franchise fee A fee charged by local governments for exclusively providing a service to the public. Franchise fees are often associated with compensation from the provider for access to public rights-of-way for its service lines.

Freeport exemption A common form of a personal property tax exemption extended to manufacturers for their raw and finished goods that are temporarily held in inventory before being moved across state borders.

Full-cost pricing A pricing strategy that includes both direct costs (production and distribution) and indirect costs associated with service provision. Normally, this approach is used for utility services where a reasonable return on investment is legally and administratively justified.

Full disclosure A three-step procedure, also called truth in taxation or truth in millage, whereby governments (1) determine the tax rate that yields the same tax levy as in the preceding year, (2) publish that tax rate in the local newspaper, and (3) adopt a tax rate to generate sufficient tax revenues to balance the current operating budget. This procedure effectively eliminates the potential for a tax windfall whenever property is reappraised, because it shifts responsibility for increases in the tax levy away from reappraisal and onto the legislative body, which sets the tax rate.

Full-value assessment   A legal requirement that appraisals must be set at the estimated market value, with the only adjustments being for partial exemptions such as a homestead exemption. Although twenty states and the District of Columbia nominally have a full-value assessment standard, relatively few states actually maintain their assessments at this standard.

General sales tax   A tax levied on a broad range of goods and services usually at the point of sale. The tax is specified as a percentage of the transaction price. In most cases, tax liability falls on the buyer rather than the vendor, but the vendor collects the tax on behalf of the taxing jurisdiction.

Graduated tax rate   The division of taxable income into brackets, with each increment subject to a separate tax rate. In a graduated rate structure, higher brackets are subject to progressively higher tax rates. Total tax liability equals the sum of each bracket's liability.

Gross income   All income subject to taxation, both earned and unearned, except that income excluded by law from the tax base.

Gross receipts tax   A broad-based benefits tax that is usually levied on investor-owned utility companies for their use of public rights-of-way or for their exclusive franchise to provide services to consumers in that municipality. These taxes (or, in some cases, fees) are usually levied at a percentage of the value of the gross receipts collected by the utility company from consumers in the jurisdiction.

Growth community   A low revenue effort community that has capacity for more but pursues a laissez-faire economic principle toward tax effort in the hope that it will stimulate economic development. Growth communities are characterized by modest revenue effort coupled with a modest level of locally provided public services.

Homestead exemption   A tax relief measure that permits local governments to exempt from the tax base a portion of the appraised value of qualifying residential property, which lowers the effective tax burden of residential property owners and shifts it onto other types of property. The adjustment may be a fixed dollar amount per residential property or a percentage of value.

Horizontal equity   The equal distribution of the revenue burden among persons or businesses in comparable circumstances. In theory, in a perfectly horizontally equitable world, taxpayers in the same income bracket would bear the same income tax liability. Many adjustments to the tax base or tax liability, however, undermine horizontal equity in order to achieve other social or economic goals.

Impact fee   A charge to developers for the cost of off-site capital improvements needed to serve a new development. Impact fees provide up-front financing for the expansion of public facilities, such as water and sewer treatment facilities or arterial roads, needed to serve a new development.

Income elasticity   The relationship between revenue yield of a tax and changes in income. When a tax is income elastic, revenue yield increases (decreases) at a greater rate than growth (decline) in the local economy as measured by changes in income. Conversely, when a tax is inelastic, revenue yield is less responsive to economic growth and decline.

Income tax credit A tax credit for lower-income households used to offset the taxes paid on food purchases. Although it reduces the sales tax's regressivity, it has not been a popular tax relief measure among most state legislatures, probably because of the relatively lower burden of local sales taxes. The income credit does for sales taxes what the circuitbreaker does for local property taxes.

Indirect costs Expenses resulting from support services provided by one department to another. Indirect, or overhead, costs include administration, accounting, personnel, purchasing, legal, and other staff services.

Intangible property A category of personal property, such as stocks, taxable bonds, and bank accounts, that does not have physical form and substance. *See* Tangible property.

Land write-down A technique used by local governments to sell a redeveloped property in a tax increment district at a cost to the private investor that is lower than the cost to redevelop the property. The predevelopment costs of the land are recouped through the tax increment fund over the life of the project.

Legal liability The person or business entity defined in law as responsible for the tax or fee. State and local laws establish legal liability in order to facilitate tax enforcement.

License An authorization, issued under a government's regulatory powers, for an individual or business to engage in an ongoing activity. Local governments regulate activities, such as various professions, or grant privileges, such as owning a pet, and assess a fee for the license to recover at least a portion of the cost of regulating that activity. Once the license expires, it may be renewed. *Compare with* Permit.

Local option Authority granted in state law that gives local governments discretion over defining the tax base, setting tax rates, and/or providing tax relief.

While local options enhance the appeal of a tax proposal, they increase horizontal inequities, adversely affect tax neutrality through border-city/county effects, and increase the cost of tax enforcement and compliance.

Marginal-cost pricing A pricing strategy in which prices for services are set according to the cost of producing each additional unit of a service. Economists view it as the most efficient and equitable basis for allocating the cost of public services.

Market value The price that a knowledgeable and prudent buyer would agree to pay a willing seller in a competitive and open market.

Mass appraisal A variation of the sales comparison method. Sometimes referred to as computer-assisted mass appraisal, this method for valuing property relies on statistical modeling to provide an estimate of market value, especially for single-family residential properties.

Merit goods and services Goods and services endowed with a public purpose but providing individual benefits that can be denied to those unwilling to pay for them. Some of the benefits from these goods and services accrue to the whole community, such as the improvement of business opportunities or the creation of jobs, and therefore a portion of their cost should be borne by all taxpayers. The remaining private benefits should be financed by service charges to users.

Mixed drinks tax An excise tax levied on the retail value of alcoholic drinks, especially those consumed on the premises.

Multiplier effect The multiplicative effect of a dollar of new investment in the local economy. Multiplier effects vary by type of investment but are well documented and are an important part of estimating the long-term economic impact of public and private expenditures.

Neutrality   The approach to revenue policy that places long-term economic viability over short-term political accommodation. The key to neutrality is selecting tax policies that do not interfere with or hinder market growth; this means (1) relying on flat tax rates levied on broad tax bases, (2) using benefits-based levies where feasible, (3) avoiding interjurisdictional rate differentials, and (4) being attentive to local business taxes to achieve this.

Nuisance taxes   Narrowly based (usually excise) taxes, such as theater admission taxes, occupation privilege taxes, and property taxes on intangibles, that are costly to administer, increase non-neutrality, and yield small amounts of revenue.

Outsourcing   Governments contracting with a third party to collect and enforce current and delinquent taxes and service charges. The third party may be a private firm, such as a law firm specializing in delinquent property tax collections, or another unit of government that, because of economies of scale, can collect taxes at a lower cost per account. The primary danger from private collectors is their tendency to focus on collecting from the easier accounts and ignoring the more costly accounts unless the contract is structured to prevent this from occurring.

Overlapping tax bases   A situation in which taxpayers owe taxes to a city, its overlapping county or parish, an overlapping school district, and often other overlapping special districts, such as for hospitals, fire protection, or flood control. The result is confusion for taxpayers and often competition among the overlapping local governments for revenue from the shared tax base. With the exception of the independent cities in Virginia and the city of Baltimore, Maryland, local governments in other states share overlapping jurisdiction.

Partial-cost pricing   A pricing policy that sets the price for the service at less than full cost, with the difference made up by a subsidy from general revenues. In the case of merit goods and services, a partial subsidy is justified if (1) some

of the benefits from the service accrue to the whole community, (2) the government wants to stimulate demand for the service in the community, (3) enforcement at full cost would result in widespread evasion, or (4) the service is used primarily by low-income households.

Payroll tax   An excise tax that masquerades as a type of income tax in which the tax base is the employer's payroll. Whereas employees are liable for personal income taxes, the employer bears legal liability for the payroll tax. However, except in more competitive employment markets, the incidence of the payroll tax is likely shifted to employees, especially lower-skilled ones, as lower wages.

Peak-period pricing   A pricing strategy that structures prices according to when a service is used. In cases where a service cannot be stored, peak demand means that production and delivery capacity must be built to satisfy peak usage. Charging the same rate to all users regardless of time of use means that off-peak-period users subsidize peak-period users. Peak-period pricing, when it varies by the cycles of service usage such as by hour, day, or season, approximates the marginal-cost pricing strategy advocated by economists.

Penalty and interest   Separate charges imposed for failure to pay a tax or utility charge by the due date. The penalty charge is the punitive assessment for failure to meet the due date, and interest compensates the local government for the lost investment income from revenue. Penalties may be at a fixed amount or they may escalate the longer the debt remains unpaid; interest is assessed as a percentage of the outstanding balance and accrues each month the debt remains unpaid.

Permit   Use of a local government's regulatory powers authorizing an individual or business to undertake a one-time activity or task. Permits usually grant a privilege for a fixed period of time, such as a building permit or a parade permit. Local governments may charge a fee for the permit as compensation for regulating the activity. *Compare with* License.

Personal exemption   An adjustment to the tax base for each dependent in a household, often granted under personal income tax laws in order to promote horizontal equity. Larger households incur more living expenses, so tax codes often include a fixed dollar amount that is deducted from the adjusted gross income in the process of computing taxable income. Personal exemptions also promote vertical equity.

Personal property   Mobile property that is not attached permanently to real estate, including tangible property (such as furniture, equipment, inventory, and vehicles) and intangible property (such as stocks, taxable bonds, and bank accounts).

Point of sale   The jurisdiction in which a sale occurs. In the case of the general sales and some excise taxes, consumers may live in one jurisdiction but make their taxable purchases in another, creating an apportionment issue for policy makers. Most states resolve the issue by giving the sales tax revenue to the jurisdiction where the sale occurs—that is, the point of sale. However, in order to reduce border-city/county effects, some states may designate the jurisdiction of residence as the recipient of the revenue.

Price elasticity of demand   A measure of the impact that a change in tax or service charge rates has on the demand for a particular product or service. For example, a moderate increase in the occupancy tax for hotels and motels in a tourist community will likely have little effect on occupancy rates. However, the same increase in a nontourist community will likely have a greater effect on hotel occupancy rates, especially if there are nearby communities (substitutes) with lower tax rates.

Private goods and services   Consumer goods and services that are sold in discrete units for a price and whose benefits nonbuyers are effectively excluded from enjoying. Government may undertake production of an otherwise private good

because the opportunity for profit is insufficient to attract a private firm or because the large capital investment naturally limits provision to a monopolist. Government can finance private goods and services through charges to users or through general revenues.

Privilege tax   A type of excise tax levied on the privilege of conducting a particular type of business or transaction. Examples include occupational privilege taxes levied on particular professions or individual employees, admission taxes, deed transfer taxes, and bank franchise taxes.

Progressive distribution   *See* Graduated tax rate.

Property (or *ad valorem*) tax   A tax based on the assessed value of a property, either real estate or personal property. Tax liability falls on the owner of record as of the appraisal date. Although its role in local revenue structures continues to decline generally, the property tax remains the primary source of revenue for municipalities and counties.

Property tax rate   A rate, set either by a local governing board or in state law, that when applied to a property's assessed value represents a taxpayer's liability. The approved rate may be the sum of several separate rates, including those for operations (or the general fund) and for debt service (interest and principle, also called "sinking funds") for the portion of the general obligation debt coming due in the current budget year.

Proportional distribution   A distribution of the tax or service charge burden such that the effective tax rate remains flat across the income spectrum. That is, lower-income households incur a tax burden that takes the same percentage of their income (or wealth) as it does higher-income households.

Proprietary powers   Statutory powers of local governments that allow them to provide business-like services, such as water, sewage treatment, and electric power, from which they derive income as owners. As a proprietor, government may also levy a reasonable charge on users of these services and earn a reasonable rate of return on its investment.

Public goods and services   Goods and services produced by government that cannot be sold in units and that provide benefits to all citizens. These goods and services are financed from general tax revenues and include such services as public safety and public health.

Rational nexus test   The preferred standard of three tests developed by state courts to determine an impact fee's compliance with the due process and equal protection clauses of the Constitution. This test, developed by the Wisconsin Supreme Court, holds that a rational nexus must exist between a new development and the off-site improvements financed with an impact fee. Such a nexus exists if the population growth from new development creates the need to expand existing facilities (the "needs test") and home owners paying the fee are also the ones benefiting from the expanded facilities (the "benefits test").

Real property   Immobile property including land, natural resources above and below the ground, and fixed improvements to the land.

Regressive distribution   A tax or service charge whose distribution is such that the effective rate decreases as household income increases, thus burdening lower-income households more heavily than higher-income ones.

Regulatory powers   A broad umbrella of power given to local governments by state law to promote health, safety, and general welfare. Local governments use these powers to regulate land use, issue licenses and permits, and in some cases levy impact fees. Such powers are inherently broad, and state courts have recognized that it is impossible for legislatures to enumerate all of them.

Return-on-investment pricing   A pricing strategy used particularly with utility services that allows local governments to earn a profit comparable to that earned by privately owned utilities. The profit

may be retained in the utility or transferred to the general fund as compensation to the "owners" of the utility.

Right-of-way tax   *See* Gross receipts tax.

Sales comparison method   A method for appraising real and some personal property that relies on recent sales as an indicator of what buyers and sellers are negotiating for settlement prices. It is most widely used by appraisers for single-family residences in cases where there have been a number of verifiable arms-length sales that can provide a benchmark for appraising value for comparable properties.

Sales price   The amount of money (or other goods or services) exchanged for a property or good or service. In legal parlance, sales price is often referred to as the consideration given for the item or service.

Sales tax holiday   A temporary (two-to four-day) moratorium on state and local sales taxes, usually in August, that exempts the sales tax on back-to-school items such as clothing, supplies, and even computer hardware and software.

Sectoral change   Shifts in the importance of different sectors of the economy brought on by changes in technology and economic development. In the United States, the movement in employment away from manufacturing and toward service industries constitutes a fundamental sectoral shift in the national economy.

Security deposit   As a tool for enhancing collection of utility charges, local governments often require new customers to provide a deposit up front prior to providing service. Once the user establishes a record of timely payment, the deposit may be refunded with accrued interest.

Selective sales tax   *See* Excise tax.

Senior tax freeze   A tax relief measure that freezes the property tax liability of a household once either spouse turns 65.

As with most across-the-board relief measures, the senior tax freeze introduces significant horizontal and vertical inequities as well as reducing the property tax's neutrality, while also shifting the tax burden to younger households, including first-time home buyers.

Setoff provision A local government's withholding of compensation from contractors who are delinquent in paying their property taxes or utility services charges.

Special assessment A levy on property owners for the increased property value created by the installation of nearby public improvements. Special assessments differ from other benefits-based levies in that the maximum assessment is the increase in property value created by the improvements, regardless of the extent to which the beneficiaries use the facility. Historically, special assessments have been used for street improvements, water and sewer lines, curbs, sidewalks, and storm drainage improvements.

Spillover benefits Benefits from a public service or a tax incentive that affect an area beyond the borders of the local government providing the service or incentive. The cost, however, is borne by the taxpayers in the community where the service or incentive is provided.

Split tax roll A generic term describing the result of different tax rates being applied to different classes of taxpayers. For example, home owners may pay one (usually lower) rate on their primary residence, while businesses pay another (usually higher) rate on their property. In more recent incarnations of this concept, a split tax roll or two-tiered rate structure targets tax relief to home owners and is a tool for bringing equity to education funding.

Standard (or itemized) deductions
See Tax deduction.

Step-down method An indirect costing method that considers the benefits that support services derive from each other. Support services are ranked according to the amount of service each provides to all other support services, and then the benefits of each support service are apportioned to all lower-ranked support services. This approach makes at least some adjustment for the benefits that support services derive from each other before indirect costs are allocated to line activities, including those for which charges are levied.

Strategic plan A management tool to guide local governments in their economic development program. Each plan should identify (1) the community's economic strengths and weaknesses, opportunities and threats; (2) the goals, measurable objectives, and strategies to obtain those objectives; and (3) measurable benchmarks for assessing the progress toward achieving the community's economic development goals.

Street rental fee *See* Gross receipts tax.

Substitution effect A generic term that estimates how the behavior of consumers or taxpayers may change in the wake of a price or tax change.

Sumptuary (or sin) tax A type of excise tax that is levied to discourage consumption of certain classes of goods by rendering their cost prohibitive. Examples are taxes on tobacco, alcohol, gasoline, and diesel fuel.

Tangible property A category of personal property, such as furniture, equipment, and inventory, that has physical form and substance, yet is mobile.

Tax abatement A temporary reduction in the property (or sales) tax burden of a business. The purpose of the abatement is to attract new business investment to the community by increasing the business's after-tax profits.

Tax base The objects or transactions to which a tax is applied. State law or local ordinances define the tax base as well as the objects or transactions exempted from taxation.

Tax base sharing An approach to interlocal cooperation in which tax revenue from new business development is shared among municipalities in the metropolitan area. The first and most successful application of this approach for the property tax is in the Minneapolis–St. Paul area. In the case of the sales tax, North Carolina's approach to apportioning revenue between cities and counties is a form of tax base sharing.

Tax competition   A generic term that describes the rivalry among local governments, particularly those with overlapping tax bases, for tax revenue. It also describes their rivalry for new business investment.

Tax credit   A dollar amount by which a taxpayer's liability may be reduced. Credits are most often associated with personal income taxes and represent an adjustment to tax liability. In the case of an earned-income tax credit, qualifying taxpayers may receive a payment if the credit exceeds the liability.

Tax deduction   An adjustment to the personal or corporate income tax base that reduces taxable income. Two types are used: (1) a standard deduction, which provides a fixed dollar amount for each category of tax filers (single, married filing jointly, married filing separately); and (2) itemized deductions, which give tax filers with extraordinary expenses the option of deducting those expenses separately.

Tax deferral   A tax relief measure that delays tax payments by home owners until their property is sold or the estate is settled. A deferral is effectively a loan from the local government, usually at terms favorable to the taxpayer.

Tax exemption   A general term to describe the exclusion of certain types of transactions or objects from the tax base. For example, food consumed at home may be exempted from the local option sales tax; business inventory or goods held for sale in another state may be exempted from the property tax as a freeport exemption.

Tax and expenditure limitations (TELs)   A movement, begun with

Proposition 13 in 1978, that has ushered in sweeping limitations on state and local governments' taxing and spending authority. Most initiatives have targeted the property tax, particularly limiting increases in the tax base and/or capping tax rates and liability. Others have focused on providing tax relief to particular groups, particularly senior citizens.

Tax expenditures   An alternative term for tax breaks or tax loopholes, preferred by economists, that characterizes such measures as expenditures on the revenue side of the budget. Tax expenditures include any targeted reduction in the tax base, tax rate, or tax liability.

Tax exportation   The shifting of the tax burden to nonresidents. Local governments export their tax burden through such measures as hotel and motel taxes, entertainment taxes, taxes on the income or purchases of commuters, and taxes on businesses selling their products or services to customers outside the taxing jurisdiction.

Tax freeze   A property tax relief measure that freezes property assessments, property tax rates, or property tax liability.

Tax incentive   A generic term describing a number of tools used by local governments to attract business investment. The tools involve manipulation of the tax base or tax liability in order to enhance the community's attractiveness to business leaders.

Tax incidence   While the law establishes tax liability, the economic burden can be shifted either forward to consumers in the form of higher prices or backward to owners in the form of lower profits. Understanding the incidence of a tax is a prerequisite to assessing its equity and neutrality.

Tax increment district (TID)   An area, usually comprising several blocks or acres and often in a blighted condition, set aside for economic development using tax increment financing to attract business investment.

Tax increment financing (TIF) A tax incentive designed to attract business investment by the dedication of property tax revenue from the redevelopment of an area (tax increment district) to finance development-related costs in that district. Tax increment financing divides tax revenue from the area into two categories: (1) taxes on the predevelopment value of the tax base, which are kept by each taxing body; and (2) taxes from increased property values resulting from redevelopment, which are deposited by each jurisdiction in a tax increment fund and are used to finance public improvements in the redevelopment area.

Tax liability The product of tax base and tax rate. A taxpayer of record is legally responsible for the liability. Changes in either the base or the rate affect liability.

Tax lien A legal claim on assets, usually real property, that serves as collateral for any outstanding tax liabilities (or sometimes utility charges). A lien remains attached to the title of the property until the liability has been satisfied. In the event the taxpayer fails to make payment by the due date, a government may elect to foreclose on the lien by seeking a court order transferring title of the property to that government. The property is then sold at a tax sale, and the proceeds are used to settle outstanding claims by creditors, beginning with delinquent and currently due taxes.

Tax pyramiding A nonneutral consequence of taxes that fall on each stage of a production process. Whenever a product has multiple stages in its production process, any tax (other than a value-added tax) on each stage results in a cascading (or pyramiding) effect, with taxes falling on top of taxes.

Tax rate The amount of tax applied to the tax base. The rate may be a percentage of the tax base, as in the case of the sales and income taxes. In the case of the property tax, rates are expressed in cents (such as $.45 per $100 of assessed value) or as a millage rate (such as 30 mills), where one mill equals one-tenth of a cent.

Tax roll The end product of the assessment phase that lists the owners of each property, each property's legal description and assessed value, and the liability of each owner.

Taxable income The tax base for the personal and corporate income tax after all adjustments, including deductions and exemptions, have been applied. Changes in any of these adjustments or in the exclusions from the tax base affect taxable income. In the case of a graduated income tax, taxable income is segmented into brackets.

Taxable nexus A legally defensible connection that must exist between a person or business and the transaction or property being taxed in order to establish tax liability. The U.S. Supreme Court has ruled that states cannot compel out-of-state mail order or Internet vendors to collect the sales tax unless the vendor has a physical presence in the state. Similar rules exist at the state level for the application of wage and personal income taxes on professional athletes, for example.

Taxing powers The constitutional and statutory bases whereby governments levy taxes. Local governments rely on taxing powers granted them in state law to levy a property tax, a general sales tax, excise taxes, an income tax, and even special assessments. In some states, local governments rely on their home-rule powers to levy certain taxes.

Three-factor formula A common basis used by states and local governments to apportion taxable income of multistate and multinational corporations. The three-factor formula uses a combination of total sales, payroll, and property value to apportion taxable income. Often the formula is weighted heavily toward sales as an added incentive for attracting business investment on the assumption that corporate income taxes are shifted forward to consumers as higher prices for goods and services.

Truth in millage *See* Full disclosure.

Truth in taxation *See* Full disclosure.

Two-part tariff   *See* Variable-rate pricing.

Unearned income   The portion of the income tax base generally from returns on capital as opposed to labor. Sources of unearned income include interest, dividends, realized capital gains, royalties, and rent.

Uniformity clause   A provision in many state constitutions that compels, in varying degrees, that all taxpayers—or at least those in comparable economic or social situations—be treated the same.

Use tax   A tax, adopted in tandem with the general sales tax, levied on goods brought into a jurisdiction from another jurisdiction where a sales tax is not levied or is levied at a lower rate. The use tax is designed to protect retailers in a taxing jurisdiction by discouraging consumers from making their purchases outside the jurisdiction simply to avoid its sales tax. Enforcement is difficult except on big-ticket items for which records of ownership are maintained by governments.

Use (or production) value   An approach to property valuation that is based on the property's value given its current use and not its market value (highest and best use). State law typically allows this basis of appraisal for agricultural and open space land as a way of providing tax relief to farmers who own land on the fringe of an urban area where speculation by developers often increases land value well beyond what the land is worth for agricultural purposes.

Variable-rate pricing   A pricing strategy that is a two-part tariff whereby users are charged a minimum rate for the capacity (or fixed) cost of access to the service and a variable rate based on the quantity of service used. Utility services typically use this pricing structure.

Vertical equity   The distribution of the tax burden among taxpayers in different economic circumstances. Vertical equity considers both what constitutes different circumstances and the degree to which those differences are important in terms of the distribution of the tax burden.

Name Index

Subject Index

A Revenue Guide for Local Government
Second Edition

Text type
Times Roman, Vectora

Composition
Circle Graphics
Columbia, Maryland

Printing and binding
Victor Graphics
Baltimore, Maryland

Design
Charles Mountain

Text
60# recycled offset

Cover
12 pt. bristol